LIBRARY OF NEW TESTAMENT STUDIES
647

Formerly the Journal for the Study of the New Testament Supplement Series

Editor
Chris Keith

Editorial Board
Dale C. Allison, John M.G. Barclay, Lynn H. Cohick, R. Alan Culpepper,
Craig A. Evans, Robert Fowler, Simon J. Gathercole, Juan Hernández Jr., John
S. Kloppenborg, Michael Labahn, Matthew V. Novenson, Love L. Sechrest, Robert
Wall, Catrin H. Williams, Brittany E. Wilson

Sin, the Human Predicament, and Salvation in the Gospel of John

Mathew E. Sousa

t&tclark
LONDON • NEW YORK • OXFORD • NEW DELHI • SYDNEY

T&T CLARK
Bloomsbury Publishing Plc
50 Bedford Square, London, WC1B 3DP, UK
1385 Broadway, New York, NY 10018, USA
29 Earlsfort Terrace, Dublin 2, Ireland

BLOOMSBURY, T&T CLARK and the T&T Clark logo are trademarks of
Bloomsbury Publishing Plc

First published in Great Britain 2021
This paperback edition published 2023

Copyright © Mathew E. Sousa, 2021

Mathew E. Sousa has asserted his right under the Copyright, Designs and
Patents Act, 1988, to be identified as Author of this work.

For legal purposes the Acknowledgments on p. viii constitute an extension
of this copyright page.

Cover design: Charlotte James

All rights reserved. No part of this publication may be reproduced or transmitted in any
form or by any means, electronic or mechanical, including photocopying,
recording, or any information storage or retrieval system, without prior permission
in writing from the publishers.
Bloomsbury Publishing Plc does not have any control over, or responsibility for, any
third-party websites referred to or in this book. All internet addresses given in this
book were correct at the time of going to press. The author and publisher regret any
inconvenience caused if addresses have changed or sites have ceased to exist, but
can accept no responsibility for any such changes.

Library of Congress Cataloging-in-Publication Data

Names: Sousa, Mathew E., author.
Title: Sin, the human predicament, and salvation in the gospel of John / Mathew E. Sousa.
Description: London; New York: T&T Clark, 2021. | Series: The library of
New Testament studies, 2513-8790; 647 | Includes bibliographical
references and index. | Summary: "Mathew E. Sousa demonstrates that in
certain respects, John's doctrine of salvation fails to align with its
customary depiction in Johannine scholarship"– Provided by publisher.
Identifiers: LCCN 2021005425 (print) | LCCN 2021005426 (ebook) |
ISBN 9780567699190 (hardback) | ISBN 9780567699237 (paperback) |
ISBN 9780567699206 (pdf) | ISBN 9780567699220 (epub)
Subjects: LCSH: Bible. John–Criticism, interpretation, etc. | Sin–Biblical teaching. |
Salvation–Biblical teaching.
Classification: LCC BS2615.52.S658 2021 (print) |
LCC BS2615.52 (ebook) | DDC 226.5/06–dc23
LC record available at https://lccn.loc.gov/2021005425
LC ebook record available at https://lccn.loc.gov/2021005426

ISBN: HB: 978-0-5676-9919-0
PB: 978-0-5676-9923-7
ePDF: 978-0-5676-9920-6
ePUB: 978-0-5676-9922-0

Series: Library of New Testament Studies, volume 647
ISSN 2513-8790

Typeset by Newgen KnowledgeWorks Pvt. Ltd., Chennai, India

To find out more about our authors and books visit www.bloomsbury.com
and sign up for our newsletters.

Contents

Preface	vii
Acknowledgments	viii
List of Abbreviations	ix

1 Introduction — 1
   The Human Predicament in John's Gospel: Assessing the Claims of Scholarship — 1
      Considering Experience — 9
      Considering Christian Theology — 10
   Thesis, Method, and Program — 16

2 Life and Light, Darkness and Ignorance of God: The Prologue as Introduction to the Human Predicament and Its Solution — 21
   The Incarnation of Life and Light in the Darkness — 22
      The Extent of the Darkness — 30
      The Mission of Jesus — 32
   The Problem of Ignorance of God — 41
   Conclusion — 47

3 Illness, Disability, and Death: The Man with a Disabling Illness at Bethzatha and Jesus's Consequent Monologue — 49
   The Man at Bethzatha, Illness, and Disability — 52
      Illness and Disability in the Wider Narrative of John's Gospel — 60
      Summary and Implications — 63
   To Pass from Death into Life — 65
      Death as a Bodily and Relative Reality — 65
      Death as a Way of Life — 67
   Conclusion — 69

4	Sin and Its Effects: The Case of "the Jews" Who Believe and Fall Away	71
	Sin and the Believers Who Fall Away	73
	Doing Wrong, Having Guilt, and the Nature of Liberation from Sin	86
	Conclusion	93
5	Conclusions and Reflections	95

Bibliography	101
Index of Modern Authors	111
Index of Ancient Sources	114
Index of Subjects	129

Preface

Some years ago, while studying the Bible and Christian theology as an undergraduate student at Azusa Pacific University, my thinking on the matter of salvation began to change. I had been raised and had come to faith in a Protestant, non-fundamentalist Christian home, but had come to understand salvation as, in essence, a forensic status that is conferred on those who believe in Jesus. Looking back, the idea that a person is "saved" in the moment she or he decides in favor of Christ must have been conveyed through various channels, perhaps more implicitly than explicitly and even unintentionally at times. During my undergraduate education I was urged to rethink in certain respects this soteriological perspective. Christian theological traditions were introduced to me—particularly Wesleyan and Eastern Orthodox theology—that speak of salvation as a process of moral and physical transformation. Salvation was presented as a personal as well as communal reality. As my theological education continued at Fuller Theological Seminary I increasingly found myself persuaded by the soteriology of these theological traditions. They raised new questions in my mind concerning what the NT says about Jesus as the realization and basis of salvation, on the one hand, and about the human predicament, on the other. My interest in these matters led me especially to the Gospel of John, perhaps because of the way I found John's presentation of these matters to be explained in Johannine scholarship.

The present study is a product of this theological formation. It formally began with a suspicion that John's soteriology does not align in certain respects with how it is regularly construed in Johannine scholarship. After additional work and reflection it became clear that an issue of major importance was and is the human predicament in the Gospel of John, which is typically interpreted in scholarship in light of a presumed emphasis in John's Gospel on Jesus's mission as one of "revelation" above all else. The plight is regularly described in ways that prioritize mental perception to the detriment or even exclusion of ethics and human corporeality. The present study finds John to paint a rather different picture. The study demonstrates that, for John, salvation consists of far more than the emergence of belief in a moment of "decision." The human predicament, according to John's delineation of it, is a way or manner of life, a mode of existence that is not wholly rectified or resolved for John in the moment one comes to believe in Jesus. The plight as well as its solution pertain for John to ethics and to the quality or condition of human corporeality. Salvation, in John's view of things, is a process that involves the transformation of what believers *do* and *how* they live in relationship with God and others.

Acknowledgments

Many people supported me in bringing this book to fruition, and I wish now to express my gratitude. Constant throughout the long journey of research and writing have been the love, commitment, and patience of my wife, Casey. She has provided encouragement in times of difficulty and enthusiasm at points of success. As a postsecondary counselor for students with disabilities, she also has been an important sounding board for working through the matter of disability in John's Gospel. Our children, Lukas and Brooke, have been patient throughout this process too, as research and writing have at times been all-consuming. They have been a daily source of laughter and joy.

I am grateful to Chris Keith for accepting this book for publication in LNTS and to the team at Bloomsbury T&T Clark for their assistance during the publication process. Catrin Williams provided insightful feedback that has led to various improvements in the book's argument. Engaging the questions and suggestions of Marianne Meye Thompson and Joel Green over the course of research and writing has made the book far better than it would be otherwise. I am grateful for their good counsel. John Behr introduced me to key voices on the Christian doctrine of theosis and guided my thinking on such matters as the incarnation and atonement in Orthodox theology. Michael Gorman provided helpful comments on an earlier version of the manuscript.

This study is a product also of the faith that my parents, Joan and Ernie Sousa, have fostered in me. At an early age they began telling me about God's love and faithfulness, urging me to trust in and seek after God. I am grateful for their love and various means of support. My grandfather, E. Dale Cooksey, was generous in his support as well. To a certain degree he made it possible for me to write this book. I am grateful also to my parents-in-law, Glen and Debbie Brush, and to my in-laws as a whole, who have offered encouragement and whose care of Lukas and Brooke on various occasions has provided additional time for research and writing. Glen and Debbie also generously provided the laptop on which the manuscript was completed. Time for research and writing was generously provided as well by Kristen and Kevin Gray, who cared for Lukas on a weekly basis during the book's early stages. Finally, after eight years of labor, I feel compelled to say that, with thankfulness as well as hope, I regard the completion of this work to be a personal indication of the faithfulness of God. My intention for this work has always been, ultimately, that it be an offering to the Lord, and I continue to hope that in some small way it might contribute to the life of God's people.

Abbreviations

Ancient Texts[1]

Ad Thal.	Maximus the Confessor, *Quaestiones ad Thalassium*
Amb.	Maximus the Confessor, *Ambiguorum Liber*
Apoll.	Gregory of Nyssa, *Antirrheticus adversus Apollinarium*
C. Ar.	Athanasius, *Orationes contra Arianos*
In Jo.	Cyril of Alexandria, *Commentarius in Joannem*
Comm. Jo.	Origen, *Commentarii in evangelium Joannis*
De Beat.	Gregory of Nyssa, *De beatitudinibus*
Decr.	Athanasius, *De decretis*
Dial. Trin.	Cyril of Alexandria, *De Trinitate dialogi*
Eccl. hier.	Dionysius the Areopagite, *De ecclesiastica hierarchia*
Ep.	Gregory of Nazianzus, *Epistulae*
Ep. Adelph.	Athanasius, *Epistula ad Adelphium*
Ep. Serap.	Athanasius, *Epistulae ad Serapionem*
Haer.	Irenaeus, *Adversus haereses*
Hom. Jo.	John Chrysostom, *Homiliae in Joannem*
Inc.	Athanasius, *De incarnatione*
Or.	Gregory of Nazianzus, *Orationes*
Or. catech.	Gregory of Nyssa, *Oratio catechetica magna*
Or. dom.	Gregory of Nyssa, *De oratione dominica*
Or. dom.	Maximus the Confessor, *Expositio orationis dominicae*
Paed.	Clement of Alexandria, *Paedagogus*
Protr.	Clement of Alexandria, *Protrepticus*
Rom.	Ignatius of Antioch, *Epistula ad Romanos*
Serm.	Augustine, *Sermones*
Strom.	Clement of Alexandria, *Stromateis*
Super ev. Joh.	Thomas Aquinas, *Super evangelium S. Ioannis lectura*
Syn.	Athanasius, *De synodis*
V. Mos.	Gregory of Nyssa, *De vita Moysis*

---

[1] For all other abbreviations of ancient texts, see Billie Jean Collins, Bob Buller, John F. Kutsko, et al., *The SBL Handbook of Style: For Biblical Studies and Related Disciplines*, 2nd ed. (Atlanta, GA: SBL Press, 2014).

Modern Texts

AB	Anchor Bible
AnBib	Analecta Biblica
ANF	*Ante-Nicene Fathers*
BDAG	Danker, Frederick W., Walter Bauer, William F. Arndt, and F. Wilbur Gingrich. *Greek-English Lexicon of the New Testament and Other Early Christian Literature*. 3rd ed. Chicago: University of Chicago Press, 2000 (Danker-Bauer-Arndt-Gingrich)
BETL	Bibliotheca Ephemeridum Theologicarum Lovaniensium
Bib	*Biblica*
BNTC	Black's New Testament Commentaries
CBQ	*Catholic Biblical Quarterly*
CCSG	Corpus Christianorum: Series Graeca. Turnhout: Brepols, 1977–
CEB	Common English Bible
CEV	Contemporary English Version
CTQ	*Concordia Theological Quarterly*
CTR	*Criswell Theological Review*
CurBR	Currents in Biblical Research
DJG	*Dictionary of Jesus and the Gospels*. Edited by Joel B. Green, Jeannine K. Brown, and Nicholas Perrin. 2nd ed. Downers Grove, IL: Intervarsity Press, 2013
EBib	*Etudes bibliques*
ESV	English Standard Version
EvQ	*Evangelical Quarterly*
FC	Fathers of the Church
GNO	Gregorii Nysseni Opera
HBT	*Horizons in Biblical Theology*
HNT	Handbuch zum Neuen Testament
HTR	Harvard Theological Review
ICC	International Critical Commentary
Int	*Interpretation*
ISV	International Standard Version
JBL	*Journal of Biblical Literature*
JETS	Journal of the Evangelical Theological Society
JSJ	Journal for the Study of Judaism in the Persian, Hellenistic, and Roman Periods
JSNT	Journal for the Study of the New Testament
KD	Kerygma und Dogma
L&N	Louw, Johannes P., and Eugene A. Nida, eds. *Greek-English Lexicon of the New Testament: Based on Semantic Domains*. 2nd ed. New York: United Bible Societies, 1989
LCL	Loeb Classical Library
LNTS	The Library of New Testament Studies
NABR	New American Bible, Revised Edition

NASB	New American Standard Bible
Neot	*Neotestamentica*
NET	New English Translation
NICNT	New International Commentary on the New Testament
NIV	New International Version
NJB	New Jerusalem Bible
NLT	New Living Translation
NovTSup	Supplements to Novum Testamentum
NRSV	New Revised Standard Version
NTL	New Testament Library
OECS	Oxford Early Christian Studies
OTP	*Old Testament Pseudepigrapha*. Edited by James H. Charlesworth. 2 vols. New York: Doubleday, 1983, 1985
PG	Patrologia Graeca. Edited by Jacques-Paul Migne. 162 vols. Paris, 1857–86
QD	Quaestiones Disputatae
RNT	Regensburger Neues Testament
RSV	Revised Standard Version
SC	Sources chrétiennes
SJT	*Scottish Journal of Theology*
SNTSMS	Society for New Testament Studies Monograph Series
TDNT	*Theological Dictionary of the New Testament*. Edited by Gerhard Kittel and Gerhard Friedrich. Translated by Geoffrey W. Bromiley. 10 vols. Grand Rapids, MI: Eerdmans, 1964–76
TJ	*Trinity Journal*
TS	*Theological Studies*
TynBul	*Tyndale Bulletin*
WBC	Word Biblical Commentary
WMANT	Wissenschaftliche Monographien zum Alten und Neuen Testament
WUNT	Wissenschaftliche Untersuchungen zum Neuen Testament
ZKT	*Zeitschrift für katholische Theologie*
ZNW	*Zeitschrift für die neutestamentliche Wissenschaft und die Kunde der älteren Kirche*

1

Introduction

The Human Predicament in John's Gospel: Assessing the Claims of Scholarship

What may be termed the "plight" or "predicament" of human beings in the Gospel of John is an issue that is frequently acknowledged and broached in Johannine scholarship, especially in literature devoted to John's soteriology, anthropology, and theology.[1] Perhaps as a consequence, there is some variation within scholarship in how this predicament is described. Rudolph Bultmann speaks of the human predicament in John's Gospel as "existence in bondage" to the collective power of sin, the devil, and death, which holds sway over the *kosmos* as "the world of man."[2] Bultmann frequently describes this existence in bondage as "blindness."[3] Cornelis Bennema speaks of the human predicament in John's Gospel as a "spiritual oppression" that is caused by the devil, sin, and death, and that manifests itself in various physical, social, and religious ways.[4] Craig Koester summarizes the plight in John's Gospel as "separation from God" (which is caused by sin and death as well as by human limitations).[5]

Interestingly, in some studies that focus specifically on John's soteriology it is difficult to determine how the human predicament should be understood, because

---

[1] The pronouncement in John's Gospel that Jesus is "the Savior of the world" (4:42; cf. 3:17; 12:47; 20:30-31) is just one indication that, for John, there is a "predicament" in which human beings find themselves as well as a "solution." For some implications of the phrase "Savior of the world," see Craig R. Koester, " 'The Savior of the World' (John 4:42)," *JBL* 109 (1990): 665–80; Warren Carter, *John and Empire: Initial Explorations* (New York: T&T Clark, 2008), 188–91.
[2] Rudolf Bultmann, *Theology of the New Testament*, trans. Kendrick Grobel, 2 vols. (New York: Scribner's Sons, 1951–5; repr., Waco, TX: Baylor University Press, 2007), 2:15–17. George Allen Turner speaks similarly of the plight in John's Gospel as comprising "the world" (as a hostile environment), "sin," and "death" ("Soteriology in the Gospel of John," *JETS* 19 [1976]: 271–7).
[3] Bultmann finds that, for John, "all were blind" before the Revealer's advent; in the Revealer's call each person must decide "whether he is willing to acknowledge his blindness and be freed from it or whether he wants to deny it and persist in it" (*Theology*, 2:24).
[4] Cornelis Bennema, "The Sword of the Messiah and the Concept of Liberation in the Fourth Gospel," *Bib* 86 (2005): 35–58.
[5] Craig R. Koester, "What Does It Mean to Be Human? Imagery and the Human Condition in John's Gospel," in *Imagery in the Gospel of John: Terms, Forms, Themes, and Theology of Johannine Figurative Language*, ed. Jörg Frey, Jan G. van der Watt, and Ruben Zimmermann, WUNT 200 (Tübingen: Mohr Siebeck, 2006), 403–20 (see esp. 405–8).

here discussions devoted to the topic are lacking and descriptions are peripheral to other concerns.[6] In certain treatments of John's soteriology the nature of the plight receives no attention at all and, thus, seems to be assumed.[7] It is the case more generally that John's portrayal of the human predicament, or at least such aspects of it as "sin" and "death," does garner some amount of attention from those variously interested in John's soteriology, anthropology, and theology, although a full description of the plight and its various aspects is often lacking.[8] For many interpreters, the paramount importance of "revelation" presumed for John's soteriology seems to dictate the way in which John's portrayal of the human predicament is conceived and explained.[9] This observation will now be discussed more fully.

Notwithstanding the variation just noted in how scholarship describes the human predicament in John's Gospel, there is consensus that, for John, "sin" and "death" largely define this predicament. Sin and death collectively represent the crux of the matter. A common assertion (or in some cases assumption) in scholarship, though, is that sin in the Fourth Gospel amounts to "unbelief."[10] This idea seems to take shape in one of two ways: (1) "sin" in John's Gospel is deemed *not* to be a moral or ethical category; or (2) "sin" in John's Gospel is deemed to be the source and cause of immoral behavior, and it is rectified when one "believes" in response to divine revelation. In

---

[6] An example here is Cornelis Bennema's *The Power of Saving Wisdom: An Investigation of Spirit and Wisdom in Relation to the Soteriology of the Fourth Gospel*, WUNT 2/148 (Tübingen: Mohr Siebeck, 2002). Of the twenty-two "main soteriological themes in the Johannine literature" that Bennema considers (110–12), not one represents the plight from which human beings are saved (Bennema later explains the plight in John's Gospel, however, in his essay, "The Sword of the Messiah"). Other works that do not investigate or offer a focused discussion of the human predicament in John's Gospel, although they concern John's soteriology, include Mary Margaret Pazdan, "Discipleship as the Appropriation of Eschatological Salvation in the Fourth Gospel" (PhD diss., University of St. Michael's College, 1982), and Jimmy Ward Dukes, "Salvation Metaphors Used by John and Paul as a Key to Understanding Their Soteriologies" (PhD diss., New Orleans Baptist Theological Seminary, 1983).

[7] See, e.g., Charles H. Talbert, "The Fourth Gospel's Soteriology between New Birth and Resurrection," in *Getting "Saved": The Whole Story of Salvation in the New Testament*, ed. Charles H. Talbert and Jason A. Whitlark (Grand Rapids, MI: Eerdmans: 2011).

[8] D. Moody Smith, in *The Theology of the Gospel of John* (New Testament Theology [Cambridge: Cambridge University Press, 1995]), devotes about six pages to the human condition in John (under the subheading "The Revelation of the Glory to the World"), which he describes as "a state of alienation and condemnation characterized by darkness (1:5; 12:46), death (5:19–27; 8:37, 44), sin (8:21, 34), slavery (8:34–36), and falsehood (8:44)" (81). Smith does not explain how such aspects as "sin" and "death" are to be conceived with respect to John, however. Smith writes, "The portrayal of the world, and thus of the human condition, not only accords with what we find in the New Testament generally, but summarizes and, indeed, accentuates its desperate quality"; Smith goes on to qualify this statement, though, by explaining that "the familiar Pauline polarity of righteousness and sin, or human sin versus God's righteousness, is not found in John" (81). For a somewhat different reading of righteousness and sin in John's Gospel, see Matthew Vellanickal, *The Divine Sonship of Christians in the Johannine Writings*, AnBib 72 (Rome: Biblical Institute Press, 1977).

[9] On the importance of revelation in the Fourth Gospel, Smith (following Rudolph Bultmann and John Ashton) writes, "The fundamental question or issue of the Gospel can be stated as the nature of revelation" (*Theology*, 75). For a brief critique of this general assessment see Susan E. Hylen, *Imperfect Believers: Ambiguous Characters in the Gospel of John* (Louisville, KY: Westminster John Knox, 2009), 9–12.

[10] This view is rather ubiquitous in scholarship, but see in particular Rainer Metzner, *Das Verständnis der Sünde im Johannesevangelium*, WUNT 122 (Tübingen: Mohr Siebeck, 2000).

each case, the interpretation of sin informs and is informed by the interpretation of such matters as "ignorance" and "knowledge" of God, "darkness" and "light," as well as "death" and "life," since such matters directly or indirectly relate to sin in John's Gospel. Consequently, in each case the interpretation of sin and the human predicament more broadly shapes as well as reflects a certain reading of John's soteriology and theology as a whole.

An example of the first line of interpretation, which finds "sin" to lack moral and ethical significance for John, is the study of Rainer Metzner: *Das Verständnis der Sünde im Johannesevangelium*. Metzner finds that "sin" is for John "neither a nomistic nor a moral category. It does not adequately allow itself to be comprehended as the violation of a generally accepted human value-system."[11] For Metzner, the Christological determination of "sin" in John's Gospel, in conjunction with the Johannine lawsuit motif, indicates that sin should be understood "trans-morally" and in accordance with John's theology of revelation: sin is "an expression of a fundamental blindness and hostility of the world to the will of God coming to bear in the Revealer. ... Sin is the one denial of the world to the messenger of God, manifested in its opposition to the revelation of God."[12] In finding "sin" to lack moral or ethical significance for John, because it designates "unbelief," Metzner follows interpreters such as E. F. Scott,[13] Thomas Knöppler,[14] and Alois Stimpfle.[15] Christina Urban apparently

---

[11] Metzner, *Sünde*, 354. For a reassessment of how "ethics" should be defined with respect to John's Gospel, see Ruben Zimmerman, "Is There Ethics in the Gospel of John? Challenging an Outdated Consensus," in *Rethinking the Ethics of John: "Implicit Ethics" in the Johannine Writings*, ed. Jan G. van der Watt and Ruben Zimmermann, WUNT 291 (Tübingen: Mohr Siebeck, 2012), 44–80. Zimmerman argues that certain forms of ancient ethical discourse have as their focus not specific instruction for matters of daily life, but broader, more fundamental guidelines "pertaining to life in its entirety" (61). The Fourth Gospel accords with the latter in the sense that it is primarily concerned "with living one's life as a whole" (55). "John does not want to solve individual problems of daily life itself. Instead he wants to carry out ethical work at a more fundamental level that enables the reader in the end to find a happy life, or in Johannine terminology, an 'eternal life,' which nevertheless starts from daily life" (79).

[12] Metzner, *Sünde*, 352, 354.

[13] During his exposition of "the work of Christ" in John's Gospel Scott says the following:

> To the mind of John ... sin in itself involves no moral culpability. ... Sin is in itself a mere privation, and only assumes the darker character when the freedom offered through Christ is refused. There can be no deliverance from sin, in the Pauline sense; for the real sin which merits condemnation is nothing else than disbelief in Christ. ... The "sin" from which Christ has offered us deliverance is the natural incapacity of man to possess himself of the higher life. He is separated from God, not by a principle of moral evil which has won mastery over him, but by the inherent constitution of his being, as a creature of this world, "born of flesh." (E. F. Scott, *The Fourth Gospel: Its Purpose and Theology* [Edinburgh: T&T Clark, 1908], 220–2)

[14] "The ἁμαρτία-concept, according to the understanding of the Fourth Evangelist expressed in Jesus's word [9:3, 41], is no ethical category, but is determined by the missing relationship both to God and also to Jesus: ἁμαρτία means spiritual blindness toward God and Jesus" (Thomas Knöppler, *Die theologia crucis des Johannesevangeliums: Das Verständnis des Todes Jesu im Rahmen der johanneischen Inkarnations- und Erhöhungschristologie*, WMANT 69 [Neukirchen-Vluyn: Neukirchener Verlag, 1994], 76). Knöppler goes on to say, "Beyond the lack of belief in Christ and the affiliation with the non-godly side, the Johannine understanding of sin is determined by this, that ethical-moral impulses [Momente] play no role, rather the definite decay of sinners unto death represents a decisive element" (80).

[15] "Sin means not a misconduct in the areas of decency and custom, morality and (divine) law, but the state of unbelief, that is, lack of knowledge [Erkenntnislosigkeit]" (Alois Stimpfle, "'Ihr seid schon

agrees.[16] So do Udo Schnelle[17] and Michael Theobald.[18] Michael Labahn considers how John's respective delineations of "sin" and "law" may contribute to Johannine ethics and, on the basis of previous research, concludes the same: "aside from a few exceptions in 1 John, 'law' and 'sin' do not appear to function as moral categories in the Johannine writings."[19]

This line of interpretation has major implications for John's soteriology and theology. If sin is found *not* to be a moral or ethical category for John and, thereby, *not* to signify immoral actions and wayward behavior, then human behavior becomes irrelevant to the human predicament and, also, to its solution. What people *do* becomes insignificant in John's view of things.[20] It would seem to follow that human corporeality or embodiment is of no consequence for John.[21] Jesus, according to John, has come to save human beings from "sin," but sin understood *not* as immoral actions and conduct but as a lack of mental perception, as "spiritual blindness." Those who reject Jesus and his revelation continue in their faulty perception, which may now be described as "unbelief," while those who believe in Jesus are liberated from their ignorance and, thus, saved. Salvation is essentially (or perhaps entirely) "realized" in the emergence of

---

rein durch das Wort' (Joh 15,3a): Hermeneutische und methodische Überlegungen zur Frage nach 'Sünde' und 'Vergebung' im Johannesevangelium," in *Sünde und Erlösung im Neuen Testament*, ed. Hubert Frankemölle, QD 161 [Freiburg: Herder, 1996], 122).

[16] Urban argues that "sin" in John's Gospel is so determined by John's Christology and anthropology (specifically the possibility of being in relationship with God through Jesus or, rather, continuing to be "of oneself") that it has no "ethical dimension" (Christina Urban, *Das Menschenbild nach dem Johannesevangelium: Grundlagen johanneischer Anthropologie*, WUNT 2/137 [Tübingen: Mohr Siebeck, 2001], 361–7; see also 399, 409–10, 414, 448).

[17] "The Johannine understanding of sin exhibits a clear theological profile: sin is neither a legal nor a moral category. Instead, the predominant use of the word in the singular points to the fact that John understands sin in a general, comprehensive sense: *sin is unbelief, lack of faith*" (Udo Schnelle, *Theology of the New Testament*, trans. M. Eugene Boring [Grand Rapids, MI: Baker, 2009], 725; italics original). Interestingly, Schnelle finds that, for John, the basis of such unbelief is self-love and self-interest: "The world strives after its own glory and lacks love for God" (724; see also 721). How, for Schnelle, this love of "self" rather than of God (cf. Deut 6:5) and others (cf. Lev 19:18) can be deemed *not* to pertain to morality and ethics I do not know.

[18] "The Christological intensification, which the Evangelist already gives to the term [sin] in the first place, is unmistakable: 'sin'—rejection of God—means in the actual sense to reject Jesus, who embodies divine wisdom. ... The point of the Johannine understanding of sin is thus not ethical, but Christological" (Michael Theobald, *Das Evangelium nach Johannes: Kapitel 1–12*, RNT [Regensburg: Friedrich Pustet, 2009], 577). "The freedom disclosed by Jesus's word according to John 8:31 and following is meant not *ethically* ... but *ontologically*" (591; italics original).

[19] Michael Labahn, "'It's Only Love'—Is That All? Limits and Potentials of Johannine 'Ethic'—a Critical Evaluation of Research," in van der Watt and Zimmerman, *Rethinking the Ethics of John*, 32.

[20] Jack T. Sanders:

> Here is not a Christianity that considers that loving is the same as fulfilling the law (Paul) or that the good Samaritan parable represents a demand (Luke) to stop and render even first aid to the man who has been robbed, beaten, and left there for dead. Johannine Christianity is interested only in whether he believes. "Are you saved, brother?" the Johannine Christian asks the man bleeding to death on the side of the road. "Are you concerned about your soul?" "Do you believe that Jesus is the one who came down from God?" "If you believe, you will have eternal life," promises the Johannine Christian, while the dying man's blood stains the ground. (*Ethics in the New Testament* [Philadelphia, PA: Fortress, 1975], 100)

[21] In the NT, the idea that ethics pertain to "the body" and vice versa is clearly expressed in 1 Cor 6:12–20. See also, e.g., Matt 5:29–30; 6:22–23; Luke 11:33–36; Rom 12:1.

belief.²² The preponderance of this line of interpretation becomes all the more evident when one observes that, within scholarship, immoral behavior is seldom identified and emphasized as a key component of the human predicament in John's Gospel.

Differing to varying degrees from this assessment, other interpreters likewise explain "sin" in the Fourth Gospel as "unbelief," but explain sin as pertaining to morality and human behavior in the sense that "unbelief" is the source and cause of wayward conduct. Jan van der Watt, for example, finds that "sin" in John's Gospel is in essence "not accepting (believing in) God as he is revealed in and through Jesus"; the human predicament is "a lack of spiritual knowledge and blindness."²³ "This existential situation," van der Watt continues, "results in hatred for and rejection of the Son and the Father by the opponents of Jesus, and consequently, in their evil behaviour."²⁴ Sin, for John, is to be understood "as the negative position and attitude of a person. ... This existential position forms grounds for doing wrong things."²⁵ In describing "sin" or "unbelief" as the cause of immoral actions and behavior, van der Watt more or less follows interpreters such as Raymond Brown²⁶ and Craig Koester.²⁷ Dorothy Lee

---

[22] Jörg Frey, in his *Die johanneische Eschatologie*, vol. 1, *Ihre Probleme im Spiegel der Forschung seit Reimarus*, WUNT 96 (Tübingen: Mohr Siebeck, 1997), details the development of the scholarly opinion that John presents an eschatology that is purely or essentially realized. Frey himself argues *against* the idea that John holds a purely present eschatology (see, in particular, Jörg Frey, *Die johanneische Eschatologie*, vol. 3, *Die eschatologische Verkündigung in den johanneischen Texten*, WUNT 117 [Tübingen: Mohr Siebeck, 2000]; Jörg Frey, "Eschatology in the Johannine Circle," in *Theology and Christology in the Fourth Gospel: Essays by the Members of the SNTS Johannine Writings Seminar*, ed. Gilbert van Belle, Jan G. van der Watt, and P. J. Maritz, BETL 184 [Leuven: Peeters, 2005], 47–82).

[23] Jan G. van der Watt, "Salvation in the Gospel according to John," in *Salvation in the New Testament: Perspectives on Soteriology*, ed. Jan G. van der Watt, NovTSup 121 (Leiden: Brill, 2005), 107. Van der Watt finds John to present a "positive picture" of the "disciples of Moses" or "the Jews" in the sense that John's portrayal of their religious activities indicates "a *zealous, devoted* people who serve God in the ways they knew or believed to be the best. ... Right or wrong, they seem to be genuine about their religion. The idea of a well-organized religious group, who seriously try serving God through their cultic activities, is portrayed" (105–6; italics original). The problem with Jesus's opponents is therefore their lack of perception or spiritual "blindness." Schnelle seems to offer a rather different explanation: "The core of unbelief is not ignorance or incapability but the intentional rejection of a blatantly obvious factual reality. ... Precisely because Jesus speaks the truth and is himself the truth, many do not believe in him" (*Theology*, 721; cf. 725).

[24] Van der Watt, "Salvation," 107.

[25] Jan G. van der Watt, *Family of the King: Dynamics of Metaphor in the Gospel according to John* (Leiden: Brill, 2000), 323–4. Integral perhaps to van der Watt's construal (and to those like his) is the idea that behavior can be separated from ontology: "The primary concern in the Gospel is not sinful actions, but the sinful being of a particular person" (324). Such an idea seems also to shape Urban's reading of John's Gospel: "the question of the *being of humanity* belongs genuinely and first of all in the anthropological and not in the ethical discussion" (*Menschenbild*, 412; italics original; see also 126–35, 412 n.328).

[26] On John 8:21–30 Raymond E. Brown writes, "We note that 'sin' is in the singular in vs. 21, for in Johannine thought there is only one radical sin of which man's many sins (plural in vs. 24) are but reflections. This radical sin is to refuse to believe in Jesus and thus to refuse life itself" (*The Gospel according to John (I-XII): Introduction, Translation, and Notes*, 2nd ed., AB 29 [Garden City, NY: Doubleday, 1983], 350). Brown goes on to write, "The revelation that the Son of God has brought, which is the truth, has set free those who believe in it" (362).

[27] Koester, after explaining (rightly) that the phrase "children of light" in John 12:36 has "ethical connotations," says that for John "those who believe in Jesus believe in God (12:44), and this relationship is the basis for conduct congruent with God's will. Conversely, sinful actions emerge out of unbelief, which is the fundamental form of sin" (*Symbolism in the Fourth Gospel: Meaning,*

appears to agree: sin and evil are for John "bound up with a failure of recognition, an incomprehensible absence of knowledge"; "sin" may therefore be defined as "unbelief," as "a fundamental disorientation in relationship to God underlying acts of wrongdoing, that can be removed only by the divine miracle of incarnate love."[28]

In certain cases both views (i.e., that "sin" for John does and does *not* pertain to immoral behavior) seem to be espoused simultaneously. Bultmann, for instance, describes "sin" as "unbelief" and as "blindness," and he says that, for John, "one might almost say: the sin of 'the Jews' lies not in their ethics, as in Paul, but in their dogmatics."[29] Bultmann indicates elsewhere, though, that sin is for John the source and cause of immoral behavior: "being in darkness, the world is simultaneously *in falsehood*. For it is this illusion about itself, not some immoral conduct, that is the lie—an illusion, however, which is no mere error in thought, but the illusion of a false self-understanding out of which any immoral conduct that may develop proceeds to grow."[30]

Regardless of whether one is deemed consistent in his or her analysis, though, an important result of finding "unbelief" in John's Gospel to be the source and cause of immoral behavior is that human behavior becomes wholly consequent on and determined by a moment (and dualism) of decision.[31] If "sin" is for John "unbelief," then it follows that, when a person "believes," the source and cause of wayward behavior is addressed and rectified.[32] The problem of what human beings *do*, according to this line of interpretation, is resolved for John in the emergence of faith. This calls

---

Mystery, Community, 2nd ed. [Minneapolis, MN: Fortress, 2003], 165). Koester says elsewhere, "Th[e] primary sin of unfaith is expressed in the many 'sins' or wrongful actions that people commit" (*The Word of Life: A Theology of John's Gospel* [Grand Rapids, MI: Eerdmans, 2008], 66).

[28] Dorothy Lee, *Flesh and Glory: Symbol, Gender, and Theology in the Gospel of John* (New York: Crossroad, 2002), 168, 188–9. Lee asserts, however, that John "is not concerned primarily with sin as a series of discrete acts of moral transgression, but rather with the theological and spiritual root of evil within the human heart" (188). In her discussion of sin and gender, Lee explains (somewhat curiously) that it is important "to move away from an understanding of sin that is primarily moral to a theological apprehension" (195).

[29] Bultmann, *Theology*, 2:27.

[30] Bultmann, *Theology*, 2:18; italics original. Bultmann says further, "The conduct of every man … corresponds to his origin, i.e. to what he is, his essence"; sin "is not an occasional evil occurrence; rather, in sin it comes to light that man in his essence is a sinner" (2:24–25). Faith "is the admission that one has hitherto languished in blindness, has been enmeshed in the 'works' of the devil, and has now come over from death into life" (2:25).

[31] "Each man is, or once was, confronted with deciding for or against God; and he is confronted anew with this decision by the revelation of God in Jesus. The cosmological dualism of Gnosticism has become in John a *dualism of decision*" (Bultmann, *Theology*, 2:20; italics original). On the importance of this "decision" in John's soteriology see also Walter Grundmann's discussion of John in the article, "ἁμαρτάνω, ἁμάρτημα, ἁμαρτία," *TDNT* 1:305–8. See as well Karl Schelkle, "John's Theology of Man and the World," in *A Companion to John: Readings in Johannine Theology (John's Gospel and Epistles)*, ed. Michael J. Taylor (New York: Alba House, 1977), 127–40; Benjamin E. Reynolds, "The Anthropology of John and the Johannine Epistles: A Relational Anthropology," in *Anthropology and New Testament Theology*, ed. Jason Maston and Benjamin E. Reynolds, LNTS 529 (London: T&T Clark, 2018), 121–39.

[32] "Sin is classified as not to accept Jesus for who he truly is. Once Jesus is accepted or rejected, the person's attitude and actions are determined accordingly" (Jan G. van der Watt, "Ethics of/and the Opponents of Jesus in John's Gospel," in *Rethinking the Ethics of John*, 190). In John's Gospel "the implication of receiving life is that it is realized straight away" (van der Watt, *Family of the King*, 206).

into question the extent to which John may be said to present salvation as a process of bodily transformation (if such a characterization is thought at all to be suitable), since the believer's moral renewal or sanctification is "realized" in the moment she or he *begins* to believe in Jesus.[33] One could perhaps argue, on the basis of Christian experience, then, either that John offers a rather naïve portrait of the Christian life (i.e., one in which no immoral, devious, or self-serving conduct occurs in the lives of believers) or that, in light of John's Gospel, something is terribly amiss in the life of the Christian community. How "sin," following the emergence of belief, factors into salvation as an ongoing process and experience is here a question apparently not applicable to the Fourth Gospel.

Assessments of the human predicament in John's Gospel have these same implications when sin is *not* characterized as "unbelief." This is because scholars who find this characterization to be inapt still seem to maintain that, for John, salvation from sin is realized in the emergence of belief. J. Terence Forestell, for example, refines the common assessment of "sin" in John's Gospel when he writes, "Although many commentators assert that unbelief is the only sin in John, it would be more accurate to say that unbelief manifests a state of sin in which man lives"; "evil actions simply manifest a deeper spiritual state which the fourth gospel calls sin."[34] In the Fourth Gospel, "sin" should be viewed as "a way of existence characterized by murder, hatred, lying and self-exaltation. It is a state of alienation which results in division and hatred among men."[35] For Forestell, though, because "sin" in John's Gospel is a "spiritual state" from which evil actions arise, the result is that the problem of sin and evil behavior is resolved for John in the emergence of belief: "Sin is destroyed in John by the very gift of eternal life," and, for John, "eternal life or salvation does not lie in the future. It is the present possession of all those who believe in Christ."[36] According to Forestell, what remains to be realized for believers following their acceptance of Christ, in John's view of things, is greater contemplation of Christ's glory, not moral and physical transformation.[37]

---

[33] Joel B. Green, in his book *Body, Soul, and Human Life: The Nature of Humanity in the Bible* (Studies in Theological Interpretation [Grand Rapids, MI: Baker, 2008]), offers an account of salvation in the NT as an embodied, relationally embedded process of transformation (see 87–180). Interestingly, aside from one page (141), the Gospel of John is conspicuously absent in this account.

[34] J. Terence Forestell, *The Word of the Cross: Salvation as Revelation in the Fourth Gospel*, AnBib 57 (Rome: Biblical Institute, 1974), 148, 152.

[35] Forestell, *Word of the Cross*, 198. Forestell goes on to say here, "Attendant upon this state of alienation and at its source is ignorance of God or a false knowledge of God."

[36] Forestell, *Word of the Cross*, 148, 119. Cf. 15, 17–19, 153, 156, 192.

[37] Forestell, *Word of the Cross*, 126–7. Forestell contends that the texts in John that speak of a future bodily resurrection (e.g., 5:28–29; 6:39–40, 44, 54; cf. 12:48), and thus of bodily renewal and transformation, are "additions to the primitive gospel" and, therefore, should not significantly factor into Johannine soteriology (133–4). Consequently, Forestell finds that "the Easter Message in John is primarily a message of life with God beyond the grave and not one of bodily resurrection"; in John's view of things "physical death and resurrection become of incidental importance" (96, 204). Conversely, Frey finds that, despite John's emphasis on the presence of eternal life for those who believe, "the reality of physical death remains a problem for the disciples." "It is hard to understand how exegetes can claim that 'death' has become totally irrelevant. ... In my view, this demonstrates a serious disregard of the bodily reality of life, a reality which was shared by the Johannine community as well" ("Eschatology," 80 n.102).

Martin Hasitschka also finds to be inadequate the characterization of sin in John's Gospel as "unbelief": "Sin is according to John ... not to be understood so much in a moral/ethical sense and also is not simply to be equated with unbelief, but is basically a power that enslaves human beings."[38] Unlike Forestell, though, Hasitschka at times suggests that, for John, liberation from sin consists of a process. The future verbs in John 8:32 (γνώσεσθε, ἐλευθερώσει), for example, indicate that liberation should be viewed "as promised and not yet fully realized."[39] Liberation from sin occurs for John, according to Hasitschka, through the gift of a new, salvific relationship with God, which for believers "is already a reality, even if the full redemption from the consequences of sin is still to come, and people must still suffer under these consequences."[40] Note here, though, that it is sin's "consequences" that are found to persist for John in the process of salvation. Although Hasitschka concludes that, for John, these consequences of sin (particularly death) persist for believers following the moment of decision, Hasitschka seems to maintain that *sin itself* does not: the occurrences in John's Gospel of ἁμαρτία in the singular, according to Hasitschka, signify a "fundamental offense," a "basic attitude" toward God (which is also a power) *that is the source of all sinful actions* (denoted by ἁμαρτία in the plural).[41] This "basic attitude," Hasitschka explains, is defined in John's Gospel as love of "the darkness" rather than "the light" and as hatred of "the light" (3:19).[42] Evidently, then, the problem of sin and evil behavior is resolved for John in the moment one comes to believe in Jesus, since it is here that one's "basic attitude" of ungodliness and hatred of the light comes to an end.[43]

Anastasia Scrutton follows Forestell in describing "sin" in John's Gospel as "a mode of existence that is the opposite of spiritual life."[44] Sin is for John "an attitude of ungodliness, which exhibits itself in immoral actions."[45] Interestingly, Scrutton also finds John's soteriology to consist of a "process," a point that distinguishes her reading from that of Forestell and aligns it with that of Hasitschka. Like Hasitschka, though, Scrutton seems to uphold the idea that, for John, sin is defeated and destroyed in the emergence of belief. This is because, according to Scrutton, "sin" in John's Gospel is "an attitude of ungodliness" that is the source or cause of evil behavior. Sin, for John, is *not* to be identified with immoral actions, Scrutton emphasizes, because immoral actions

---

[38] Martin Hasitschka, "Befreiung von Sünde nach dem Johannesevangelium," in *Sünde und Erlösung im Neuen Testament*, ed. Hubert Frankemölle, QD 161 (Freiburg: Herder, 1996), 107.

[39] Martin Hasitschka, *Befreiung von Sünde nach dem Johannesevangelium: Eine bibeltheologische Untersuchung*, Innsbrucker theologische Studien 27 (Innsbruck: Tyrolia, 1989), 245 n.159.

[40] Hasitschka, *Befreiung*, 166.

[41] Hasitschka, *Befreiung*, 202–4, 239–40, 278; Hasitschka, "Befreiung," 96, 99.

[42] Hasitschka, *Befreiung*, 203 n.52.

[43] Like Hasitschka, Vellanickal speaks of salvation for John as consisting of a process: salvation involves "growth and development to full maturity" and is "a dynamic process of a continuous heading towards becoming children of God" (*Divine Sonship*, 103, 160–1). Also like Hasitschka, though, Vellanickal evidently regards sin as destroyed for John in the emergence of belief: in John's Gospel sin is a "diabolical power" that (1) is exhibited "concretely and fundamentally" in "unbelief"; and (2) is the result of "diabolic sonship," an affiliation with and origin from the devil that seems to be undone when one is born anew as a child of God (252–63, 286–94).

[44] Anastasia Scrutton, "'The Truth Will Set You Free': Salvation as Revelation," in *The Gospel of John and Christian Theology*, ed. Richard Bauckham and Carl Mosser (Grand Rapids, MI: Eerdmans, 2008), 366.

[45] Scrutton, "Salvation," 368.

"are not sin itself, but the consequence of sin."⁴⁶ The implication here is that salvation from sin—an "ungodly attitude"—is realized for John when one believes in response to divine revelation.

Whether scholars define "sin" in John's Gospel as "unbelief" (which is commonplace) or not, then, there seem to be two general lines of interpretation concerning the relationship in John's Gospel between sin (which involves, among other things, "ignorance" of God, "the darkness," and "death") and salvation: (1) sin is not a moral or ethical category, a conclusion that effectively makes human behavior irrelevant both to the human predicament and to its solution; or (2) sin (as "unbelief," an ungodly attitude, or something similar) is the source and cause of immoral behavior, a conclusion that makes sin—in conjunction with the behavior that results from it—a thing of the past for those who "believe." In each case, salvation is "realized" for John in the emergence of faith, at least with respect to what believers *do*. Both lines of interpretation consequently raise questions about the extent to which John may be said to present salvation as a process of bodily transformation, since in each case John is found to prioritize mental perception to such a degree that human behavior, in John's view of things, is either irrelevant or wholly determined by a moment of decision. A few scholars (e.g., Hasitschka) depart somewhat from these lines of interpretation in the sense that they do not equate sin in John's Gospel with "unbelief" and, also, find John to present salvation as a process, but these scholars nevertheless seem to maintain that the problem of sin *itself* is resolved for John in the emergence of faith. As a result, the implications noted above still stand. Whether, for John, sin's power is not destroyed in the emergence of belief, but instead factors into salvation as an ongoing process and experience, is a question scholars either find John to answer in the negative or assume John answers in the negative. It would appear, in light of the conclusions of scholarship, then, that John is uninterested in human morality, paints a rather naïve portrait of the Christian life, or suggests that something is terribly wrong in the life of the Christian community (for here sin and wrongdoing should be nonexistent).

Considering Experience

Do these lines of interpretation do justice to the Gospel of John? Might John have something to say about sin in the lives of those who believe, for instance? Some scholars, ostensibly on the basis of personal experience, have voiced similar concerns with respect to the Fourth Gospel. Walter Grundmann finds that, in John's Gospel, sin is destroyed when a person decides in favor of Christ (following Bultmann et al.), and Grundmann observes as a consequence that John's portrayal of sin and salvation constitutes "a contradiction to the reality of the Christian community, which in practice is not without sin. Here is a serious problem."⁴⁷ Grundmann attempts to alleviate the

---

[46] Scrutton, "Salvation," 366–7. Scrutton explains that salvation according to a revelatory model is not "primarily moral," and that "while ethical behavior and moral striving may *result* from the salvation of the individual, moral perfection is not viewed as the means to salvation or the way by which salvation is accomplished" (362; italics original).

[47] Grundmann, *TDNT* 1:307.

difficulty by referring to statements in 1 John (2:1; 5:16) that speak of sin as an enduring influence and factor in the lives of believers.[48] Yet, because of Grundmann's conclusion about sin in John's *Gospel*, the apparent contradiction Grundmann observes between the Gospel and the experience of the Christian community remains.

Craig Koester perceives a possible contradiction between the Fourth Gospel's anthropology and human experience when he asks whether John's portrait of the human condition bears "any resemblance to human life as it is actually lived."[49] Koester explains that John's use of imagery "accents the differences between belief and unbelief and between life and death, but when taken alone these contrasts can seem simplistic. One might conclude that people either know nothing of God or they know him completely, that they are either in the darkness or are fully enlightened."[50] Koester finds such an assessment of John's Gospel to be inadequate, on the basis of John's portrayal of Nicodemus, the Samaritan woman, and the man born blind, and Koester concludes that, although "separation from God" is overcome for John through faith, this separation "does not fully go away" in the lives of believers. Its denouement will occur only when the faithful "see Jesus face to face." Yet, because Koester explains sin as "unbelief," it seems that here once again John is understood to present the problem of sin as rectified or resolved in the emergence of belief (rather than as, say, an aspect of the experience of separation from God that "does not fully go away" in the moment one believes).

Considering Christian Theology

There are perhaps Christian theological traditions that conceive of salvation in ways that align with the soteriology scholars commonly find in the Gospel of John, according to which salvation from sin (if not the plight as a whole) is realized in the moment one comes to believe in Jesus. But, there are certainly Christian theological traditions with which such a soteriology does not align, and that consequently may be found—in concert with personal experience—to call into question the interpretations of John reviewed above. In Eastern Orthodox theology, for example, the human predicament is often described as *the way* human beings live in relationship with God and one another, the rectification of which is found to consist of a soteriological process that involves, among other things, ascetic struggle.[51] Here, the human predicament is wholistic and

---

[48] Richard B. Hays takes a similar approach in his book, *The Moral Vision of the New Testament: A Contemporary Introduction to New Testament Ethics* (San Francisco, CA: HarperOne, 1996), 154–5 (cf. 150).
[49] Koester, "What Does It Mean to Be Human?" 417.
[50] Koester, "What Does It Mean to Be Human?" 417.
[51] About this soteriology and the ascetic struggle it is found to involve, Andrew Louth writes:

> Th[e] reconstitution of human nature is something impossible without the grace of God, without everything implied in God the Word's living out what it is to be human, and thereby on the one hand showing us what it is to be truly human, and on the other experiencing and overcoming the accumulated power of evil that has manifested itself in human nature and human affairs—ultimately experiencing and overcoming the power of death itself. This reconstitution of our human nature is therefore something beyond our human powers—no self-help will be anywhere near adequate—but on the other hand it is something that

comprehensive in scope. It necessarily involves human behavior and the condition or state of bodily life. This assessment of the human plight is discerned ultimately in the light of Jesus, who is understood to be the realization and embodiment of what it means to be human. Jesus, according to this theological tradition, is the image and likeness of God in whose image and pattern human beings have been created. Jesus is therefore not only or merely "the revealer"—Jesus is the incarnation of and measure for the way human beings are to live in relationship with God and one another. This soteriology is called "theosis," and in the Christian "West" there is renewed interest in this ecclesial teaching.[52] It is an ancient ecclesial teaching that gained prominence initially in the

> involves the most profound commitment of our human powers; it is not a change in which we will be passively put right—some sort of moral and spiritual surgery—it is a change that requires our utmost cooperation, that calls for truly ascetic struggle. No theology can call itself Orthodox in the true sense that does not embrace such an ascetic commitment. ("The Place of Theosis in Orthodox Theology," in *Partakers of the Divine Nature: The History and Development of Deification in the Christian Traditions*, ed. Michael J. Christensen and Jeffery A. Wittung [Grand Rapids, MI: Baker, 2007], 37)

[52] On the history and/or theology of the Christian teaching of theosis, see Jules Gross, *The Divinization of the Christian according to the Greek Fathers*, trans. Paul A. Onica (Anaheim, CA: A & C Press, 2002); trans. of *La divinization du chrétien d'après les pères grecs: Contribution historique à la doctrine de la grâce* (Paris: Gabalda, 1938); Andreas Theodorou, "Die Lehre von der Vergottung des Menschen bei den griechischen Kirchenvätern," KD 7 (1961): 283–310; Myrrha Lot-Borodine, *La Déification de l'homme selon la doctrine des Pères grecs* (Paris: Cerf, 1970; repr., Paris: Cerf, 2011); Vladimir Lossky, *In the Image and Likeness of God* (Crestwood, NY: St. Vladimir's Seminary Press, 1974); Georgios I. Mantzaridis, *The Deification of Man: Saint Gregory Palamas and the Orthodox Tradition*, trans. Liadain Sherrard, Contemporary Greek Theologians 2 (Crestwood, NY: St. Vladimir's Seminary Press, 1984); Christos Yannaras, *The Freedom of Morality*, trans. Elizabeth Briere, Contemporary Greek Theologians 3 (Crestwood, NY: St. Vladimir's Seminary Press, 1984); John D. Zizioulas, *Being as Communion: Studies in Personhood and the Church*, Contemporary Greek Theologians 4 (Crestwood, NY: St. Vladimir's Seminary Press, 1985); Panayiotis Nellas, *Deification in Christ: Orthodox Perspectives on the Nature of the Human Person*, trans. Norman Russell, Contemporary Greek Theologians 5 (Crestwood, NY: St. Vladimir's Seminary Press, 1987); Vladimir Lossky, *The Mystical Theology of the Eastern Church* (Crestwood, NY: St Vladimir's Seminary Press, 1997); John Meyendorff, *A Study of Gregory Palamas*, trans. George Lawrence (Crestwood, NY: St. Vladimir's Seminary Press, 1998); Christos Yannaras, *Elements of Faith: An Introduction to Orthodox Theology*, trans. Keith Schram (Edinburgh: T&T Clark, 1991); John Behr, *The Mystery of Christ: Life in Death* (Crestwood, NY: St. Vladimir's Seminary Press, 2006); Stephen Finlan and Vladimir Kharlamov, eds., *Theōsis: Deification in Christian Theology*, PTMS 52 (Eugene, OR: Pickwick, 2006); John D. Zizioulas, *Communion and Otherness: Further Studies in Personhood and the Church*, ed. Paul McPartlan (London: T&T Clark, 2006); Christos Yannaras, *Person and Eros*, trans. Norman Russell (Brookline, MA: Holy Cross Orthodox Press, 2007); Christensen and Wittung, *Partakers of the Divine Nature*; Norman Russell, *The Doctrine of Deification in the Greek Patristic Tradition*, OECS (Oxford: Oxford University Press, 2009); Norman Russell, *Fellow Workers with God: Orthodox Thinking on Theosis*, Foundations Series 5 (Crestwood, NY: St. Vladimir's Seminary Press, 2009); Paul M. Collins, *Partaking in Divine Nature: Deification and Communion*, T&T Clark Theology (London: T&T Clark, 2010); Vladimir Kharlamov, ed., *Theosis: Deification in Christian Theology*, PTMS 156 (Eugene, OR: Pickwick, 2011). For evidence of renewed interest in theosis in the Christian "West," see, e.g., Veli-Matti Kärkkäinen, *One with God: Salvation as Deification and Justification* (Collegeville, MN: Liturgical Press, 2004); Myk Habets, "Reforming Theōsis," in Finlan and Kharlamov, *Theōsis*, 146–67; Myk Habets, *Theosis in the Theology of Thomas Torrance*, Ashgate New Critical Thinking in Religion, Theology, and Biblical Studies (Burlington, VT: Ashgate, 2009); Mark S. Medley, "Participation in God: The Appropriation of Theosis by Contemporary Baptist Theologians," in Kharlamov, *Theosis*, 205–46; Jordan Cooper, *Christification: A Lutheran Approach to Theosis* (Eugene, OR: Wipf and Stock, 2014). On the teaching's depreciation in the West, Louth writes, "For whatever reasons, the doctrine of deification ceased to have a central role in Western theology from about the twelfth century, though it had a continuing place among the mystics, with

Greek patristic tradition and that gives shape to modern Orthodox theology.[53] Early church fathers who are commonly regarded as proponents include Irenaeus of Lyons, Clement of Alexandria, Athanasius of Alexandria, the Cappadocians (Basil of Caesarea, Gregory of Nazianzus, and Gregory of Nyssa), and Maximus the Confessor.[54]

With respect to the matter at hand, what makes this theological tradition particularly relevant is the fact that the teaching of theosis is in part the product of the church's interpretation of and reflection on the Gospel of John.[55] Proponents of theosis frequently draw on John's Gospel (by means of citations and allusions) to express, clarify, and/or substantiate the teaching.[56] Some excerpts from proponents of the teaching will serve to illustrate this point. We will hear presently from Irenaeus and Maximus the Confessor.

Irenaeus (born ca. 150), in the course of arguing in his *Adversus haereses* that the crucified Jesus and the divine Word are one and the same person, explains that those

---

all the marginalization, and suspicion, and also allure, that such relegation entailed" ("The Place of Theosis," 33). For a historical survey of theosis in the West see Collins, *Partaking in Divine Nature*, 111–70.

[53] Louth: "the doctrine of deification in Orthodox theology is not some isolated *theologoumenon*, but has what one might call structural significance. ... [D]eification, by the place it occupies in Orthodox theology, determines the shape of that theology" ("The Place of Theosis," 43).

[54] Significant texts include Irenaeus, *Haer.* 3.4.2, 3.6.1, 3.16.9, 3.18.1, 3.19.1, 4.38.4, 5.1.1, 5.16.2; Clement of Alexandria, *Protr.* 1, 11–12, *Paed.* 1.5, 1.6, 1.12, 3.1, *Strom.* 5.10, 7.16; Athanasius, *Inc.* 9, 13, 16, 54, *C. Ar.* 1.9, 2.69–70, 3.20, 3.34, *Decr.* 14, *Ep. Serap.* 1.24, *Syn.* 51, *Ep. Adelph.* 4; Gregory of Nazianzus, *Or.* 1.5, *Ep.* 101; Gregory of Nyssa, *Or. dom.* 5, *De Beat.* 5, *Apoll.* 11, 53, *Or. catech.* 25–26, 32, 35, 37, *V. Mos.* 2; Maximus the Confessor, *Or. dom.* 5, *Amb.* 7, 42, *Ad Thal.* 2, 21–22, 54, 64. See also Cyril of Alexandria, *Dial. Trin.* 7.639–644, *In Jo.* 1.9.91–93, 4.2.363, 12.1.1088; Dionysius the Areopagite (Pseudo-Dionysius), *Eccl. hier.* 1.3, 2.2.1, 3.3.11–12.

[55] On this point see Gross, *Divinization*, 2, 80–92; Theodorou, "Die Lehre von der Vergottung des Menschen," 286–9; David L. Balás, "Divinization," in *Encyclopedia of Early Christianity*, ed. Everett Ferguson, 2nd ed. (New York: Garland, 1997), 338–40; Russell, *Deification*, 11, 87–9; Russell, *Fellow Workers with God*, 58–9; Stephen Thomas, *Deification in the Eastern Orthodox Tradition: A Biblical Perspective*, Gorgias Eastern Christian Studies 2 (Piscataway, NJ: Gorgias Press, 2007), 2, 163–8; Collins, *Partaking in Divine Nature*, 38, 46–7; Stephen Finlan, "Deification in Jesus' Teaching," in Kharlamov, *Theosis*, 21–41 (see especially 31–5); Athanasios Despotis, "From Conversion according to Paul and 'John' to Theosis in the Greek Patristic Tradition," *HBT* 38 (2016): 88–109. Maurice F. Wiles says the following about the importance of the Gospel of John for the soteriology and theology of the Greek patristic tradition:

> The dominant conception of salvation in the whole tradition of early Greek theology is the bridging of the gap between the human and the divine, the mortal and the immortal, in the person of the God-man Christ Jesus. The nature of the union of human and divine in his person is thus directly related to the nature of the salvation that he brought. ... Moreover, if there is any one major strand of New Testament thought from which this whole tradition springs it is the thought of the Fourth Gospel. (*The Spiritual Gospel: The Interpretation of the Fourth Gospel in the Early Church* [Cambridge: Cambridge University Press, 1960], 148)

[56] It is worth noting that the Christian teaching of theosis, as developed particularly by patristic and Orthodox theology, is by no means monolithic or uniform. Proponents of the teaching formulate their contentions and points of emphasis in light of and in conversation with their respective contexts. Strictly speaking, there is not one Christian doctrine of theosis but many. Nevertheless, that there is in fact much accord and continuity between the various proponents of theosis becomes evident when the primary sources are examined. As such, in speaking of "the Christian teaching of theosis" I refer to and prioritize the continuity of this theological tradition, to no exclusion of the various conceptual and semantic differences belonging to this tradition. On this continuity, see, e.g., Russell, *Fellow Workers*, 26, 30, 172.

who assert that Jesus was only a mere man deprive themselves of God's "gift of grace" (*Haer.* 3.19.1, cited below). This grace, Irenaeus goes on to say, is the divine work of "adoption," which consists of God's fashioning of believers in the image and likeness of God. This divine work brings about liberation for human beings from Adam's disobedience and its consequences, and it is possible only because the divine Word "became flesh." Irenaeus is worth quoting here at length:

> But again, those who assert that He was simply a mere man, begotten by Joseph, remaining in the bondage of the old disobedience, are in a state of death; having been not as yet joined to the Word of God the Father, nor receiving liberty through the Son, as He does Himself declare: "If the Son shall make you free, you shall be free indeed." But, being ignorant of Him who from the Virgin is Emmanuel, they are deprived of His gift, which is eternal life; and not receiving the incorruptible Word, they remain in mortal flesh, and are debtors to death, not obtaining the antidote of life. To whom the Word says, mentioning His own gift of grace: "I said, You are all children of the Highest, and gods; but you shall die like human beings." He speaks undoubtedly these words to those who have not received the gift of adoption, but who despise the incarnation of the pure generation of the Word of God, defraud human nature of promotion into God, and prove themselves ungrateful to the Word of God, who became flesh for them. For it was for this end that the Word of God was made a human being, and He who was the Son of God became the Human One, that human nature, having been taken into the Word, and receiving the adoption, might become the Son of God. For by no other means could we have attained to incorruptibility and immortality, unless we had been united to incorruptibility and immortality. But how could we be joined to incorruptibility and immortality, unless, first, incorruptibility and immortality had become that which we also are, so that the corruptible might be swallowed up by incorruptibility, and the mortal by immortality, that we might receive the adoption of children.[57]

Here, Irenaeus cites and evokes the Fourth Gospel (John 8:36, 10:34, and 1:14 are respectively quoted or paraphrased) in order to express and underscore the salvific significance of Jesus's divinity: the Word's incarnation provides the basis of God's gift to human beings of adoption and liberation from the bondage of sin and death. Those who receive God's gift of adoption are "united" with the Son's life and become fashioned in the divine image and likeness (cf. *Haer.* 5.1.3). And, importantly, integral to this soteriology is the point that the life of the incarnate Word *interprets* human sinfulness and death: the "antidote" that is the incarnate Word's own incorruptibility and immortality, which believers are said to "receive" and "attain," illumines human corruptibility and mortality as a problem. The flesh's becoming Word (i.e., "that human nature ... might become the Son of God") is an important reason why the Word has

---

[57] *Haer.* 3.19.1 (SC 211:370–375; *ANF* 1:448–49). Throughout the present study, translations of early church fathers not under copyright (such as *ANF*) have been modified where necessary for the purpose of gender inclusivity.

become flesh.[58] This Christological and soteriological perspective, according to which Jesus's mode of life is the *telos* that sets in relief the human predicament, is developed further in *Haer*. 5.16.2 (cited below). Note here that Irenaeus again draws on the Gospel of John to explain and substantiate this perspective. The Word of God, who "from the beginning even to the end" (5.16.1) forms and prepares human beings for life,

> was manifested when the Word of God was made a human being, assimilating Himself to humanity, and humanity to Himself, so that by means of their resemblance to the Son, human beings might become precious to the Father. For in times long past, it was *said* that the human being was created after the image of God, but it was not [actually] *shown*; for the Word was as yet invisible, after whose image the human being was created. Wherefore also humanity did easily lose the similitude. When, however, the Word of God became flesh [σὰρξ ἐγένετο ὁ λόγος τοῦ θεοῦ], He confirmed both of these: for He both showed forth the image truly, since He became Himself what was His image; and He re-established the similitude after a sure manner, by assimilating man to the invisible Father through means of the visible Word.[59]

For Irenaeus, the Word of God, the divine Son of the Father, is the measure of human life because he is the image and likeness of God, *in whose image and pattern* human beings have been created. When, therefore, "the Word of God became flesh," the extent to which human beings have lost "the similitude" was revealed through the dissimilarity of human beings with God's image and likeness, and especially through their hostility toward him. The vocation to which human beings are called is to be fashioned freely in the image and likeness of God, which is the Son, and so it is by means of their resemblance to the Son, Irenaeus says, that human beings "become precious to the Father."

A similar reading of the Fourth Gospel is found in the work of Maximus the Confessor (d. 662). During his response to the presbyter Thalassius regarding certain interpretive difficulties in the book of Jonah (*Ad Thal*. 64), Maximus describes three "laws" he finds to be at work in God's economy, the first two of which ("the natural law" and "the scriptural law") culminate in the third ("the law of grace").[60] This third law, the law of grace, serves to direct believers toward their proper manner and pattern of life, which is Christ, in whose image and likeness human beings have been created.[61] Maximus finds John 15:13 to summarize this life:

---

[58] Irenaeus's conception of an asymmetrical "exchange" in the person of Christ is articulated perhaps most famously in the preface of *Haer*. 5 (*ANF* 1:526): here we are exhorted to follow "the only true and steadfast Teacher, the Word of God, our Lord Jesus Christ, who did, through his transcendent love, become what we are, that He might bring us to be even what He is Himself."

[59] *Haer*. 5.16.2 (SC 153:216; *ANF* 1:544; trans. modified).

[60] Paul M. Blowers provides a concise and helpful explanation of these laws in the introduction to *On the Cosmic Mystery of Jesus Christ: Selected Writings from St Maximus the Confessor*, trans. Paul M. Blowers and Robert Louis Wilken, Popular Patristics Series 25 (Crestwood, NY: St. Vladimir's Seminary Press, 2003), 28–9.

[61] Blowers explains that the law of grace "leads humanity to the ultimate imitation of the love of Christ demonstrated in the incarnation, a love which raises us to the level of loving others even above

Finally, the law of grace teaches those who follow it directly to imitate God himself, who, if I may rightly say so, loves us, his virtual enemies because of sin, more than himself, such that, even though he himself transcends every essence and nature, he consented to enter our human essence without undergoing change, and, while retaining his transcendence, to become a man and willingly to interact as one among men. He did not refuse to take our condemnation on himself, and indeed, the more he himself became a man by nature in his incarnation, the more he deified us by grace, so that we would not only learn naturally to care for one another, and spiritually to love others as ourselves, but also like God to be concerned for others more than for ourselves, even to the point of proving that love to others by being ready to die voluntarily and virtuously for others. For as the Lord says, "There is no greater love than this, that a man lay down his life for his friend."[62]

For Maximus, Christ's incarnation allows human beings to become like God and love others—even their enemies—more than themselves, so much so that believers in Christ, by means of the grace of deification, become cruciform. Like Irenaeus, Maximus finds the Gospel of John to present Jesus as the incarnation and realization of the life—the way of living—that is the solution to and diagnosis of the human predicament.

These excerpts from Irenaeus and Maximus serve here as a sample of an ancient and ongoing tradition of John's reception that understands John's soteriology in terms of, and as advocating, theosis.[63] In light of this interpretive tradition, the question of the extent to which Johannine scholarship has satisfactorily traced John's presentation of sin, the human predicament, and salvation gains further significance. Of course, it may simply be that the Gospel of John offers a different soteriology than that of certain streams of Christian theology. But the fact that the ecclesial teaching of theosis, for instance, is in part the product of the church's reading of the Gospel of John raises questions about the true character of John's soteriology and theology.[64] Do the lines of interpretation we have traced in Johannine scholarship accurately reflect John's delineation of sin and the human predicament more broadly? Might John's portrayal of both the plight and its solution indicate that, for John, salvation consists of far more than the emergence of belief in a moment of decision?

---

ourselves, a sure sign of the radical grace of deification" ("Introduction," in *On the Cosmic Mystery of Jesus Christ*, 29).

[62] *Ad Thal.* 64 (CCSG 22:237; trans. Blowers).

[63] For additional instances of such readings of John, see, e.g., Origen, *Comm. Jo.* 19.1; Athanasius, *Inc.* 14, *C. Ar.* 3.19–23; John Chrysostom, *Hom. Jo.* 11.1; Augustine, *Serm.* 31.6, 77.9; Cyril of Alexandria, *In Jo.* 1.9.91–93; Dionysius the Areopagite (Pseudo-Dionysius), *Eccl. hier.* 2.1, 2.2.1; Maximus the Confessor, *Ad Thal.* 2, 6; Thomas Aquinas, *Super ev. Joh.* 15.2; Gregory Palamas, *Triads* 3.1.30; Lossky, *Mystical Theology*, 162; Zizioulas, *Being as Communion*, 146–7 (cf. 67–122); Behr, *The Mystery of Christ*, 107–8 (cf. 38–9).

[64] Other studies on the Gospel of John that in some way consider the potential of theosis as an interpretive aid include David Crump, "Re-examining the Johannine Trinity: Perichoresis or Deification?" *SJT* 59 (2006): 395–412; Andrew J. Byers, *Ecclesiology and Theosis in the Gospel of John*, SNTSMS 166 (Cambridge: Cambridge University Press, 2017); and Michael J. Gorman, *Abide and Go: Missional Theosis in the Gospel of John*, Didsbury Lectures Series (Eugene, OR: Cascade, 2018). See also Kent Brower, *Holiness in the Gospels* (Kansas City, MO: Beacon Hill, 2005), 64, 74–6.

Thesis, Method, and Program

The present study demonstrates that, in fact, John's portrayal of the human predicament aligns more with certain streams of Christian theology, such as Orthodox theology, than with the conclusions of scholarship reviewed above. What human beings *do*, in John's view of things, is neither irrelevant nor wholly determined by a moment of "decision." These points are corollaries of my thesis, though. If, for John, Jesus is "the way" that leads to the Father (14:4–5), the way that is "truth" and "life" (14:6), then it seems that Jesus is for John the measure or point of reference for the way human beings are to live, and that Jesus shows to be false the way of "the world," inasmuch as the world's inhabitants do not affirm, follow, and resemble him. My thesis is this: the human predicament in the Gospel of John is a way or manner of life. This way of life has the following characteristics: (1) it consists of ignorance of and unfaithfulness to God, of illness or bodily infirmity, and of death; (2) it is the way of "the world," that is, of human beings as a whole; (3) it was the way of "the world" prior to Jesus's advent; and (4) it continues to affect or influence human beings following the emergence of belief, inclining believers toward ensuing behavior and thinking that is akin to that which has preceded. The sinful inclination of human beings, for instance, is not destroyed for John in the moment one believes.[65] So too do the realities of illness and death persist in the lives of believers. All of this indicates, consequently, that salvation is for John a process that involves the transformation of *what believers do* and *how they live in relationship with God and others*.

On the basis of our exegetical analysis, assessments that find "sin" in John's Gospel to be defeated or resolved when a person "believes" (hence sin as "unbelief"), and to be void of significance with respect to morality and human behavior, will be shown to be wide of the mark. It will be shown that John portrays a human predicament that has traversed the bounds of "spiritual blindness" or "ignorance" narrowly conceived, indicating the insufficiency of such characterizations. In addition to John's delineation of "sin," then, what the Gospel says about ignorance and knowledge of God, "darkness" and "light," as well as "death" and "life," will be considered and examined, given that these matters are interrelated and are integral to John's portrayal of the human predicament. The question of "disability" in John's Gospel will be explored as well, given

---

[65] In light of the fact that John's Gospel, on multiple occasions, depicts disciples of Jesus as eventually abandoning him (see, e.g., 6:60–66; 13:27), Marianne Meye Thompson writes:

> If it is true that those who have faith have "passed from death to life," it is also true that some of those who had once been Jesus' disciples abandoned, deserted, and betrayed him. It is apparently not the initial moment of faith that determines whether one has "passed from death to life"; it is the ending of the story that counts. ("When the Ending Is Not the End," in *The Ending of Mark and the Ends of God: Essays in Memory of Donald Harrisville Juel*, ed. Beverly Roberts Gaventa and Patrick D. Miller [Louisville, KY: Westminster John Knox, 2005], 72)

> Thompson goes on to ask, "How then does one explain those who abandon Jesus?" (74). I argue below that, for John, it is the wayward manner of life human beings embody and perpetuate, prior to belief in Jesus, that continues to influence human beings subsequent to belief's inception, and that can lead to the dissipation of belief if one does not keep Jesus's word.

that Jesus is shown on more than one occasion to deliver someone from (what we now understand and refer to as) "disability."⁶⁶ Furthermore, since the human predicament relates directly to its "solution" and vice versa, throughout our analysis we will strive not to lose sight of the solution to the human predicament in John's Gospel, which is undoubtedly Jesus (1:29; 4:42; 6:35; 8:12; 11:25; 14:6, 19c). John's portrayal of Jesus and his mission will come into focus especially in Chapter 2, during our analysis of John's prologue. It would prove difficult in fact to examine the human predicament in John's Gospel *without* considering Jesus, since Jesus is for John "the light" that contrasts "the darkness," "life" in the face of "death," and the one who "knows" God vis-à-vis a world that does not. As we will see below, it seems that, for John, the human predicament is discerned ultimately in light of Jesus: the world and, in particular, God's "own" people do not live and do as Jesus does.⁶⁷

With regard to exegetical method, our goal is to read the Gospel of John cooperatively and competently, to allow John to form our readerly competence.⁶⁸ Accordingly, narrative criticism will be utilized so as to attend to John's narrative cues and features (such as sequence, duration, structure, and characterization). Both the speech and actions of Jesus (the narrative's key figure), and of other characters in John's Gospel, will be a focus of our attention.⁶⁹ The prologue will hold considerable sway

---

⁶⁶ A definition of "disability" is provided in Chapter 3.

⁶⁷ To find the Fourth Gospel to portray Jesus in this way results, on the one hand, in disagreement with Wayne A. Meeks's opinion that John "does not provide a plausible and universalizable model for behavior" ("The Ethics of the Fourth Evangelist," in *Exploring the Gospel of John: In Honor of D. Moody Smith*, ed. R. Alan Culpepper and C. Clifton Black [Louisville, KY: Westminster John Knox, 1996], 318 n.13) and, on the other hand, in agreement with Vellanickal's point that, in John's Gospel, the life of Jesus is the measure of the life of all those who confess and follow him ("the measure of sonship to God is the life of sonship in Christ" [*Divine Sonship*, 262]). Udo Schnelle makes a point similar to that of Vellanickal: for John, Jesus

> is pure humanity. ... If believers remain in the Word Jesus Christ, they will participate in his abundant life. When they receive the love of the Son of God, they become true human beings themselves and thus become human to each other. The human realization of God in Jesus Christ ... makes possible for John the self-realization of human beings in the way of love. (*The Human Condition: Anthropology in the Teachings of Jesus, Paul, and John*, trans. O. C. Dean Jr. [Minneapolis, MN: Fortress, 1996], 116)

Note also the reading of C. H. Dodd, who observes that John's distinctive language of mutual indwelling refers to "a personal relation with a living God, mediated through a concrete historical personality, in whom that relation is original and perfect"; Jesus is for John "archetypal at least in the sense that his relation to the Father is the archetype of the true and ultimate relation of men to God. ... He was the true self of the human race, standing in that perfect union with God to which others can attain only as they are incorporate in Him" (*The Interpretation of the Fourth Gospel* [Cambridge: Cambridge University Press, 1953; repr., Cambridge: Cambridge University Press, 1988], 197, 244, 249). See further Franz Mussner, *ZΩH: Die Anschauung vom "Leben" im Vierten Evangelium, unter Berücksichtigung der Johannesbriefe*, Münchener theologische Studien, historische Abteilung (München: Karl Zink, 1952), 74–90, 110–11, 143–4; Hasitschka, *Befreiung*, 167, 418–19; cf. Fredrik Wagener, *Figuren als Handlungsmodelle: Simon Petrus, die samaritische Frau, Judas und Thomas als Zugänge zu einer narrativen Ethik des Johannesevangeliums*, WUNT 2/408 (Tübingen: Mohr Siebeck, 2015), 563, 566–7.

⁶⁸ On the reader's role to receive texts cooperatively and complete them competently in the generation of meaning, see Umberto Eco, *The Role of the Reader: Explorations in the Semiotics of Texts* (London: Hutchinson, 1981).

⁶⁹ Richard A. Burridge emphasizes the importance of appreciating both the words and actions of Jesus in the Gospel narratives in his *Imitating Jesus: An Inclusive Approach to New Testament Ethics* (Grand

for the interpretation of John's Gospel as a whole.[70] Additionally, certain sensibilities of linguistic analysis will guide our assessment of various terms and themes in John's Gospel.[71] Consideration of the sociohistorical environment and cultural matrix in which the Gospel of John was produced, particularly texts that possess a thematic and linguistic affinity with John (e.g., the Johannine Epistles), will be a constant, given that the Gospel of John is a cultural product.

In the chapters that follow, then, we will turn our attention to passages in the Gospel of John in which a human "predicament" or "plight" may be said to come to the fore. We will begin in Chapter 2 with John's prologue (1:1–18). The prologue introduces a number of the narrative's key themes (such as "life," "light," "darkness," and ignorance of God) and in certain ways constitutes a synopsis of the narrative as a whole (e.g., both Jesus's rejection and reception are described throughout vv. 4–18). Most importantly, it is in these opening lines that John introduces both the human predicament and its solution. In Chapter 3 we move forward in John's narrative to Jesus's healing of a man with a disabling illness at Bethzatha and Jesus's consequent discourse (5:1–29). Here, the matters of illness or bodily infirmity, disability, and death come into focus. That Jesus restores the man both physically and socially and proceeds to speak of the Father and Son's unified intention to deliver human beings from death (to which illness can lead) suggests that illness, disability (in a qualified sense), and death are interrelated aspects of the human predicament for John. This point is confirmed, as we will observe, by John's wider portrayal of Jesus's activity and mission.[72] In Chapter 4 we then turn to

---

Rapids, MI: Eerdmans, 2007), 19–32. This emphasis follows from Burridge's earlier work on the genre of the canonical Gospels (*What Are the Gospels? A Comparison with Greco-Roman Biography*, 2nd ed., The Biblical Resource Series [Grand Rapids, MI: Eerdmans, 2004]). Richard Bauckham modifies Burridge's assessment of the Gospel of John by arguing that the Fourth Gospel most closely parallels ancient historiography (*The Testimony of the Beloved Disciple: Narrative, History, and Theology in the Gospel of John* [Grand Rapids, MI: Baker, 2007], 16–21, 93–112). On the related matter of whether John's Gospel is Christocentric or theocentric, see Marianne Meye Thompson, *The God of the Gospel of John* (Grand Rapids, MI: Eerdmans, 2001).

[70] Recent endorsements for privileging the prologue as an interpretive key include Martin Hengel, "The Prologue of the Gospel of John as the Gateway to Christological Truth," in Bauckham and Mosser, *John and Christian Theology*, 265–94; Christopher W. Skinner, "Misunderstanding, Christology, and Johannine Characterization: Reading John's Characters through the Lens of the Prologue," in *Characters and Characterization in the Gospel of John*, ed. Christopher W. Skinner, LNTS 461 (London: T&T Clark, 2013), 111–25; John Painter, "The Prologue as an Hermeneutical Key to Reading the Fourth Gospel," in *Studies in the Gospel of John and its Christology: Festschrift Gilbert Van Belle*, ed. Joseph Verheyden et al., BETL 265 (Leuven: Peeters, 2014), 37–60.

[71] Specifically, James Barr's point that it is at the level of the sentence and its larger "literary complex" that the sense of a word should ultimately be deduced (*The Semantics of Biblical Language* [London: Oxford University Press, 1961], 262, 269–70) will be important in tracing John's presentation of, for example, "sin."

[72] Concerning John's accounts of Jesus's miracles or signs, Bultmann explains that, originally, "their point lay in the miracle they report, but for the evangelist they take on a symbolic or allegorical meaning" (*Theology*, 2:3). Jean Zumstein expresses this view more recently when he states that, in John's Gospel, "the actions done by Jesus have no meaning in themselves. … [T]hey point beyond themselves to the one who did them in order to reveal through them his distinctive significance" ("The Purpose of the Ministry and Death of Jesus in the Gospel of John," in *The Oxford Handbook of Johannine Studies*, ed. Judith M. Lieu and Martinus C. de Boer [Oxford: Oxford University Press, 2018], 332–3). See also Michael Theobald, "Theologie und Anthropologie: Fundamentaltheologische Aspekte des johanneischen Offenbarungsverständnisses," ZKT 141 (2019): 44–63 (specifically 54–5). The present

Jesus's words about the destructive and coercive influence of "sin," which Jesus offers as he converses with his fellow "Jews" during Tabernacles (8:21–59). "Sin" is here the topic of an extended discussion for the first time (cf. 1:29; 5:14), so it is in connection with this passage that we will consider and examine John's delineation of sin in detail. The dialogue here between Jesus and some fellow "Jews" who believe in him (8:31 and following) will prove crucial in fact for understanding sin in John's Gospel. The study will then conclude in Chapter 5 with a summation of the conclusions reached and some reflection on their implications for John's soteriology and theology.

study challenges this line of interpretation in the sense that it finds John's accounts of Jesus's healings to bear significance beyond the revelatory or symbolic function commonly attributed to them.

2

Life and Light, Darkness and Ignorance of God: The Prologue as Introduction to the Human Predicament and Its Solution

From among the many theological convictions that John's prologue introduces and develops, two in particular will be emphasized in the reading that follows. First, Jesus is the incarnation and realization in the world of true and everlasting life. Jesus, for John, is the inauguration in the world of steadfast love and faithfulness, of the way of life that is "light" and knowledge of God. This life, as that which comes into existence in the world in the person of Jesus, culminates in resurrection from death to life without end. Jesus is therefore the realization of the way human beings are to live in relationship with God and one another. Jesus, for John, is the measure and fulfillment of human life, in the light of which the life of God's "own" people and "the world" as a whole is shown and judged to be false. The human predicament is ultimately discerned and defined in the Gospel of John, then, in the light of Jesus, who is the "solution."

As we will see below, this feature of John's Christology and soteriology may be seen at the very least to qualify the contention, ubiquitous in scholarship, that in John's Gospel Jesus is "the revealer" who saves human beings from a lack of mental perception—commonly described as "ignorance" of God, "spiritual blindness," or something similar—by revealing God. For John, Jesus is undoubtedly "the revealer" in the sense that he reveals God and the way that leads to everlasting life with God. But defining Jesus's mission in John's Gospel simply as one of "revelation" does not do justice to John's presentation of Jesus, for, as our analysis of John's prologue and narrative will demonstrate, Jesus is here shown to do *more* than simply "reveal." We will observe as well that Jesus's mission or soteriological purpose is shown to consist of more than God's "encounter" with and "invitation" to human beings, and to involve more than a purely forensic "atonement." Such characterizations seem in fact to neglect a—if not *the*—principal aspect of Jesus's mission in John's Gospel, which is this: Jesus realizes and establishes in himself, that is, in his "flesh," the relationship with God and way of life that is true and everlasting, which he does so as to be the source or basis of this life in others.

This feature of John's Christology and soteriology sets in relief the human predicament, which leads us to observe and stress a second point. The Johannine themes of "the darkness" and "ignorance" of God, which are introduced in John's prologue and signal a human plight or predicament, attribute to human beings a way of life that is wayward and misguided, a manner of life that contrasts and opposes that of Jesus and, thus, God. "Darkness" (when figurative in meaning) and expressions of a failure on the part of human beings to "know" God describe the character of human beings, the character of the world into and on account of which Jesus is sent. For John, Jesus has come into the world so that human beings may not "remain" or "continue" in the darkness (12:46) and instead know God (17:3), so "the darkness" and "ignorance" of God are ultimately causes, not consequences, of Jesus's advent. They refer to a wayward behavioral pattern on the part of human beings that both preexisted and prompted Jesus's advent.

In demonstrating these points, a rather unique version, evidently, of the "incarnational" interpretation of John 1:3c–4 ("What has come into existence in him, was life") will be advanced. The moral and ethical implications of "light" and "darkness" and of knowledge of God (or lack thereof) will also be highlighted, based on (among other things) the local and wider cotext of John's Gospel. The point that "the darkness" and "ignorance" of God mutually attribute to human beings a behavioral pattern and way of living that is wayward and misguided, and that preexisted and prompted Jesus's advent, will be important to bear in mind when, in Chapters 3 and 4, we turn to the matters of "death" and "sin" in John's Gospel.

The Incarnation of Life and Light in the Darkness

Let us start at the beginning. John's prologue famously commences with the introduction of the Word and his relation to God (τὸν θεόν), and with a description of the Word's role and work in the creation of all things "in the beginning" (vv. 1–3b). Following this, an indication of a problem or predicament appears: the "light," which is the Word and his life (v. 4), "shines in the darkness, and the darkness did not overcome it" (ἡ σκοτία αὐτὸ οὐ κατέλαβεν [v. 5]).[1] In order to apprehend the sense of this "darkness," we must first examine that which it contrasts and opposes, that is, the light and life of the Word (v. 4).

The respective connotations of "life" and "light" in v. 4 depend in part on how vv. 3c–4 are punctuated: should a full stop immediately *follow* the words ὃ γέγονεν in v. 3c (so that the sentence of v. 4 begins, "In him was life") or instead *precede* them (so that the sentence, now spanning vv. 3c–4, begins, "What has come into existence in him, was life")?[2] Although reasonable arguments can be made for either alternative, the internal

---

[1] All translations of biblical texts are my own unless noted otherwise.
[2] There are perhaps other possibilities for the placement of the stop, but translators and commentators routinely affirm one of these two alternatives. Most of the earliest and highly regarded manuscripts (e.g., p⁶⁶, ℵ, A, B, etc.) do not contain punctuation here (on p⁷⁵ see Ed L. Miller, *Salvation-History in the Prologue of John: The Significance of John 1:3/4*, NovTSup 60 [Leiden: Brill, 1989], 37–9). I supply

and external evidence appears to favor the latter reading: the staircase parallelisms of vv. 1–2 and vv. 4–5,³ the internal symmetry of v. 3a–b,⁴ and the testimony of such early church fathers as Clement of Alexandria, Tertullian, and Origen suggest a full stop before ὃ γέγονεν.⁵ Thus we read in vv. 3c–4a: "What has come into existence in him, was life" (ὃ γέγονεν ἐν αὐτῷ ζωὴ ἦν).⁶

At this early juncture, the reference to this emergence of "life," particularly the connotation of ζωή itself, is rather ambiguous. Is the creation of life "in the beginning" (cf. Gen 1) to be understood here?⁷ Many think so.⁸ The prologue begins with God and his Word at the beginning of creation, which is narrated in the imperfect and aorist tenses (vv. 1–3b). The Word's role in the work of creation becomes explicit in v. 3: "all things came into existence (ἐγένετο) through him, and without him not one thing came into existence (ἐγένετο)" (v. 3a–b). The aorist forms of γίνομαι here, in

---

a comma after "him" to distinguish more clearly what I regard to be the relative, substantival clause (on the comma's placement, see Miller, *Salvation-History*, 14, 26, 77–8).

³ "Staircase" parallelism refers to instances "where one line picks up the last principal word of the preceding line" (Brown, *John (I–XII)*, cxxxii). If in v. 3c a stop is placed before ὃ γέγονεν, then such parallelism becomes evident in vv. 3b–c (and thereby accords with that in vv. 1–2 and 4–5) in the sense that it is the subject of the verb γίνομαι in v. 3b and in v. 3c that, while different in each case, ends and commences each line: ... ἐγένετο οὐδὲ ἕν [or οὐδέν]. ὃ γέγονεν. ... The verb γίνομαι would seem to be the key or principal word of this staircase parallelism (cf. ζωή in v. 4 [... ζωὴ ἦν, καὶ ἡ ζωὴ ἦν ...]; σκοτία in v. 5 [... ἐν τῇ σκοτίᾳ φαίνει, καὶ ἡ σκοτία ...]).

⁴ J. Ramsey Michaels (*The Gospel of John*, NICNT [Grand Rapids, MI: Eerdmans, 2010], 51 n.25) displays the symmetry in this way:

πάντα / δι' αὐτοῦ / ἐγένετο,
καὶ χωρὶς αὐτοῦ / ἐγένετο / οὐδὲ ἕν.

⁵ The external evidence for this punctuation also includes C, D, Wˢ, the Old Latin b, Syrus Curetonianus, and Irenaeus (Latin trans.). Modern translations that affirm this reading include the CEB, CEV, NABR, NJB, NLT, and the NRSV; modern commentators include Brooke Foss Westcott (*The Gospel according to St. John: The Greek Text, with Introduction and Notes*, ed. A. Westcott [Grand Rapids, MI: Eerdmans, 1954], 4, 8); J. H. Bernard (*A Critical and Exegetical Commentary on the Gospel according to St. John*, ed. A. H. McNeile, vol. 1, ICC [Edinburgh: T&T Clark, 1928], 3–4); Rudolf Bultmann (*The Gospel of John: A Commentary*, trans. G. R. Beasley-Murray [Oxford: Blackwell, 1971], 36–9); Brown (*John (I–XII)*, 3, 6–7); R. Alan Culpepper (*The Gospel and Letters of John*, Interpreting Biblical Texts [Nashville, TN: Abingdon, 1998], 113, 117); George R. Beasley-Murray (*John*, 2nd ed., WBC 36 [Nashville, TN: Nelson, 1999], 1–2); and Frederick Dale Bruner (*The Gospel of John: A Commentary* [Grand Rapids, MI: Eerdmans, 2012], 3–4, 14–17, 45–7). See also Bruce Vawter, "What Came to Be in Him Was Life (Jn 1,3b–4a)," *CBQ* 25 (1963): 401–6. Kurt Aland provides a detailed argument for this punctuation on the basis of both the external and internal evidence ("Eine Untersuchung zu Joh 1, 3–4: Über die Bedeutung eines Punktes," *ZNW* 59 [1968]: 174–209). Miller finds the external evidence in particular to favor this punctuation, and he finds this reading to be significant for the interpretation of John's Gospel because John 1:1–5 consequently expresses a "salvation-historical perspective": vv. 1–5 depict a chronological progression of God's relationship with and salvific activity in the world, which culminates in the incarnation (vv. 3c–4) (*Salvation-History*, 11–15, 90–109).

⁶ Concerning the text-critical question in v. 4 involving ἦν, although there are good internal and external reasons to read ἐστιν, the ἦν is better attested and seems to be the more difficult reading.

⁷ In John 1:1–3b, an allusion to the creation account of Genesis is suggested by the opening phrase ἐν ἀρχῇ (John 1:1; cf. Gen 1:1), by the additional occurrence of ἐν ἀρχῇ in v. 2, and by the reference in v. 3a to the time when "all things came into existence" (πάντα ... ἐγένετο; cf. Gen 2:4).

⁸ For a brief review of this line of interpretation see Miller, *Salvation-History*, 59–62. Of those interpreters who place the stop before ὃ γέγονεν and, then, find ζωή in v. 4a to refer to creation, Miller cites, in particular, Albin August Van Hoonacker, M.-E. Boismard, and Ignace de la Potterie.

conjunction with the preceding introduction of the Word (vv. 1–2), locate this creation of all things "in the beginning" (vv. 1–2). In what immediately follows this description of the Word's work at the beginning of creation (v. 3a–b), however, the verb γίνομαι occurs again but now in the perfect tense (ὃ γέγονεν ... [v. 3c]), which distinguishes what is said to have "come into existence" here (i.e., "life") from the creation of all things in the beginning (vv. 1–3b). This change in tense suggests that the story John is telling has now transitioned from the beginning of creation (in vv. 1–3b) to a new scene (in v. 3c and following).[9] A new scene is suggested also by the fact that, while in v. 3b John says that all things came into existence "through him" (δι' αὐτοῦ), in vv. 3c–4a John says that ζωή has come into existence "in him" (ἐν αὐτῷ).

Perhaps most important for interpreting the connotation of ζωή (v. 4a), though, and most suggestive of a transition here (in vv. 3c–4a) from the beginning of creation to a new scene is how ζωή is immediately described (v. 4b): "and that life was the light (φῶς) of human beings." In the Gospel of John it is Jesus, the Word become flesh (v. 14), who is this light: "I am the light (φῶς) of the world," Jesus later says; "The one who follows me will not walk in the darkness, but will have the light of life" (8:12). Indeed, in John's Gospel Jesus is "the light" (3:19–21; 9:5; 11:9–10; 12:35–36, 46) as well as "the resurrection and the life" (ζωή [11:25]); he is "the way and the truth and the life" (ζωή [14:6]). Jesus, John explains, has been granted by the Father to have "life in himself" (ἐν ἑαυτῷ [5:26]; note ἐν αὐτῷ in 1:4a), just as the Father does (cf. 1:1). Jesus has come to impart the true and everlasting life (ζωή) that he himself *is* (6:32–35, 48–55). Jesus's followers will therefore live because of him (6:57; 14:19).

To understand the emergence of life described at the outset of John's Gospel (1:3c–4) as referring to the life that emerges in the person of Jesus, in and through his advent, is suggested also by the First Epistle of John: the life (ζωή) that "has appeared" (ἐφανερώθη), which the Johannine community has beheld and proclaims, is "the eternal life that was with the Father," Jesus Christ, the Son of the Father (1 John 1:2–3; cf. ἐφανερώθη in 1 John 3:8).[10] God has given the children of God "eternal life, and this life is in his Son" (ἐν τῷ υἱῷ αὐτοῦ [1 John 5:11]; note again ἐν αὐτῷ in John 1:4a). In light of the ensuing narrative of John's Gospel and, also, in light of the witness of 1 John, then, the scene that, at the outset of John's Gospel, seems to follow that of God and his Word at the beginning of creation (1:1–3b) is the incarnation of God's Word (1:3c–5). In Jesus, who is the divine Word and Son of the Father, life "has come into existence" (v. 3c).[11]

---

[9] Miller makes a similar point: "the perfect γέγονεν ... stands in unmistakable contrast to the two instances of the aorist ἐγένετο in vs. 3. ... We conclude that the shift from the aorist ἐγένετο (twice) in vs. 3 to the perfect γέγονεν in vs. 4a [sic] probably signals the introduction of a new thought" (*Salvation-History*, 81–2).

[10] On the importance of considering the Johannine Epistles for the interpretation of John's Gospel, Frey writes, "The Epistles are the only source which allows a closer look at the community or circle of communities in which the Gospel originates. ... [W]hatever the sequence of the edition of the Gospel and the Epistles was, the Johannine Epistles are the closest commentary on the Gospel, historically and theologically" ("Eschatology," 61).

[11] Although readers (or listeners) unfamiliar with John's Gospel (its proclamation, narrative, and theology) and with the historical milieu in which it was produced (as evinced by, e.g., the Johannine Epistles) would perhaps be unable at this juncture in the Gospel to identify the Word, its life and light, with Jesus, the ensuing narrative of John impels model readers, regardless of prior knowledge,

How can it be that life everlasting (ζωή), divine life, may be said to have *come into existence* in Jesus? Based on John's frequent description of Jesus as the one who has come from God "into the world" (1:9-10; 3:17; 6:33-35; 8:42; 11:27; 12:46; etc.), it seems that, for John, the life of God (ζωή) may be said to have "come into existence" (v. 3c) in the sense that, in the person of Jesus, this life has now come into existence *in the world, as a human being.*[12] In Jesus, the life of God has become "flesh" (σὰρξ ἐγένετο [v. 14a]). The Word's incarnation brings true and everlasting life into existence where it did not exist formerly. Only so, only by means of the Word's incarnation, has this life "appeared" (1 John 1:2), has it been "revealed" (John 1:14b, 18; 14:7-11).[13] This life "continues to shine" (φαίνει) in the darkness (v. 5) because, although Jesus was met in the world by an opposition that would eventually bring about his death (hence the imperfect ἦν [2x] in 1:4), Jesus is "the resurrection and the life" (11:25; 20:26-28), the divine Word and Son of the Father. Because Jesus lives, all those who believe and remain in him will live because of him (6:57; 14:19). They will become "children of light" (12:36). The Word's incarnation of true and everlasting life is thus of ongoing and everlasting significance (hence the perfect γέγονεν in v. 3c).

In accordance with the wider cotext of John's Gospel, then, the "life" (ζωή) that, in the incarnate Word, has come into existence in the world and become human (1:3c-4), signifies "eternal life," life without end (cf. 3:15-16, 36; 6:40, 50-51, 58; 10:28).[14] But the fact that the Word and his life are said to be the "light" of human beings (1:4b, 9) suggests that ζωή signifies also, simultaneously and as such, a certain manner or

---

to make the connection expounded above as the narrative unfolds and is apprehended. Van der Watt concludes somewhat similarly that, in light of what follows in John's prologue and narrative, "the best way to explain the metaphorical dynamics in v. 4 is to see ἡ ζωή [v. 4b] as personified. Life is then the vehicle of a submerged metaphor, of which the submerged tenor is Jesus (i.e. Jesus is life)" (*Family of the King*, 236).

[12] To explain further, because the Word was with God in the beginning (v. 1), "before the world was made" (17:5), and because the life of the Word is the life of God (cf. 1:1, 18; 5:26), "what has come into existence in him" (ὃ γέγονεν ἐν αὐτῷ) refers not to the coming into existence of the life of the Word *itself*, but to the coming into existence of the life of the Word *in the world* (1:9-10; cf. again 3:17, 19; 12:46; 16:28). Jesus is the Word become "flesh" (σὰρξ ἐγένετο; 1:14; cf. 6:51). That is, in Jesus (who is one person; cf., e.g., 1:1, 4, 18; 5:26; 8:12, 58; 12:41; 17:5; 20:28) the life of God has come into existence in the world as a human being. In Jesus the life of God has become human.

[13] Miller, who likewise places the stop before ὃ γέγονεν in v. 3c, notes that the verb γίνομαι can bear "a kind of ontological-existential signification ('to be,' 'to become,' 'to come into being')" as well as "a historical-temporal signification ('to come to pass,' 'come on the scene,' 'appear,' 'happen,' 'occur')" (*Salvation-History*, 79). Miller decides between these senses and prefers the latter, translating γέγονεν in v. 3c as "has appeared." In doing so, though, he recognizes that γίνομαι now bears a sense in v. 3c different from its two immediately preceding occurrences in vv. 3a and 3b: "it does not follow from the fact that the ἐγένετο in vs. 3 bears the first of these meanings that γέγονεν in vs. 4 [*sic*] must also" (79). This is of course true, but it is perhaps the case that the impetus for Miller's decision to veer from the "ontological" sense of γέγονεν in v. 3c (which is again the sense of the preceding occurrences) is, at least in part, a supposed difficulty of understanding how γίνομαι in v. 3c can bear its ontological sense when ζωή is the predicate nominative. In my view, it is John's emphasis on the Word's "becoming flesh," on Jesus's coming from the Father "into the world" to be and impart life, that makes the ontological sense of γίνομαι not only comprehensible but preferable. For John, Jesus is not merely the historical "appearance" or manifestation of life. Jesus *is* life (11:25; 14:6); he is the incarnation of life (1:14; 6:48-51). It is Jesus's incarnation of life that makes life manifest in the world.

[14] Significantly, although the Father and Son are said to have this life (ζωή) in themselves (5:26), the same is never said about believers. Life may be said to be "in" believers (cf. 6:53) only insofar as Jesus is "in" them and insofar as believers abide "in" Jesus.

way of life.¹⁵ In Israel's Scriptures, as well as in the literature of Second Temple Judaism, "light" (אוֹר; φῶς) is often associated with the "way" or "path" of the righteous; it at times signifies (figuratively) righteousness, goodness, and truth, while "darkness" (e.g., אֲפֵלָה; σκότος) signifies (figuratively) the way and life of the wicked.¹⁶ Proverbs 4:18-19 LXX, for instance, tells us that "the ways of the righteous shine like light ... but the ways of the ungodly are dark."¹⁷ The pattern for this righteous and faithful way of life is God's law, which is light: "For the commandment of the law is a lamp and a light, and a way of life (ὁδὸς ζωῆς), reproof and discipline" (Prov 6:23 LXX; cf. the MT). The psalmist similarly declares that the Lord's "word" (דָּבָר; λόγος) "is a lamp for my feet and a light for my path" (Ps 119:105 [118:105 LXX]; cf. v. 1); blessed are those who "will walk in the light" of the Lord's countenance (Ps 89:15 [88:16 LXX]). According to Job 24:13 the wicked, by contrast, are those who "rebel against the light, they do not know its ways, and do not abide in its paths." In Isa 26:9 LXX we are told that the Lord's commandments are "a light on the earth" from which the earth's inhabitants may learn righteousness. The people of God, consequently, are to live in such a way that they become "a light to the nations" (Isa 42:6).

"Light" and "darkness" often have similar connotations in Second Temple literature.¹⁸ In 1QS III, 20-21, we are told that the righteous (בני צדק) are those who "walk in the ways of light," while the wicked are those who "walk in the ways of darkness" (cf. also the "sons of light" in, e.g., III, 13). In the Testament of Zebulun the Lord is proclaimed as "the light of righteousness" (9:8; cf. Num 6:24-26; Pss 27:1; 31:16; Isa 60:19-20); the Lord's people must therefore choose "either the darkness or the light, the law of the

---

¹⁵ Otto Schwankl makes a similar point:

> The concepts of life and light go closely together. ... Life and light are indeed almost, but not completely identical. Through the light is the life once again qualified. The light is thus a special mode of life; it is "life with level [Niveau]," qualified life. The term "light" is a parameter of life that indicates the quality that is attributed to the life. (*Licht und Finsternis: Ein metaphorisches Paradigma in den johanneischen Schriften*, Herders Biblische Studien 5 [Freiburg im Breisgau: Herder, 1995], 89; see also Otto Schwankl, "Die Metaphorik von Licht und Finsternis im johanneischen Schrifttum," in *Metaphorik und Mythos im Neuen Testament*, ed. Karl Kertelge, QD 126 [Freiburg im Breisgau: Herder, 1990], 142)

Schwankl, though, finds ὃ γέγονεν in v. 3c (which he takes with v. 4) to refer to creation, which in the Word has "life" (v. 4a). In v. 4b, "light" attributes to "life" a special mode or quality: they jointly describe a "spiritual" life that derives from the Word, and to which the Word directs human beings (*Licht und Finsternis*, 89-90). The Word's incarnation and victory over the darkness are then described in v. 5.

¹⁶ For this connotation of "light" (אוֹר; φῶς) in Israel's Scriptures, see, e.g., Pss 37:3-6 (36:3-6 LXX); 43:3 (42:3 LXX); 89:14-16 (88:14-16 LXX); 97:10-11 (96:10-11 LXX); 119:105 (118:105 LXX; cf. v. 1); Prov 6:23; Hos 10:12 LXX (cf. MT); Mic 7:9; Isa 2:2-5; 26:9 LXX; 49:6; 62:1 LXX (cf. MT); for "light" and "darkness" (אוֹר and אֲפֵלָה/חֹשֶׁךְ; φῶς and σκότος [cf. σκοτεινός and σκοτίζω]), see, e.g., Ps 112:4 (111:4 LXX); Prov 4:18-19; Eccl 2:13; Isa 5:20; 9:2 (1), 6-7 (5-6); 42:6-7, 16. On the connotations of "light" and "darkness" in Israel's Scriptures and their import for the NT, see Elizabeth R. Achtemeier, "Jesus Christ, the Light of the World: The Biblical Understanding of Light and Darkness," *Int* 17 (1963): 439-49. For "light" and "darkness" in Second Temple literature see below.

¹⁷ αἱ δὲ ὁδοὶ τῶν δικαίων ὁμοίως φωτὶ λάμπουσιν ... αἱ δὲ ὁδοὶ τῶν ἀσεβῶν σκοτειναί (cf. Prov 4:18-19 MT).

¹⁸ See, e.g., Wis 5:6; 7:26; Sir 24:27; 1 En. 3:6-8; 108:14-15; T. Benj. 5:3; T. Gad 5:1; T. Jos. 10:3; 20:2; T. Levi 14:4; 19:1; T. Naph. 2:10; T. Zeb. 9:8; T. Job 43:6; 1QS II, 24-III, 7; III, 13-23; 1QM XIII, 1-16; Philo, *Leg.* 1.17-18, 46-47; *Det.* 101; *Deus* 3, 122-123; *Ebr.* 157; Sib. Or. 14:4-9.

Lord or the works of Beliar" (T. Levi 19:1). In the Testament of Benjamin it is said that "the darkness flees" from the person whose mind or understanding is shaped by "the light of good works" (T. Benj. 5:3). Noteworthy as well is the concluding vision of *1 Enoch*, in which it is disclosed that, following the last days, "the righteous ones shall be resplendent. (The sinners) shall cry aloud, and they shall see the righteous ones being resplendent" (1 En. 108:14–15).[19]

Such an association of "light" with righteousness, faithfulness, and truth, and of "darkness" with waywardness and evil, is found also in the Fourth Gospel.[20] That the darkness opposes the light is conveyed initially in John 1:5: the darkness did not "overcome" or "overtake" (κατέλαβεν) the light, indicating that this darkness was hostile and inimical toward the light (cf. καταλάβῃ in 12:35). More to the point, though, is Jesus's declaration in 3:19 that, although "the light" has come into the world, human beings "loved the darkness (ἠγάπησαν ... τὸ σκότος) rather than the light, because their works were evil" (ἦν γὰρ αὐτῶν πονηρὰ τὰ ἔργα). "The darkness," as described here, consists of "evil works," and these works were an important reason why human beings rejected the light upon his advent in the world. This suggests that, prior to the advent of the light, the life of human beings was defined by waywardness and evil, that is, by "the darkness."[21] The darkness then fostered the world's rejection of the light. In "hating" and not "coming" to the light (v. 20), despite the light's advent in the world (vv. 17, 19), human beings continue to walk and live in the darkness (cf. 12:46). "The darkness" here, together with "evil works" (v. 19), doing "evil" (ὁ φαῦλα πράσσων

---

[19] *OTP* 1:89. Hans Conzelmann, in his article "φῶς κτλ," in *TDNT*, observes that in Second Temple literature "light and darkness become moral qualities" (9:324). Conzelmann then goes on to explain "light" in John's Gospel, though, in terms of "revelation": "The identification of light with revelation and of the revelation of the Revealer means the exclusion of all metaphysical and cosmological speculation. ... Light is a pure concept of existence. Its knowledge ... can be fully indicated by defining it as faith and perception" (9:350).

[20] For "light" and "darkness" in the Johannine literature see Dodd, *Interpretation*, 201–12; Schwankl, "Die Metaphorik"; Schwankl, *Licht und Finsternis*; van der Watt, *Family of the King*, 235–9, 245–60; Lee, *Flesh and Glory*, 166–74; Koester, *Symbolism*, 141–73; Marianne Meye Thompson, "'Light' (φῶς): The Philosophical Content of the Term and the Gospel of John," in *The Prologue of the Gospel of John: Its Literary, Theological, and Philosophical Contexts. Papers Read at the Colloquium Ioanneum 2013*, ed. Jan G. van der Watt, R. Alan Culpepper, and Udo Schnelle, WUNT 359 (Tübingen: Mohr Siebeck, 2016), 273–83. Van der Watt in particular emphasizes the ethical connotations of "light" and "darkness" in John's Gospel, but he explains them only by means of the language of "revelation" and mental perception: "As the one having the divine existence in himself, [Jesus] serves as the example (revelation) of how Christians should live. As life he is the light in the sense that he illustrates (reveals) and brings the divine alternative of existence to men" (*Family of the King*, 236; see also 250, 255, 296–303). John's description of Jesus as "the light" in 1:4 is "an ethical statement. Light makes it possible for people to see and act correctly" (236–7; cf. van der Watt's idea that, for John, "once Jesus is accepted or rejected, the person's attitude and actions are determined accordingly" ["Ethics of/and the Opponents of Jesus," 190]). Schnelle, while commenting on the foot washing scene in John 13, explains that to describe Jesus in John's Gospel merely as the "example" of how to live is inadequate: "If Jesus were exclusively the example, human beings would again be left to their own abilities in that they would have to emulate his example as best as they could. This would run counter to the movement of God's prevenient love. Human beings cannot imitate Jesus, because Jesus' deed alone is the basis of human existence and human action" (*The Human Condition*, 117). Schnelle goes on to explain that human beings "can, however, join the love movement initiated by God and in it be in accord with Jesus. ... Thus the love of Jesus ... is the presupposition and enabling of the disciples' service of love" (117–18).

[21] On the extent or scope of the darkness in John's Gospel see below.

[v. 20]), "hating" the light (v. 20), and so on, therefore attributes to human beings a way of life that is wayward and evil. Those who "do the truth" (v. 21), by contrast, "come" to the light (v. 21).

This conception of "the darkness" as a way of life that contrasts and opposes the light, because the former consists of waywardness and evil, is evident also in 8:12: those who "follow" Jesus (ὁ ἀκολουθῶν ἐμοί), the light of the world, "will not walk in the darkness, but will have the light of life." Jesus here juxtaposes two ways of life that are diametrically opposed to one another. To "follow" Jesus, "the light," means to believe in him (cf. 1:12; 3:16–18; 10:26–27; 12:36) and love him (cf. 3:19; 8:42; 16:27; 21:15–17); it means to keep his word (8:31, 51; 14:23–24) and commandments (14:15, 21; 15:10). Jesus's followers (μαθηταί) are to love one another as Jesus has loved them (13:34–35; 15:12–14), following his example (ὑπόδειγμα [13:15]). In doing so they follow and know "the way" to the Father (14:4–6). To "walk in the darkness" is to live in a manner that is wholly opposite: it is to be lost (12:35). Jesus's followers are to live in such a way that they become "children of light" (υἱοὶ φωτός) who eschew "the darkness" (12:35–36).

What most clearly evinces that, in John's Gospel, "the light" and "the darkness" each designate a certain way or manner of life, though, is the manner of life that Jesus, "the light," himself exemplifies. In contrast to the world (the works of which are "evil" [7:7; cf. 3:19]) and, in particular, "the Jews" (οἱ Ἰουδαῖοι),[22] who do not know God,[23] and who do not have "the love of God" in them (5:42; cf. Deut 6:5; Lev 19:18), Jesus knows and loves God,[24] does God's will,[25] and is "full of grace and truth," that is, full of steadfast love and faithfulness.[26] Jesus is "devout" (θεοσεβής),[27] keeps God's commandments (15:10), and is "the Holy One of God" (ὁ ἅγιος τοῦ θεοῦ).[28] Jesus lives sacrificially for

---

[22] Throughout this study "the Jews" will remain in quotations in order to indicate that the designation refers to the Ἰουδαίοις as particularly portrayed in the Fourth Gospel. On this portrayal and the sense of οἱ Ἰουδαῖοι in John's Gospel see below (in connection with 1:11).

[23] 1:10–11; 7:28; 8:19; 8:55; 15:21; 16:3; 17:25; but cf. 4:22.

[24] 7:29; 8:55; 10:15; 14:31; 17:25; see also 8:49.

[25] 4:34; 5:19, 30; 6:38; 8:28–29; 10:17–18; 12:49–50.

[26] 1:14; cf. vv. 16–17. The phrase χάρις καὶ ἀλήθεια here seems to correspond to חֶסֶד וֶאֱמֶת ("steadfast love and faithfulness") in the MT (see, e.g., Gen 24:27; 24:49; 32:11; 47:29; Exod 34:6; Josh 2:14; 2 Sam 2:6; 15:20; Pss 25:10; 40:11 [10]; 86:15; 115:1; Prov 3:3; 20:28; cf. Hos 4:1; Mic 7:20; Zech 7:9); translations of חֶסֶד וֶאֱמֶת in the LXX include δικαιοσύνη καὶ ἀλήθεια (Gen 24:27; 32:11); ἔλεος καὶ δικαιοσύνη (Gen 24:49); ἐλεημοσύνη καὶ ἀλήθεια (Gen 47:29; Prov 20:28); ἔλεος καὶ ἀλήθεια (Josh 2:14; 2 Sam 2:6; 15:20; Pss 24:10; 39:11); ἐλεημοσύνη καὶ πίστις (Prov 3:3). For reasons why John may have preferred χάρις to the alternatives listed above see Marianne Meye Thompson, *John: A Commentary*, NTL (Louisville, KY: Westminster John Knox, 2015), 34. James A. Montgomery shows χάρις to be a fitting translation of חֶסֶד ("Hebrew *Hesed* and Greek *Charis*," *HTR* 32 [1939]: 97–102). On this point Andrew T. Lincoln asserts, "John's Greek phrase is a valid translation of the Hebrew [חֶסֶד וֶאֱמֶת], and so 'full of grace and truth' is to be seen as the prologue's equivalent of 'abounding in steadfast love and faithfulness'" (*The Gospel according to Saint John*, BNTC 4 [Peabody, MA: Hendrickson, 2005], 106). This sense of χάρις καὶ ἀλήθεια (John 1:14, 17) as "steadfast love and faithfulness" (corresponding to חֶסֶד וֶאֱמֶת) is demonstrated more fully by Lester J. Kuyper, "Grace and Truth: An Old Testament Description of God, and Its Use in the Johannine Gospel," *Int* 18 (1964): 3–19. Brown helpfully notes that "the Word of God who comes down from heaven in Rev 19:11–13 is called 'faithful and true [*pistis ... alēthinos*],' which is probably another reflection of the *ḥesed* and '*emet* motif" (*John (I-XII)*, 14). This understanding of χάρις καὶ ἀλήθεια (1:14) as connoting "steadfast love and faithfulness" will factor significantly in our analysis below.

[27] 9:31; cf. ἀκούω in 11:41–42; cf. also 12:28.

[28] 6:69; cf. "the Holy One of Israel," who is faithful and true (Ps 71:22 [70:22 LXX]; Isa 49:7 LXX).

the sake of others: he gives his flesh (σάρξ) for the life of the world (6:51).[29] Jesus offers himself (i.e., his ψυχήν) for the well-being of his friends (15:13; see also 10:11, 15, 17–18; 12:25).[30] According to 1 John Jesus is "the righteous one" (2:1; cf. 2:29) who is without sin (3:5; cf. John 8:46). As such, Jesus is "the light" that contrasts and opposes "the darkness" (John 1:4–5; 3:19–21; 8:12; 12:35, 46). Jesus is "the light" that human beings are to believe in and follow, so that they may become "children of light" (John 12:36; cf. 1:12–13; 3:3–7; 15:8). Such children, according to 1 John, are no longer to "walk in the darkness"; rather, they are to "do the truth" (1 John 1:6–7; cf. John 3:21; 8:12) and "do righteousness" as Jesus does (1 John 2:29).

With respect to the connotations of "light" and "life" in John 1:4–5, then, the wider cotext of John's Gospel as well as the testimony of 1 John suggest that "light" here attributes to the Word and his life a certain pattern, character, or manner.[31] The sense in which "the darkness" (v. 5) is contrary to this life is suggested also. "Light" signifies a way of life that is righteous, faithful, and true, while "darkness" signifies a way of life that is wayward, disobedient, and evil.[32] Shortly after vv. 4–5 the quality of the light and his life is made explicit in v. 14: in beholding his "grace and truth," his steadfast love and faithfulness, the Johannine community beheld his "glory" (δόξα [2x]), the glory of the divine Son of the Father.[33] This seems integral to John's presentation of Jesus as "the

---

[29] In 6:51 σάρξ seems to foreground Jesus's humanity as that which is offered unto death and resurrection (cf. σῶμα in 2:21; 19:38, 40; 20:12).

[30] It is the noun ψυχή that occurs when Jesus speaks of "laying down" (τίθημι) his life (10:11, 15, 17–18; 15:13; cf. 12:25; 13:37–38). Louw and Nida explain that ψυχή together with τίθημι is idiomatic and conveys the sense, "to die, with the implication of voluntary or willing action—'to die voluntarily, to die willingly'" (L&N 1:266 [23.113]). Since Jesus says that, as the Father has ζωήν in himself, the Son (as granted by the Father) likewise has ζωήν in himself (5:26; Jesus *is* in fact this ζωή [6:35; 11:25; 14:6]), the ψυχή that Jesus willingly and voluntarily offers unto death seems to signify his humanity, his σῶμα (2:19–22; 19:38–40; cf. σάρξ in 6:51; πνεῦμα in 19:30). Van der Watt finds similarly that ψυχή in John "seems to refer to physical life" (*Family of the King*, 241 n.424). Jesus says in 10:17–18 that he lays down his ψυχήν in order to take it up again: "I have power to lay it down, and I have power to take it up again" (10:18; cf. 2:19–22; 20:9, 20, 27).

[31] Schwankl emphasizes that, because of their ambiguity, terms such as "life" and "light" in John 1:4 should be determined by the "macrotext" of John's Gospel: "one can therefore 'actually' understand [such terms] only when one has read the whole Gospel" (*Licht und Finsternis*, 98).

[32] "Light" and "darkness" carry similar connotations in Paul's exhortation to the Ephesians not to associate with those who oppose and disobey God: "for you were formerly darkness" (ἦτε γάρ ποτε σκότος) Paul tells them,

but now are light in the Lord (νῦν δὲ φῶς ἐν κυρίῳ). Walk as children of light, for the fruit of the light is in all goodness and righteousness and truth (ὁ γὰρ καρπὸς τοῦ φωτὸς ἐν πάσῃ ἀγαθωσύνῃ καὶ δικαιοσύνῃ καὶ ἀληθείᾳ) ... and do not take part in the unfruitful works of the darkness, but instead even expose them. (Eph 5:8–11)

See also Matt 5:14–16; Luke 11:33–36; Acts 26:18; Rom 13:11–14; 1 Pet 2:9.

[33] Richard Bauckham offers a similar assessment of the "glory" beheld in the incarnate Word (1:14): "The glory is the radiance of the character of God, the grace and truth about which Moses heard [in Exod 34:6–7], but which the disciples of Jesus have seen in his human person and life" (*Gospel of Glory: Major Themes in Johannine Theology* [Grand Rapids, MI: Baker, 2015], 52). On the Fourth Gospel's presentation of the "glory" of Jesus more broadly, Margaret Pamment concludes that, for John, "glory" refers to the selfless love and unmerited generosity of God ("The Meaning of *Doxa* in the Fourth Gospel," *ZNW* 74 [1983]: 12–16). Dorothy Lee explains the "glory" of Jesus in the Gospel of John in this way: "The 'children of God' who gaze upon the glory in the flesh—in the incarnation and the 'signs' ministry, on the cross and in the risen body—see in outline the shape of

light." Jesus is true and everlasting life become "flesh," become human.³⁴ In Jesus this life "has come into existence" in the world, as a human being. As such, Jesus "shines" in the darkness and reveals life.³⁵

The Extent of the Darkness

The figurative connotation of "the darkness" in John's Gospel attributes to human beings a way or manner of life that is wayward and evil.³⁶ The darkness contrasts and opposes the life—which is "light"—that the incarnate Word brings into existence and reveals. It is important to recognize, though, that, for John, the incarnation of the Word was prompted in part by the fact that *all* human beings, prior to the Word's incarnation, were walking and living in darkness.³⁷ Jesus makes this point clear when he says the following about his soteriological purpose: "I have come as light into the world, in order that (ἵνα) every person who believes in me may not remain (μείνῃ) in the darkness" (12:46). The ἵνα-clause here expresses the purpose and result of Jesus's

---

their own salvation. Only flesh restores flesh. ... Only God's humanity heals humanity" (*Flesh and Glory*, 60).

34 "Johannine theology is shaped by the idea of the divine assuming form: in Jesus Christ, God really became human and made true human existence possible" (Schnelle, *The Human Condition*, 118).

35 Andrew T. Glicksman, like van der Watt and others, explains that in John's Gospel "Christ's identity as light has important ethical implications because, as the light, he reveals what constitutes proper behavior" ("Beyond Sophia: The Sapiential Portrayal of Jesus in the Fourth Gospel and Its Ethical Implications for the Johannine Community," in van der Watt and Zimmerman, *Rethinking the Ethics of John*, 92). While I agree with this assessment, the point I stress here is that John seems to indicate in the prologue (1:3c–4, 14–18) and in what follows (see, e.g., 6:48–51; 11:25; 14:6; 17:19) that Jesus, as "the light," not merely "reveals" what is good and true but *is* goodness and truth itself. This sense of light accords not only with those instances in the OT and in Second Temple literature in which "light" signifies God's faithfulness and goodness (see, e.g., Pss 4:6; 27:1 [cf. 26:1 LXX]; 44:3; T. Zeb. 9:8; cf. Num 6:24–26; Pss 31:16; 80:3; Deut 31:17–18) but also with those instances in ancient Greek philosophical and poetic literature in which "light" represents "the good itself, wisdom, truth, and ultimately the divine" (Thompson, "'Light,'" 274).

36 Van der Watt finds "the darkness" in 1:5 to refer metaphorically to the "way of existence" of Jesus's opposition; in 8:12 "the darkness" signifies a "specific reality of life with specific ethical qualities ... which stands in contrast to the life in the light" (*Family of the King*, 256–7). Forestell describes "the darkness" in John's Gospel as "a moral atmosphere in which men walk and from which Christ, the light of the world, rescues them" (*Word of the Cross*, 111; but cf. 150 n.14).

37 Forestell seems to assert a rather different view when he says the following: "Nowhere in the gospel is it affirmed that all men were in darkness before the coming of Christ. Rather the gospel presupposes a predisposition in some to the revelation that came with Christ" (*Word of the Cross*, 150 n.14; but cf. 111). Forestell's contention here aligns his reading of John with that of Scott, who says the following about the "judgment" that, for John, Christ's advent brings about for human beings:

> It needs to be observed that this judgment is not, in the first instance, an ethical one. Rather it connects itself with John's semi-Gnostic distinction of two great classes in the human race,—those who are from above and those from below,—children of light and children of darkness. The work of Christ was to sift out, as by a magnet, the purer element in mankind from the lower and grosser. ... The light has come into the world, and makes itself felt in men with an attractive or a repellent power, according to the nature that is in them. Hitherto they had been mingled together in the confused mass of humanity, but Christ effects a separation, and gathers "His own" out of the unbelieving world. (*The Fourth Gospel*, 215–16)

mission, of his coming "into the world."³⁸ Deliverance from the darkness is an aspect of Jesus's mission to "save the world" (ἵνα σώσω τὸν κόσμον [v. 47]), that is, to save the world in its entirety.³⁹ All human beings are implicated. That all human beings were living in darkness prior to Jesus's advent is made clear, furthermore, by the fact that believers are said here (v. 46) to be people whom Jesus saves. Jesus has come into the world so that those *who believe in him* may no longer "remain" or "continue" (μείνῃ) in the darkness. Jesus's words here therefore indicate that, in John's view of things, all human beings were living in darkness prior to Jesus's advent, and that Jesus's advent was prompted, at least in part, by this wayward condition of the world. To argue otherwise (i.e., that prior to the incarnation only those who would go on to reject Jesus were living in darkness) would seem to make the darkness irrelevant to Jesus's mission, since in this case the people living in darkness would *not* be the people whom Jesus saves. This would in fact contradict what Jesus repeatedly says: he delivers human beings from the darkness (8:12; 12:35–36, 46).

The origin of "the darkness," we should note, is most likely to be attributed to "the devil," who was "a murderer from the beginning" and is "the father" of falsehood (8:44).⁴⁰ That the devil is said to be "the ruler of this world" (12:31) indicates the scope of both his reign and, by association, the reign of the darkness. All human beings are again implicated. That the devil has been a murderer "from the beginning" (ἀπ' ἀρχῆς) suggests, consequently, that "the darkness" too has been a problem for human beings since "the beginning." Let us note as well that Jesus's disciples are said to be chosen (15:19) and given to him (17:6) "out of the world" (ἐκ τοῦ κόσμου). This indicates that they were formerly "of the world," that they once belonged *to* the world. In coming to believe in and follow Jesus they evidently mark the beginning of a conversion on the part of the world from "the darkness," which has gripped the world, to "the light" (cf. 17:21, in which Jesus prays for the unity and devotion of his followers to bring about the belief of "the world"). Such a conversion is perhaps to be expected, given that God loves the world (3:16) and has sent the Son in order to save the world (3:17; 12:46–47; cf. 1:29; 6:51). It is undoubtedly the case, then, that, for John, the advent of "the light" was prompted in part by the fact that all human beings, prior to the light's advent, were walking and living in darkness.⁴¹ For John, the light's advent seems to have brought the

---

[38] In their article on ἵνα BDAG explain, "In many cases purpose and result cannot be clearly differentiated, and hence ἵνα is used for the result that follows according to the purpose of the subject or of God. As in Semitic and Greco-Roman thought, purpose and result are identical in declarations of the divine will" (477).

[39] On "the world" in John's Gospel see below (in connection with John 1:10).

[40] The "devil" is later described as "the ruler of this world" (12:31; see also 14:30; 16:11; cf. διάβολος in 13:2 and σατανᾶς in 13:27). Since the devil is said to be a murderer "from the beginning" (8:44), it seems that the devil is in some way a source (hence "father" [8:38–44]) of the world's "evil deeds" (7:7). The devil seems in fact to be the personification of evil (17:15).

[41] Among those who likewise conclude that, for John, all human beings were in darkness prior to Jesus's advent are George Barker Stevens (*The Theology of the New Testament* [New York: Scribner's Sons, 1899], 187–98), Mussner (*ZΩH*, 64), Smith (*Theology*, 83), Koester (*Word of Life*, 66–7), and Andreas J. Köstenberger (*A Theology of John's Gospel and Letters: Biblical Theology of the New Testament* [Grand Rapids, MI: Zondervan: 2009], 283–4). Bultmann agrees as well: "Before the encounter with the Revealer the life of all men lies in darkness and sin" (*John*, 159; see also Bultmann, *Theology*, 2:25). For Bultmann, though, this preceding life of waywardness (one's "past") may be done away

problem of the darkness into focus, and if the light is not received and followed, the culpability or "guilt" of those who so deny the light, and who thus continue to walk in the darkness in spite of the light, is exacerbated (cf. 3:36; 9:39–41; 15:22–24). But the love of human beings for the darkness rather than the light is the consequence, at least in part, of a preceding life of waywardness (3:19–20), and even those who "do the truth" (3:21) must "come" to the light *from* the darkness in which they have lived heretofore, so that they may no longer "remain" in the darkness.[42] The fact that, in the incarnate Word, true life "has come into existence" where it did not exist formerly (1:3c–4) indicates as well that the darkness held sway over all human beings prior to Jesus's advent, for the world was devoid of true life *until* Jesus's advent.

The Mission of Jesus

In examining the problem of "the darkness" in John's Gospel we have considered what is said not only about the darkness but also about "the light." We have sought to allow our assessment of the "plight" to be informed by John's portrayal of the "solution." The question of the sense in which Jesus is this "solution" will now be addressed more fully. For John, Jesus has come into the world to deliver human beings from "the darkness" and, as we will observe, from ignorance of God, sin, illness or bodily infirmity, and death, but how does Jesus accomplish this mission? To paint with broad strokes, perhaps the most common answer to this question, at least within Johannine

> with completely, *so that such life in effect never existed*, if one decides positively in the moment of divine revelation and "believes":
>
>> Yet this sin [preceding belief] is not sin, insofar as God, by the sending of his Son, holds the whole past *in suspenso* and so makes the encounter with the Revealer the moment of true decision for men. But for this encounter there would be no sin in the definitive sense of the word (9:41; 15:24). If the encounter leads to faith, the decision is thereby made that the believer is ἐκ τῆς ἀληθείας (18:37); the believer becomes a new man, in that his past too becomes a new past, and his works can be regarded as ἐν θεῷ εἰργασμένα. If the encounter leads to unbelief, then this also decides a man's past. Now sin "remains," the anger of God "remains" (9:41; 3:36). (*John*, 159; italics original; see also 439)
>
> Significantly, Bultmann seems to conceive of "sin" here only as "guilt." If a person believes in response to the Revealer, the guilt of his or her preceding life is wiped away, and there is now a new person. But one may wonder: what about the actions that resulted in this person's "guilt"? Are not these actions also "sin"? Once a person responds positively in the moment of "decision" and believes, is this new believer now able to live in accordance with God's commandments and, thus, live without incurring "guilt"? Does John not speak to this concern? If in John's Gospel Jesus is found not only to "reveal" God but, also, to incarnate and realize the life to which all human beings are called, then the issue of *what believers do* (which pertains to inter alia morality, ethics, and "sin") becomes important, for Jesus's followers are to resemble him in how they live in relationship with God and others.

[42] In John 3:19–21, while it is said that the light "has come into the world" (v. 19), this (or something like this) is not said about the darkness. The darkness is simply assumed. It is *from* the darkness, then, that people "come to the light" (ἔρχεται πρὸς τὸ φῶς), as 12:46 makes clear (cf. also 6:44, which stresses the inability of human beings—apart from the work of the Father—to come to the Son, an inability presumably due at least partially to the wayward condition of human beings). Those who hate and reject the light do *not* "come" and, thus, "remain" in the darkness. Relevant as well to the matter at hand is a point that comes to the fore later in John's narrative: Jesus's followers must be "cleansed" or purified (13:3–11; 15:3; cf. 20:23), which implies that, prior to belief, they were "stained" or tainted by "sin" (cf. 9:39–41; 15:22–24).

scholarship, is that Jesus accomplishes his mission by revealing God. For John, Jesus is "the revealer," the divine envoy of God who presents human beings with an invitation to, and a "decision" about, a relationship with himself and, through him, the Father.[43] Another answer that frequently appears in scholarship adds a more objective element (soteriologically speaking) to the reading just described: yes, Jesus reveals God, but he also *atones*. In and through Jesus's words and deeds God is revealed to the world, but the death of Jesus is not only the culmination or final act of this revelation, for Jesus's death also atones for, and so takes away, the sin of the world.[44]

Yet there is another answer that, interestingly, some interpreters seem to approach but not reach, verge on but not lay hold of: for John, Jesus is the archetype and source of salvation in the sense that Jesus realizes in himself, that is, in his "flesh," the relationship with God and way of life that he reveals and offers to the world.[45] Here, Jesus may be said to "atone" in the sense that, in and through his coming and going, Jesus accomplishes the life to which God calls or invites human beings.[46] William

---

[43] For this line of interpretation, see, e.g., Scott, *The Fourth Gospel*, 206–33; Bultmann, *Theology*, 2:3–69; Ernst Käsemann, *The Testament of Jesus: A Study of the Gospel of John in Light of Chapter 17*, trans. Gerhard Krodel (Philadelphia, PA: Fortress, 1968); Wayne A. Meeks, "The Man from Heaven in Johannine Sectarianism," *JBL* 91 (1972): 44–72; Forestell, *Word of the Cross*; R. Alan Culpepper, *Anatomy of the Fourth Gospel: A Study in Literary Design* (Philadelphia, PA: Fortress, 1983), 86–89; van der Watt, *Family of the King* (see esp. 296–302); van der Watt, "Salvation"; Bennema, *Saving Wisdom* (see esp. 112–23); Bennema, "The Sword of the Messiah"; John Ashton, *Understanding the Fourth Gospel*, 2nd ed. (Oxford: Oxford University Press, 2007); Michaels, *John*, 39–42; Francis J. Moloney, *Love in the Gospel of John: An Exegetical, Theological, and Literary Study* (Grand Rapids, MI: Baker, 2013); William Loader, *Jesus in John's Gospel: Structure and Issues in Johannine Christology* (Grand Rapids, MI: Eerdmans, 2017); Zumstein, "Purpose." Cf. Smith, *Theology*, 115–22.

[44] Importantly, scholars who find the Johannine Jesus to atone generally seem to understand this atonement only as a forensic work and not also as the basis or source of moral and physical transformation for believers in Jesus. See, for example, Theophil E. Müller, *Das Heilsgeschehen im Johannesevangelium: Eine exegetische Studie, zugleich der Versuch einer Antwort an Rudolf Bultmann* (Zürich: Gotthelf-Verlag, 1961); George L. Carey, "The Lamb of God and Atonement Theories," *TynBul* 32 (1981): 97–122; Bruce H. Grigsby, "The Cross as an Expiatory Sacrifice in the Fourth Gospel," *JSNT* 15 (1982): 51–80; Leon Morris, "The Atonement in John's Gospel," *CTR* 3 (1988): 49–64; Max Turner, "Atonement and the Death of Jesus in John—Some Questions to Bultmann and Forestell," *EvQ* 62 (1990): 99–122; Knöppler, *Theologia crucis*, 67–101; Metzner, *Sünde*, 128–58; Jörg Frey, "Die '*theologia crucifixi*' des Johannesevangeliums," in *Kreuzestheologie im Neuen Testament*, ed. Andreas Dettwiler and Jean Zumstein, WUNT 151 (Tübingen: Mohr Siebeck, 2002), 169–238; Charles A. Gieschen, "The Death of Jesus in the Gospel of John: Atonement for Sin?" *CTQ* 72 (2008): 243–61. For a review of scholarship on the death of Jesus in John's Gospel, see John Dennis, "Jesus' Death in John's Gospel: A Survey of Research from Bultmann to the Present with Special Reference to the Johannine Hyper-Texts," *CurBR* 4 (2006): 331–63.

[45] Gregory of Nyssa, while not commenting on the Gospel of John specifically, explains the mission of Jesus in this way:

> The method followed in our salvation did not owe its efficacy so much to instruction imparted by teaching as to the very acts of Him Who entered into fellowship with humanity, seeing that He has made life an accomplished fact, in order that, through the flesh which He assumed and at the same time deified, all that is akin to it and of the same nature with it might therewith be saved. (*Or. catech.* 35 [GNO 3.4, p. 86]; trans. J. H. Srawley, *The Catechetical Oration of St. Gregory of Nyssa*, Early Church Classics [London: Society for Promoting Christian Knowledge, 1917], 101; trans. modified)

[46] In certain respects Bultmann's reading of John points in this direction. Bultmann finds the death of Jesus to be for John "the last demonstration of the obedience (14:31) which governs the whole life of Jesus"; "nothing compels us to conclude that the evangelist sees [Jesus's] sacrifice only in Jesus's

Loader, for instance, seems at times to approach such conclusions in his exposition of Johannine Christology. Loader argues that, for John, Jesus is "the revealer" in the sense that his mission is one of "encounter and invitation. He offers a relationship with himself and thus with God."[47] "The relationship of mutual love between Father and Son," Loader goes on to say, "is the source and the pattern for the relationships of love which are the goal and content of salvation."[48] Given that John is here found to conceive of salvation as a relationship with God that derives its "pattern" and very existence from the relationship Jesus shares with the Father, the conclusion that, for John, part of Jesus's mission is to realize and establish this relationship with the Father *in the world*, on behalf and for the benefit of human beings, seems but a small step. Loader approaches but never arrives at such a conclusion, however. In fact, Loader seems to disapprove of the idea that, for John, Jesus is in anyway "the human being *par excellence*."[49]

A case for this third reading of Jesus's mission in John's Gospel, which finds Jesus to be not merely "the revealer" but the archetype and source of salvation, is in certain respects found in C. H. Dodd's *The Interpretation of the Fourth Gospel*, and there are parallels between Dodd's exposition of John's Christology and soteriology and those of other Johannine scholars.[50] More can be said in support of this third alternative,

---

death rather than in his whole ministry" (*Theology*, 2:52–54). Bultmann goes on to explain that, for John, Jesus's death "is to be understood in connection with his life as the completion of his work. His life-work as a whole is sacrifice" (2:55).

[47] Loader, *Jesus in John's Gospel*, 291. Loader finds that, for John, "the gift of salvation is primarily to be seen as a relationship within which human beings have life and have it in abundance as they open themselves to the Son and the Father. In this they do not cease to be human beings ... they become human beings as they were created to be" (298). John's Gospel may be said consequently to offer a "soteriology of relationship" (300–1).

[48] Loader, *Jesus in John's Gospel*, 316. Cf. Forestell: "The believing disciple will live by the same divine life with which the risen Christ lives in communion with the Father" (*Word of the Cross*, 116). Forestell goes on to say, in regard to John's eschatology, that eternal life should be understood

> as communion with God in knowledge and love, [which for believers] can begin now and continue beyond the physical dissolution of man's present body. ... According to the Fourth Gospel Jesus has already lived out this career. All his disciples are to follow him in this career. ... The individual eschatology of the wisdom tradition is fulfilled in Jesus who as man is the just one *par excellence*. (132–3)

Moloney explains that the Gospel of John "makes clear that God has a relationship with the Son, and that he has sent the Son so that others may enter that same relationship and continue the mission of Jesus (17:18, 20; 20:21)" (*Love*, 68). Forestell and Moloney stress, in similarity with Loader, though, that Jesus's mission is to *reveal* God and the relationship with God that is salvific.

[49] Loader, *Jesus in John's Gospel*, 206.

[50] Dodd, while investigating the matter of "knowledge of God" in John's Gospel, says the following:

> The knowledge which Christ has of God is [in 7:28–29 and 8:54–55] associated on the one hand with His divine commission and on the other hand with His obedience to the divine word. It is the fulfillment of the prophetic ideal; for, as we have seen, the fact that the prophet is known by God implies as its correlative that the prophet shall know God too, while yet no prophet fully claims such knowledge. In Christ therefore we have, realized, the archetype of that true relation of man to God which is henceforth made possible in him. We may observe that this is implied already in the Synoptic saying, Matt 11:27. ... Where the Johannine statement advances beyond this is in representing Christ as occupying the place of God both as subject and as object in that divine-human relation of which His own relation with the Father is the archetype. (*Interpretation*, 166; see also 160, 187, 194–7, 244–9, 262, 282)

though. The following observations demonstrate that, for John, Jesus realizes and establishes in himself, that is, in his "flesh," the relationship with God and way of life that is true and everlasting, and that Jesus does this so as to be the source or basis of this life in others. An appreciation of this feature of John's Christology and soteriology (i.e., of this aspect of John's portrayal of Jesus as the "solution") sheds light on the matter of the plight or predicament from which Jesus saves human beings in John's Gospel, particularly "sin" and "death."

To be noted, first, is what we have already concluded from John's prologue: true and everlasting life, the divine way of living, has come into existence in the world *in Jesus* (ἐν αὐτῷ), who incarnates this life (vv. 3c–4). In the person of Jesus the life of God has become "flesh," become human (v. 14). The soteriological significance of this incarnation and realization of life in the world is then conveyed, perhaps most clearly within the prologue, in the statement that the Johannine community "received" (ἐλάβομεν) from Jesus's "fullness" (v. 16), that is, from the fullness of steadfast love and faithfulness they beheld in him (vv. 14, 17; cf. vv. 12–13).[51] Although the law was given through Moses, "grace and truth," steadfast love and faithfulness, came into existence in the world (ἐγένετο) through Jesus, the incarnate Word (v. 17).

Moving forward in John's narrative, the point that Jesus's mission involves realizing in himself (i.e., in his "flesh") the life that human beings receive and attain through believing and living in him is conveyed also during Jesus's monologue about the good shepherd: "the Father loves me," Jesus says, "on account of this, that I lay down my life, in order that (ἵνα) I may take it again. ... I have power to lay it down and I have power to take it again. This commandment I received from my Father" (10:17–18). Jesus's words here about taking or receiving again his life (ψυχήν; cf. σῶμα in 2:19–22) undoubtedly refer to his resurrection (2:19–22; 14:18–20; 20:1–29). The commandment Jesus has received from the Father, at least as stated here, then, is that he lay down his life *in order that* (ἵνα) he may arise bodily from death to life everlasting. Because Jesus, the good shepherd, will do this "on behalf of the sheep" (vv. 11, 15), and because Jesus says or implies elsewhere that the resurrection of his followers depends on and follows from his own ("Because I live, you will live also" [14:19; see also 6:57; 11:23–26]), Jesus's declaration that he lays down his life in order to take it up again (v. 17) suggests that the soteriological task he has come to accomplish is, at least in part, to realize in himself "the resurrection and the life" (11:25). Jesus's words about his purpose to take or receive again his life (vv. 17–18) further identify his resurrection as the basis for the resurrection of his followers. The point that Jesus "lays down his life" (vv. 11, 15, 17–18), we should also note, seems to define "the good" (τὰ ἀγαθά) that is said to warrant resurrection to life (5:28–29; cf. 12:25). In laying down his life and, then, rising from the dead to live eternally with the Father, Jesus establishes in himself what all those who believe, live, and abide in him will one day experience, namely, "the

---

Cf. Mussner, *ZΩH*, 74–90, 110–11, 143–4; Vellanickal, *Divine Sonship*, 248–63; Hasitschka, *Befreiung*, 167, 418–19; Schnelle, *The Human Condition*, 114–18; John Suggit, "Jesus the Gardener: The Atonement in the Fourth Gospel as Re-Creation," *Neot* 33 (1999): 161–8.

[51] For the phrase χάρις καὶ ἀλήθεια (1:14, 17) see above.

resurrection of life" (as opposed to "the resurrection of condemnation," which is said to await those who do "evil" [5:28–29]).

Later in John's Gospel, when Philip and Andrew tell Jesus about "some Greeks" who wish to see him, Jesus responds by explaining that the hour has come for the Son (i.e., ὁ υἱὸς τοῦ ἀνθρώπου) to be glorified (12:20–23). Jesus then describes himself as "the seed of wheat" (ὁ κόκκος τοῦ σίτου) that bears no fruit, and so remains alone, if it does not fall into the earth and die (v. 24). Immediately following this is the declaration that the one "who loves his life loses it," whereas the one who "disregards" or "disfavors" his life in this world "will keep it into eternal life" (v. 25).[52] With this declaration Jesus sets before his followers the life of self-denial and self-offering they are to embrace and pursue (v. 26), but the principal subject to which Jesus's words about "the one who disregards his life" (v. 25) refer is himself, the Son who is about to be "glorified" (v. 23; cf. vv. 27–33), "the seed" that has descended into the earth and soon will die (v. 24). This is made clear by the statement that immediately ensues: "If someone serves me," Jesus says, "this person must follow me; and where I am, there my servant will be also" (v. 26; cf. 14:1–4). Believers in Jesus are to follow his lead and live sacrificially for the sake of God and others (cf. 13:13–17, 34–35; 15:12–14). Believers are to resemble their good shepherd, who lays down his life (10:11, 15, 17–18). It is Jesus, then, first and foremost, who, through denying and offering himself "in this world," realizes everlasting life in the world (v. 25; cf. 20:1–29). Jesus is the one who "will keep his life" (v. 25) *par excellence*. Consequently, the life that Jesus calls others to embrace and pursue (v. 26), the life of self-denial that leads to and is eternal life (v. 25), is the life that Jesus himself lives in the world.[53] And Jesus does this, that is, he descends into the world, dies, and keeps his life, so as not to remain "alone" (μόνος), but instead bear "fruit" (v. 24). This "fruit" that Jesus has come into the world to produce, as we have already observed, is to be like Jesus himself, "the seed," inasmuch as Jesus's followers are to disregard themselves for the sake of God and others (vv. 25–26), and so bear fruit (15:1–17). In doing so they follow "the way" to the Father (14:4–6). What Jesus seems to describe here, then, with his words about "the seed" that descends into the world and dies in order to bear fruit (v. 24), and with his words about "eternal life" as that which comes in and through self-offering (v. 25), is his *inauguration* in the world of the

---

[52] For μισῶν (v. 25) as denoting the sense "disregards" or "disfavors" see BDAG 653. Cf. Matt 16:24–28; Mark 8:34–38; Luke 9:23–26; cf. also Phil 2:3–11. Van der Watt explains Jesus's words about disregarding oneself (John 12:25) in this way: "Hating one's life means to abandon one's own interests for the sake of the interests of God" ("Ethics Alive in Imagery," in Frey, van der Watt, and Zimmermann, *Imagery in the Gospel of John*, 439).

[53] The point that the life of self-denial and self-offering Jesus speaks about here (v. 25) both leads to and *is* eternal life follows from the fact that it is the way Jesus and his followers live: when people come to believe in Jesus, they are no longer "dead" in the sense that they begin to "live" (5:24–25; we will return to this point in Chapter 3 in connection with "death"). In speaking of the one who "disregards" his life (12:25), whom believers are to follow and resemble (12:26), Jesus here describes *the way* believers "live" (5:24–25; cf. 14:4–6): like the Son, believers are to deny and offer themselves for the sake of God and others, out of love for God and others and in faithfulness to God. This is the life of God—the divine way of living—that Jesus brings into existence in the world and makes "flesh" (1:3c–4, 14). It is the steadfast love and faithfulness believers behold in and receive from Jesus through living and remaining in him (1:14, 16–17).

way of life that leads to and is eternal life, which he does in order to be the source ("the seed") that produces this life in others.⁵⁴

The passage that perhaps conveys most clearly, though, the point that, for John, Jesus's mission involves making life "an accomplished fact" for human beings⁵⁵ is Jesus's prayer concerning the sanctification of his disciples: "Sanctify (ἁγίασον) them in the truth; your word is truth. Just as you sent me into the world, I also sent them into the world. And on their behalf I sanctify myself (ὑπὲρ αὐτῶν ἐγὼ ἁγιάζω ἐμαυτόν), in order that they also may be sanctified in the truth" (ἵνα ὦσιν καὶ αὐτοὶ ἡγιασμένοι ἐν ἀληθείᾳ [17:17-19]). Some contend that the verbal action ἁγιάζω signifies here is "to consecrate" (i.e., to set apart formally for or dedicate to a divine purpose)⁵⁶ rather than "to sanctify" (i.e., to cause to live in a holy and righteous manner),⁵⁷ but several factors make this reading less preferable.⁵⁸

First, Jesus's words here (17:17–19) form part of a broader petition whereby Jesus asks the Father to care for and protect his disciples (17:9–26). Toward the beginning of this petition (v. 11) Jesus addresses the Father as "Holy Father" (πάτερ ἅγιε), with the adjective ἅγιε evidently serving to elicit the Father's faithfulness to and protection of Jesus's disciples, who belong to the Father (v. 10). Accordingly, the adjective ἅγιε here (v. 11) seems to connote faithfulness and righteousness (note πάτερ δίκαιε in v. 25), suggesting that the ensuing occurrences of ἁγιάζω (vv. 17, 19 [2x]) pertain as well to acting and living in a way that is faithful and righteous.⁵⁹

Second, what Jesus asks the Father to do to his disciples in v. 17 (i.e., ἁγίασον αὐτούς …) corresponds to what Jesus does to himself (ὑπὲρ αὐτῶν ἐγω ἁγιάζω ἐμαυτόν), but Jesus has *already* been "consecrated" or "dedicated" to his mission: Jesus is he "whom the Father consecrated (ἡγίασεν) and sent into the world" (10:36).⁶⁰ This suggests that,

---

⁵⁴ Commenting on this passage, John Chrysostom explains that to love one's life is to live in accordance with and gratify one's "untoward desires," whereas to disregard one's life is not to yield to such desires: when our human nature "enjoins on us things contrary to the good pleasure of God we must vehemently turn away from it" (*Hom. Jo.* 67 [FC 41, 227]). Chrysostom goes on to explain that Jesus overcomes "the weakness of his human nature" by pursuing faithfully the will of God, which leads him to the cross (*Hom. Jo.* 67 [FC 41, 229]).

⁵⁵ Gregory of Nyssa, *Or. catech.* 35 (cited above).

⁵⁶ See L&N 1:538 (53.44). For this sense of ἁγιάζω in the LXX (cf. קדשׁ in the MT) see, e.g., Exod 19:10–23; 29:1–46; Lev 8:1–30; Num 6:10–12, Josh 7:13; 1 Kgdms 7:1; 16:5; 1 Esd 1:3; Sir 49:7; Joel 2:15–16; Zeph 1:7; Jer 1:5; 28:27–28 (51:27–28 MT).

⁵⁷ See L&N 1:745 (88.26). For this sense of ἁγιάζω in the LXX (cf. קדשׁ in the MT) see, e.g., Exod 31:12–16; Lev 11:41–45; 19:1–20:26 (esp. 20:7–8); 22:31–33; Ezek 20:10–13; 37:21–28. Cf. ἅγιος in Deut 28:9 LXX; Isa 35:8; 48:17–18 LXX; Jer 4:11 LXX; τέλειος in Deut 18:13 LXX; 3 Kgdms 8:61 (note also ὁσίως). Cf. also ἅγιος in Rom 12:1; Eph 1:4; 1 Pet 1:13–17; 2 Pet 3:11; Rev 14:12; τέλειος in Matt 5:48; 19:21; Rom 12:2.

⁵⁸ On this matter see Ignace de la Potterie, "Consécration ou sanctification du chrétien d'aprés Jean 17?" in *Le Sacré: Études et Recherches; Actes du colloque organisé par le Centre International d'Études Humanistes et par l'Institut d'Études Philosophiques de Rome*, ed. Enrico Castelli (Paris: Aubier, 1974), 333–49.

⁵⁹ Moloney puts it this way: "The use of ἅγιος in v. 11b determines the meaning of ἁγιάζω. In v. 11b it does not mean that the 'holy Father' is in some way consecrated and separated from the profane. A reader will give the same meaning to the uses of ἅγιος and ἁγιάζειν across such closely related contexts" (*Love*, 129 n.71).

⁶⁰ With respect to the sense of ἡγίασεν here (in 10:36), the point that, for John, Jesus is the divine Son of the Father who was with God and was God from the beginning (1:1–4, 14, 18; cf. 8:58; 17:5; 20:28) seems to prohibit rendering ἡγίασεν as "sanctified" or "made holy," since the implication would then

during his farewell prayer (17:17-19), Jesus speaks about something other than the "consecration" or formal "dedication" of himself and his disciples to their missions in the world, since the need for Jesus to be dedicated *again* seems unnecessary.

Third, the disciples, in coming to believe in and follow Jesus, seem *already* to have been formally "set apart" from the world (they are no longer "of the world" [vv. 6, 14, 16]) and "dedicated" to their mission in the world. They have been "chosen" (13:18; 15:16, 19) and "given" to Jesus (17:6; cf. 6:44), they have been "washed" (13:8) and "cleansed" (15:3), and they have received the commandment to love one another, the doing of which is to be a witness to "all people" (13:34-35; cf. 17:20-23). They have already entered into the labor of "reaping" what others have "sown" in the world (4:35-38; cf. ἀπέστειλα αὐτοὺς εἰς τὸν κόσμον in 17:18). These points suggest that Jesus's disciples have already been formally "consecrated" for their mission in the world and, thus, that during his farewell prayer Jesus asks the Father to do something other than "consecrate" his disciples (17:17-19).

Finally, because of Jesus's love for the Father and his fidelity to the divine purpose to which he was dedicated (10:36), it may be said that, for John, Jesus must "set himself apart" from the world (i.e., from the "profane") during his mission. But it is important to recognize that Jesus does this, that is, he sets himself apart from the world, *by the way he lives in the world*. The initial ἁγιάζω in 17:19 (ἐγὼ ἁγιάζω ἐμαυτόν) denotes ongoing or continuous action, the completion of which seems to occur neither in the moment Jesus makes this statement nor in the course of his farewell prayer as a whole (cf. 19:28-30).[61] Because the action ἁγιάζω signifies here is said to be done "on behalf of" Jesus's disciples (cf. ὑπέρ in 10:11-18; cf. also 6:51; 11:50-52; 15:13; 18:14), this action undoubtedly encompasses what Jesus *will* do (namely, lay down his life unto death) and *has been* doing.[62] The scope of the continuous verbal action ἁγιάζω

---

be that, prior to this action of the Father, Jesus was in some way *lacking* holiness and righteousness. But aside from this, in the passage in question (10:22-39) Jesus enters into a dialogue with his fellow "Jews" that quickly becomes hostile, and the point of the questions Jesus poses to his accusers (vv. 34-36, in which occurs ἡγίασεν) is to defend or justify what he has said and done against their charge of blasphemy (v. 33). It is for this reason that Jesus draws on scripture (vv. 34-35). Given this intention to warrant his words and deeds, which sense of ἁγιάζω is more relevant here: being "made holy," so as to live in a holy and righteous manner, or being formally "dedicated" to and thus authorized for a divine task? That Jesus refers to his mission (he has been "sent into the world") immediately following ἡγίασεν suggests that the latter sense (i.e., "dedicated" or "consecrated") is to be preferred (cf. Jer 1:5; Sir 49:7). Although Jesus's fellow "Jews" take offense at his words and deeds (cf. 5:16-18), the Father has dedicated or consecrated Jesus and has sent him into the world to say and do these very things. That this dialogue takes place during "the festival of Dedication" (v. 22) may further evoke the idea of "dedication" or "consecration."

[61] In this sense ἁγιάζω seems here to be what Daniel B. Wallace calls a "broad band" present tense verb (*Greek Grammar beyond the Basics: An Exegetical Syntax of the New Testament* [Grand Rapids, MI: Zondervan, 1996], 519, 521-2). See also Buist M. Fanning, *Verbal Aspect in New Testament Greek*, Oxford Theological Monographs (Oxford: Clarendon, 1990), 206 n.12.

[62] The pivotal declaration that "the one who disregards his life in this world will keep it into eternal life" (12:25), which makes clear that eternal life (and by association holiness and righteousness) comes in and through self-offering, describes the way Jesus lives *throughout* his coming and going, not merely during his passion. A particularly notable scene in this regard is the healing of a man born blind, which Jesus brings about on a "sabbath day" (9:14, 16). Prior to this, Jesus healed a man with a disabling illness on a sabbath day (5:9-10), and we are told that it was because Jesus did this on the sabbath that "the Jews" began to persecute him (vv. 16-18). Later in the narrative, but before his encounter with the man born blind, Jesus acknowledges the anger of his antagonists over this

connotes here (in 17:19) consequently diminishes the viability of rendering ἁγιάζω as "consecrate," since "consecrate" signifies an action that is more or less punctiliar.[63] The statement, καὶ ὑπὲρ αὐτῶν ἐγὼ ἁγιάζω ἐμαυτόν (17:19), by contrast, appears to describe what Jesus does throughout his coming and going, namely, realize in himself the steadfast love and faithfulness (1:14, 16–17) that leads to and is everlasting life, which Jesus does "on behalf of" human beings.[64]

For all of the reasons just listed, then, it is not the "consecration" of himself and his followers that Jesus seems to speak about in the course of his farewell prayer (17:17–19) but, rather, their mutual "sanctification."[65] Jesus appears to explain here that, in order to bring about the sanctification of his followers, he sanctifies "himself" (ἐμαυτόν). But here a question arises: how should we understand the point that Jesus sanctifies *himself*? In what sense does the mission of Jesus, the mission of the divine Son of the Father who was and is God (1:1, 18; 20:28), involve causing "himself" to live in a holy and righteous manner? Given that, for John, Jesus is the divine Word who has come into the world and become "flesh" (1:14), it is evidently this "flesh," that is, his humanity, that Jesus sanctifies in and through his coming and going.[66] Jesus will lay

---

matter: "If on the sabbath a man receives circumcision, in order that the law of Moses may not be broken, why are you angry with me because I healed a man's whole body on the sabbath?" (7:23). Jesus's words here expand on his preceding question: "Why do you seek to kill me?" (7:19). When Jesus then encounters a man blind from birth (9:1) and heals him on the sabbath (vv. 6–14), it is clear that Jesus has done so, and has made manifest the work of God (vv. 3–4), by disregarding himself for the sake of God and others. In full knowledge of the fact that healing again on the sabbath would bring on himself further persecution and, ultimately, lead to his death, Jesus heals the man anyway. About the faithfulness of Jesus in John's Gospel, Bultmann is correct: Jesus's death is for John "the last demonstration of the obedience (14:31) which governs the whole life of Jesus. ... His life-work as a whole is sacrifice" (*Theology*, 2:52, 55).

[63] De la Potterie, after reviewing the biblical notions of "consecration" and "sanctification," concludes the following:

Consecration takes place at a precise moment; it occurs always at the *beginning* of a new situation, because it is oriented essentially toward a service to be rendered (a person or a thing is "consecrated," in view of such a state, of such a task to be fulfilled, of a determined mission); sanctification, on the contrary, does not occur at a determined time; it is a continual progress toward a fulfillment, toward a final accomplishment; consecration is a punctual, initial act; sanctification is growth, which ends in the eschaton. ("Consécration ou sanctification," 340; emphasis original)

[64] About Jesus's words here (in 17:19) Westcott says the following:

The work of the Lord is here presented under the aspect of absolute self-sacrifice. He showed through His life how all that is human may be brought wholly into the service of God; and this He did by true personal determination, as perfectly man. The sacrifice of life ... was now to be consummated in death, whereby the last offering of self was made. The fruits of His victory are communicated to His disciples. By union with Him they also are "themselves sanctified in truth," through the Spirit whose mission followed on His completed work, and who enables each believer to appropriate what Christ has gained. (*St. John*, 254)

[65] Zimmermann likewise finds John's use of ἁγιάζω here to draw on "an Old Testament ethical conception as reflected, for instance, in the Holiness Code (Leviticus 19–26): the appeal for a life in holiness is based on a theonomic argumentation, cf. Lev 19:2: 'You shall be holy for I the Lord your God am holy'" ("Is There Ethics in the Gospel of John?" 71 n.103).

[66] Frédéric Louis Godet, despite making no distinction between "consecration" and "sanctification" and, thus, making them synonymous, finds Jesus's words here (in John 17:19) to convey a similar point:

down his humanity unto death and, then, will take it up again (10:17–18; cf. 2:19–22). The bread that Jesus gives for the life of the world is indeed his "flesh" (6:51).[67]

One might add to this assessment of Jesus's mission in John's Gospel, which finds Jesus to be the archetype and source of salvation, by attending to John's presentation of Jesus as the one who, in contrast to the world, "knows" and "loves" God (see, e.g., 7:29; 8:55; 14:31; 17:25). Given the characterization of "eternal life" as knowing God (17:3), the point that Jesus knows and loves the Father *par excellence* is undoubtedly significant for John's soteriology. But we have presumably demonstrated already that, for John, *how* Jesus brings about salvation is, in part, by realizing and establishing in himself— in his "flesh"—the relationship with God and way of life that is true and everlasting, which Jesus does so as to be the source or basis of this life in others. Without question, in John's Gospel Jesus reveals himself and the Father who sent him. Jesus speaks the words of the Father (17:8), which are "spirit and life" (6:63; cf. v. 68). But Jesus reveals and directs the world toward himself, it seems, partly because he is the incarnation and realization of the "solution" to the world's predicament. For John, the "gift" of salvation is indeed "the giver"; the giver is the gift.[68] And finding John to present Jesus as the "solution" of salvation in this fashion raises the question of whether John regards the human predicament to be a reality that, in various ways, persists beyond the emergence of belief, since the way Jesus lives is for John the soteriological basis, pattern, and goal for all those who believe in him. With respect to John's soteriology, we are led to ask: Are believers, for John, instantly and wholly transformed into Jesus's likeness, that is, into "children of God" (1:12–13), "children of light" (12:36), in the moment they come to believe in Jesus (i.e., when they respond positively in the "moment of decision")? Does John suggest that, in the emergence of belief, the way Jesus lives instantly becomes the way the believer lives? More specifically, is the problem of "sin," for instance, resolved for John in the moment one believes, as scholars commonly claim? In the chapters that follow we will continue to concern ourselves with such questions. But before we turn to the matter of "sin" and, also, to the matters of "illness," "disability," and "death" in John's Gospel, we must first return to John's prologue to consider how the human predicament is described there—not only as "darkness" but also as ignorance of God.

> Jesus possessed a human nature, such as ours, endowed with inclinations and repugnances like ours, but yet perfectly lawful. Of this nature He continually made a holy offering. … His human life received the seal of consecration increasingly even till the entire and final sacrifice of death. … Thereby Jesus realized in His own person the perfect consecration of the *human life*, and He thus laid the foundations of the consecration of this life in all His followers. (*Commentary on John's Gospel*, trans. Timothy Dwight, Kregel Classic Commentary Series [Grand Rapids, MI: Kregel, 1978], 898; italics original)

---

[67] As we observed in Chapter 1, this aspect of John's soteriology (i.e., that Jesus realizes in his "flesh" the divine way of living on behalf of and for the benefit of human beings) is integral to the thinking of Irenaeus: Jesus is "the Word of God, our Lord Jesus Christ, who did, through his transcendent love, become what we are, that He might bring us to be even what He is Himself" (*Haer.* 5 [*ANF* 1:526]). Cf. Athanasius: "For he [the Word of God] became human, in order that we might be deified" (*Inc.* 54 [SC 199:458]). In *C. Ar.* 3.34 Athanasius writes, "For as the Lord, by putting on the body, has become a human being, so we human beings are deified from the Word, having been taken into him through his flesh, and hereafter we inherit eternal life" (*The Orations of St. Athanasius Against the Arians: According to the Benedictine Text*, ed. William Bright, 2nd ed. [Oxford: Oxford University Press, 1884], 189).

[68] For such expression see, e.g., Loader, *Jesus in John's Gospel*, 295–6.

The Problem of Ignorance of God

The statement at the outset of the prologue that "the darkness did not overcome the light" (v. 5) reveals and brings into focus the climactic end of John's Gospel: Jesus prevails over the darkness by means of the very attempts of the darkness to defeat him, which culminate in his death. The subsequent introduction in the prologue of John the Baptist (vv. 6–8) then resumes the story of John's Gospel at its beginning, that is, at the coming of the light into the world (vv. 9–10a). The incarnation of the Word is therefore described here (vv. 9–10a) for the second time (cf. vv. 3c–4). At this juncture (v. 10) the human predicament is likewise described again, though, when we are told that the world "did not know" (οὐκ ἔγνω) the one through whom it was created (v. 10b–c: cf. v. 3a–b).[69] Immediately following this is the statement that the Word "came into what is his own (τὰ ἴδια), and his own (οἱ ἴδιοι) did not receive him" (v. 11). The words τὰ ἴδια are difficult to interpret here: they may denote the Word's "own home" (Judea or Jerusalem, perhaps)[70] or they may further describe "the world" (v. 10), reflecting the idea that the world, as God's creation (vv. 3, 10), belongs to God.[71] What is clear, in light of the story that follows, however, is that the words οἱ ἴδιοι (v. 11b) designate the particular people with whom God has uniquely established a relationship, that is, the Jewish people.[72] The announcement that God's "own" people did not receive God's

---

[69] For κόσμος in John's Gospel see Bultmann, *Theology*, 2:15–21; Smith, *Theology*, 80–5; Stanley B. Marrow, "Κόσμος in John," *CBQ* 64 (2002): 90–102; Lars Kierspel, *The Jews and the World in the Fourth Gospel: Parallelism, Function, and Context*, WUNT 2/220 (Tübingen: Mohr Siebeck, 2006); Köstenberger, *Theology*, 281–2. The first occurrence of κόσμος here in v. 10 ("He was in *the world*" [v. 10a]) seems to be neutral, with κόσμος denoting "world" in the sense of "creation" (the "inhabited world" or "world of humankind" seems too narrow given v. 10b). The second occurrence ("and *the world* was made through him" [v. 10b]) could be neutral or positive (cf. 3:16), with κόσμος denoting again "world" in the sense of "creation" or "universe." The third occurrence ("and *the world* did not know him" [v. 10c]), though, seems to be negative because of the world's failure to know the Word; κόσμος here bears a personal connotation and denotes "world" in the sense of "the inhabited world," "the world of humankind." As such, here in v. 10c "the human condition is summed up in the term *world*" (Smith, *Theology*, 80). Marrow observes that the categories "positive," "negative," and "neutral," while useful for describing the different connotations of κόσμος in John's Gospel, should not be viewed as mutually exclusive, for they often overlap ("Κόσμος," 96).

[70] BDAG 467.

[71] In Israel's Scriptures, the point that the world and all that is in it belongs to God is conveyed on several occasions. See, e.g., Exod 19:5; Deut 10:14; Ps 24:1.

[72] Throughout the Gospel of John a heritage of living in covenantal relationship with God is attributed to "the Jews" (οἱ Ἰουδαῖοι; see, e.g., 1:16–17, 19–23, 45–49; 4:22; 6:31–33; 7:22–23; 8:33). With respect to the sense and reference of οἱ Ἰουδαῖοι in John's Gospel, several possibilities have been suggested. Some contend that the designation denotes "the Jews" but has a limited reference, such as "the Jewish authorities" or "the representatives of unbelief," while others contend that οἱ Ἰουδαῖοι denotes a sense different from "the Jews," such as "the Judeans." For a survey of these possibilities and others see Stephen Motyer, *Your Father the Devil? A New Approach to John and "the Jews,"* Paternoster Biblical and Theological Monographs (Carlisle: Paternoster, 1997), 46–57; Motyer himself finds οἱ Ἰουδαῖοι to denote "the Jews" and to refer to "the religious of Judea" (54–7). On the various interpretive possibilities see also Reimund Bieringer, Didier Pollefeyt, and Frederique Vandecasteele-Vanneuville, "Wrestling with Johannine Anti-Judaism: A Hermeneutical Framework for the Analysis of the Current Debate," in *Anti-Judaism and the Fourth Gospel*, ed. Reimund Bieringer, Didier Pollefeyt, and Frederique Vandecasteele-Vanneuville (Louisville, KY: Westminster John Knox, 2001), 15–20; Kierspel, *The Jews and the World*, 13–36. In the present study a somewhat different interpretation from the ones just mentioned is espoused, one that seems to accord more aptly with the various contexts in which οἱ Ἰουδαῖοι is found in John's Gospel. In accordance with

Word upon his arrival in the world (v. 11b), then, parallels and further explains the declaration that "the world" did not know God's Word (v. 10c; cf. 7:1–7; 8:23).[73] How should we interpret this failure of human beings, particularly God's "own" people, to "know" the Word of God upon his advent in the world?

In Israel's Scriptures, the ascription to the people of God (and to those outside this people) of such a failure to "know" God occurs frequently.[74] Isaiah, for instance, opens with the declaration that, although God has brought forth a people and exalted them, "Israel does not know, and my people do not understand" (Isa 1:3).[75] Significant for our interests, though, is the point that this failure to know and understand God consists of rebellion and sin: the declaration that Israel "does not know" the Lord (Isa 1:3) parallels the preceding statement that Israel has "rebelled" against (פָּשְׁעוּ) or "rejected" (ἠθέτησαν [LXX]) the Lord (v. 2), and immediately after this ignorance is attributed to Israel (v. 3) the Lord addresses them as "sinful nation, people laden with iniquity, evil offspring, corrupt children" (v. 4). God's people are said here to have "forsaken" the Lord (v. 4). Jeremiah presents a similar conception of the people's failure to "know" God when he proclaims, voicing a lament of the Lord, "all commit adultery, [they are] an assembly of unfaithful people. They bend their tongue like their bow; falsehood and not faithfulness prevails in the land, because they go from evil to evil, and they do not know me" (Jer 9:1–2 [2–3]).[76] It is "through deceit" that the people "have refused to know me, says the Lord" (Jer 9:5 [6]).[77] In the LXX, Jeremiah says later, again offering an utterance of the Lord, "They did not know (οὐκ ἔγνωσαν), they judged neither the cause for the lowly nor the cause for the poor. Is not this you not knowing me (οὐ τοῦτό ἐστιν τὸ μὴ γνῶναί σε ἐμέ)? says the Lord" (22:16 LXX; cf. MT). In Ps 82 (81 LXX), after the Lord asks his congregants, "How long will you judge unjustly and show

---

[John 1:11, in which it is explained that the Word of God came into what is his own, "and his own people (οἱ ἴδιοι) did not receive him," the designation οἱ Ἰουδαῖοι seems to denote "the Jews" and refer to God's "own" people, the people to whom God gave the law (1:17; 5:39; 7:19) and with whom God established a covenant relationship. When οἱ Ἰουδαῖοι is understood to denote "the Jews" and to refer to God's "own" people (1:11), to God's covenant people, the point that Jesus is himself a "Jew" (Ἰουδαῖος [4:9 cf. 18:35]) becomes sensible, as does Jesus's pronouncement that "salvation is from the Jews" (4:22). To understand οἱ Ἰουδαῖοι as denoting "the Jews" and as referring to God's "own" people also accords with the point that Jesus is "the king of the Jews" (19:19–22). When "the Jews" are said to persecute Jesus (e.g., 5:16–18), are aligned with "the world" (8:23), are said to seek Jesus's death (8:37), or are shown to persuade Pilate to have Jesus crucified (18:28–19:16), the designation οἱ Ἰουδαῖοι is not "negative," strictly speaking, but tragic and ironic: the people who, above all, should have received Jesus (because they are "his own") are the very ones who persecute him and seek to bring about his death. For a somewhat similar reading of "the Jews" in John see Hylen, *Imperfect Believers*, 124–6.]

[73] Observe the parallel in syntactical structure and word selection:

καὶ ὁ κόσμος αὐτὸν οὐκ ἔγνω (1:10c)
καὶ οἱ ἴδιοι αὐτὸν οὐ παρέλαβον (1:11b).

[74] See, e.g., Exod 5:2; Judg 2:10–13; 1 Sam 2:12; Job 18:21; 36:12 (cf. LXX); Pss 14:2–4 (13:2–4 LXX); 79:6–7 (78:6–7 LXX); 82:1–7 (81:1–7 LXX); 95:8–11 (94:8–11 LXX); Isa 1:2–4; 5:13 (cf. LXX); 45:20; 48:4–8; Jer 2:8; 4:22; 9:1–5 (2–6); 22:16 LXX; Hos 4:1–2. Cf. Job 21:14; 24:11–13 ("they knew not the way of righteousness" [v. 13 LXX]); Hos 6:4–7; 8:1–4; Isa 56:11 ("they are evil, not knowing understanding" [LXX]); 59:8 ("they do not know the way of peace"). See also Wis 16:16; Pss. Sol. 2:31; Bar 4:12–13; cf. "knowing evil" (εἰδὼς κακίαν) in Pss. Sol. 17:27.

[75] MT: יִשְׂרָאֵל לֹא יָדַע עַמִּי לֹא הִתְבּוֹנָן; LXX: Ισραηλ δέ με οὐκ ἔγνω, καὶ ὁ λαός με οὐ συνῆκεν.

[76] MT (v. 2): וְאֹתִי לֹא־יָדָעוּ; LXX (v. 2): καὶ ἐμὲ οὐκ ἔγνωσαν.

[77] Cf. οὐκ ἤθελον εἰδέναι με in Jer 9:5 LXX.

partiality to the wicked?" (v. 2), and commands them to "deliver the lowly and needy" (v. 4), God declares, "they do not know and they do not understand, they walk around in darkness" (v. 5).⁷⁸

In these instances, the Greek γινώσκω or οἶδα (cf. συνίημι) and the Hebrew יָדַע express the manner of Israel's relationship with God. That is, the verbs signify (with their negations) that God's people have not "recognized" or "acknowledged" God in what they do and in how they live; they have not "known" God in the way they conduct their lives.⁷⁹ Knowledge of God, according to Israel's Scriptures, is wholistic: it involves what human beings perceive as well as do.⁸⁰ It entails living in a manner that responds positively to God's call for relationship, living in a way that acknowledges who God is in relation to the world and, in particular, to one's own creaturehood. Those who "know God" are those who "call on" the Lord (Exod 29:45–46 LXX) and "revere" God (1 Kgs 8:43); they are "upright in heart" (Ps 36:11 [10]) and "execute justice and righteousness" (1 Sam 2:10 LXX); they "love" the Lord (Ps 91:14) and devote themselves to God (Ps 46:11 [10]). David exhorts Solomon to "know the God of your father and serve him with a perfect heart and willing mind" (1 Chr 28:9). Daniel declares that the people "who know their God will stand firm and take action" (Dan 11:32). To know God entails living devotedly and in faithfulness to God, but a reoccurring pronouncement in Israel's Scriptures is that God's people have not done so; they have resembled the nations in their waywardness.⁸¹ Baruch offers a similar assessment: Jerusalem was left desolate "because of the sins of my children, because they turned away (ἐξέκλιναν) from God's law. And they did not know (ἔγνωσαν) his decrees; they neither walked in the ways of God's commandments nor treaded the paths of instruction in his righteousness" (4:12–13).⁸²

Such a wholistic conception of "ignorance" of God and, conversely, of "knowledge" of God is presented also in the Gospel of John.⁸³ Over the course of John's narrative

---

⁷⁸ MT (Ps 82:5): לֹא יָדְעוּ וְלֹא יָבִינוּ בַּחֲשֵׁכָה יִתְהַלָּכוּ; LXX (Ps 81:5): οὐκ ἔγνωσαν οὐδὲ συνῆκαν, ἐν σκότει διαπορεύονται.

⁷⁹ In Job 19:13 LXX (cf. the MT), the refusal of Job's brothers to "know" Job expresses the manner of personal relation that Job has experienced from his brethren and friends: "my brothers turned away from me, they knew strangers rather than me (ἔγνωσαν ἀλλοτρίους ἢ ἐμέ); and my friends have become unmerciful."

⁸⁰ For positive descriptions of what it means to "know" God see, e.g., Exod 29:45–46 LXX (cf. MT); 31:13; Num 12:6; Deut 4:5–6, 32–40; 1 Kgdms 2:10; 1 Kgs 8:43; 1 Chr 28:9; Pss 36:11 (10); 46:11 (10); 91:14–15; Hos 2:21–22 (19–20); 6:1–3; Isa 19:21; Jer 24:7; 31:31–34; Dan 11:32. See also Jdt 8:17–20; 4 Macc 16:23; Wis 15:3; Bar 2:30–35; Sib. Or. 2:51.

⁸¹ See, e.g., Exod 32:1–24; Num 14:1–35; Deut 32:4–27; 1 Sam 8:4–22; Pss 78:1–72; 81:8–16; 106:1–48; Isa 1:2–31; Jer 2:1–3:5; Hos 4:1–19; Amos 1:2–2:16; cf. Exod 19:5–6; 23:24–25; Lev 18:1–5, 24–30; 20:22–26; Deut 6:1–15; 7:6; 12:29–30.

⁸² By contrast, God does not "know" unrighteousness in his relationship with human beings (οὐκ ἔγνω ἀδικίαν; Zeph 3:5 LXX).

⁸³ For "knowledge of God" in John's Gospel see in particular Dodd, *Interpretation*, 151–69; C. K. Barrett, *The Gospel according to St. John: An Introduction with Commentary and Notes on the Greek Text*, 2nd ed. (Philadelphia, PA: Westminster, 1978), 162–63, 503–4. "In the Old Testament … for man to know God implies not only perception of his existence but also a relation with him of humble obedience and trust (e.g. Jer 31:34). This Old Testament usage constitutes the decisive, though not the only, factor in John's conception of knowledge" (Barrett, *St. John*, 162). James Gaffney emphasizes the shared meaning and congruence of "believing" and "knowing" in John's Gospel ("Believing and Knowing in the Fourth Gospel," *TS* 26 [1965]: 215–41).

we are informed that God's own people (1:11) do not have "the love of God" in them (5:42),[84] that they do not seek the glory that comes from God (5:44; cf. 7:18), that they do not keep the law (7:19), and that they are slaves to "sin" (8:34).[85] It is the will of someone *other* than God that they have been doing (they are "slaves" of sin because of committing sin previously [8:31–36]) and will continue to do (16:2–3), so long as they reject or do not abide in (8:31–32) God's Word.[86] This portrayal of God's own people informs and defines the "ignorance" or lack of knowledge of God that is repeatedly attributed to them (1:10–11; 7:28; 8:19, 55; 16:3). Unlike Jesus, who "knows" God and *keeps his word* (8:55; cf. 14:31; 15:10), Jesus's fellow "Jews" have *not* known God (οὐκ ἐγνώκατε αὐτόν [8:55]).[87] Consequently, God's own people have become aligned with and like "the world" (1:10–11; 7:1–7; 8:23; cf. 17:25), the deeds of which are "evil" (7:7; cf. 15:21). Because of how God's own people (i.e., "the Jews") and the world as a whole are portrayed over the course of John's narrative, then, it is clear that the ignorance of God attributed to human beings in the prologue (1:10–11) and in what follows (7:28; 8:19, 55; 15:21; 16:3; 17:25) signifies not merely a lack of mental perception concerning who God is, but a failure to live faithfully to God and do his will.[88]

Another question presents itself: is this ignorance on the part of God's own people and the world as a whole to be understood as arising concomitantly with the Word's advent in the world, or as preexisting and prompting the Word's advent? In certain

---

[84] The genitive τοῦ θεοῦ in the phrase τὴν ἀγάπην τοῦ θεοῦ (5:42) may be subjective ("God's love") or objective ("love for God"). The former reading would seem to accuse God's own people of failing to love others as God does (cf. Lev 19:2, 18; the idea that God does not love "the Jews" is ruled out by [*inter alia*] John 3:16 and 5:34b); the latter reading (which commentators generally seem to adopt) would accuse them of failing to love God (cf. Deut 6:5; 10:12). It is possible (and perhaps preferable), though, that the ambiguity of the phrase τὴν ἀγάπην τοῦ θεοῦ is intended to convey both ideas, in which case both Deut 6:5 ("Love the Lord your God with all your heart") and Lev 19:18 ("love your neighbor as yourself"), as well as the Decalogue, would be relevant. For a helpful and concise discussion of τὴν ἀγάπην τοῦ θεοῦ in John 5:42 see Brown, *John (I-XII)*, 226. For the Decalogue in John's Gospel see Jey J. Kanagaraj, "The Implied Ethics of the Fourth Gospel: A Reinterpretation of the Decalogue," *TynBul* 52 (2001): 33–60.

[85] On John 8:21–59 see Chapter 4.

[86] In the Gospel of John it is emphasized that to know or not know Jesus, the incarnate Word and divine Son of the Father, is to know or not know God (see, e.g., 7:28; 8:19; 14:7–11; 16:3; 17:3; cf. 8:42; 10:30–38; 12:44–45). For John, then, in rejecting or disobeying Jesus one demonstrates ignorance or a lack of knowledge of God.

[87] "The protagonist [of John's Gospel] is he who perfectly and unwaveringly knows, while all about him the inconstant currents of knowledge and belief have their ebb and flow, their clash and confluence" (Gaffney, "Believing and Knowing," 241). On John 8:54–55 Dodd comments that Jesus's words here "might almost come out of an Old Testament prophetic book"; in this scene Jesus "reiterates the language of the prophets, and, like them, contemplates a knowledge of God which is acknowledgment of His righteous will in action" (*Interpretation*, 158–9).

[88] Dodd finds that John 1:11 "echoes prophetic denunciations of God's own people … for unwillingness to know Him"; 1:10 "may be taken to make a corresponding statement about humanity as a whole" (*Interpretation*, 157). With respect to what, for John, constitutes "knowledge" of God, Koester provides a helpful summation: "Knowing God, in the Fourth Gospel, means relating to God. The knowledge of God includes information, but it finally presses readers beyond knowing things about God to knowing God as one knows and relates to a living being" (*Symbolism*, 290). Thompson comes to a similar conclusion: for John, knowledge of God ultimately "is not contemplation of but communion with God. Knowledge of God must therefore be interpreted as experience of God, appropriate honor of God, and acknowledgement of God in his works and response to his commands and claims" (*God*, 143).

respects this matter was already addressed during our assessment of "the darkness" in John's Gospel, and much of what was said there applies here. There is a correlation in John's Gospel between not "knowing" God and loving or walking in "the darkness" (see, e.g., 12:35), a correlation that is found also in Israel's Scriptures (see, e.g., Ps 82:5). John's attribution to human beings, particularly God's own people, of a failure to "know" God expresses the problem of "the darkness" in different but complementary terms. Accordingly, the point that the Word has come into the world so that all those who believe in him may not "remain" or "continue" in the darkness (12:46) pertains also to the problem of ignorance of God. The world's lack of knowledge of God or, put differently, its existence in "darkness" preexisted and prompted the Word's advent.[89] This point becomes clear when one considers the nature of the salvation that, for John, Jesus has come into the world to bring about, which is to "know" the only true God and the one through whom the world was created (17:2-5). That the world may come to know God and "be saved" is the ultimate aim of Jesus's advent (3:17; 12:47). In order to achieve this aim, though, Jesus himself must "know" and love God even unto death. That is, he must disregard and lay down his life "in this world" (10:17; 12:24-25), and thus sanctify himself (17:19), in order to realize in himself the knowledge and love of God that leads to and is eternal life. Jesus must bring true and everlasting life into existence in the world (1:3c-4, 14) in order to make this life possible for and available to the world (1:16-17).

A few additional remarks are now in order concerning the remainder of the prologue. The world's waywardness and ignorance of God notwithstanding (vv. 10-11), some people did receive and believe in the Word (v. 12), but to these was "given" (ἔδωκεν αὐτοῖς) new life: they received power to become "children of God" (v. 12),[90] "born of God" (v. 13).[91] These beheld Jesus's glory, that he was "full" (πλήρης) of grace and truth (v. 14), and "from his fullness" (ἐκ τοῦ πληρώματος αὐτοῦ) they received, namely,

---

[89] This ignorance of God seems, for John, to be exacerbated and magnified when one rejects or does not abide in Jesus (see, e.g., 3:36 [God's wrath "remains"]; 9:39-41; 15:22-24).

[90] In 8:39 Jesus declares to his audience that, if they were truly "children of Abraham" (τέκνα τοῦ Ἀβραάμ), they would be like Abraham and "do what Abraham did" (τὰ ἔργα τοῦ Ἀβραὰμ ἐποιεῖτε). The assumption here seems to be that one's behavior should follow from and reflect one's familial origin and heritage (on this idea see, e.g., van der Watt, *Family of the King*, 166-200). Consequently, it seems that, for John, to be "children of God" (τέκνα θεοῦ [1:12]) entails being like God and doing what God does. This conception of the children of God as those who resemble God in their manner of life follows from such OT texts as Lev 11:44-45 and 20:7-8. According to 1 John 3:1-2, "the children of God" (τέκνα θεοῦ) will one day see the Lord as he is and "will be like him" (ὅμοιοι αὐτῷ ἐσόμεθα); the author then goes on to exhort, "Children, let no one deceive you. The person who does righteousness is righteous, as he is righteous. ... By this are known the children of God and the children of the devil: every person who does not do righteousness, and who does not love his sister or brother, is not of God" (3:7-10). Cf. Luke 20:36; Rom 8:1-30; Eph 5:1-2; Phil 2:15; 1 Peter 1:14-16.

[91] On this divine generation cf. 3:3-8, in which Jesus explains that this new birth is realized through the Spirit. Cf. also 1 John 2:29, in which we are told, "If you know that he [the Son; cf. 2:1] is righteous, you know that every person who also does righteousness has been born of him" (ἐξ αὐτοῦ γεγέννηται). Pertinent as well is 1 John 4:7-8: "Beloved, let us love one another, for love is of God; and every person who loves has been born of God (ἐκ τοῦ θεοῦ γεγέννηται), and knows God (γινώσκει τὸν θεόν). The person who does not love does not know God (οὐκ ἔγνω τὸν θεόν), for God is love." God's love has been manifested in the Father's sending of the Son into the world "so that we might live through him" (ἵνα ζήσωμεν δι᾽ αὐτοῦ [v. 9]). See also 1 John 3:9; 5:18.

"grace in place of grace" (v. 16), "grace and truth" (v. 17). An implication here is that, for John, *all* human beings were in need of new life prior to Jesus's arrival, irrespective of whether some people were "children of God."[92] Whether some were "children of God" (in their elected status) or not, all human beings needed to be "born of God" and "become" children of God (cf. 3:3–8). The point that human beings lacked true life until Jesus's advent (vv. 3c-4, 9–13) is emphasized further in the announcement that, despite the gift of the law, it was through the incarnate Word that "grace and truth," steadfast love and faithfulness, "came into existence" in the world (v. 17).[93] Those who believe in Jesus *receive* this grace and truth from him (v. 16). Additionally, the point that it is to those *who believe* that Jesus gives power "to become" (γενέσθαι) children of God (v. 12) suggests that this divine generation transpires beyond the emergence of belief.[94] That is, becoming a child of God seems to be a process, because those who "believe"

---

[92] In Israel's Scriptures, the people of Israel are at times either called or described as the children of God. In Deut 14:1, for example, Moses tells the people of Israel that they are "children of the Lord your God." In Hos 1:10 we are told that, despite Israel's infidelity and sin, there will be a time when the people will be called "children of the living God." Similarly, there are instances in Second Temple literature in which "the Jews" are either called or described as children of God (see, e.g., 3 Macc 6:28–30; 7:6; cf. Wis 5:5; 2 Esd 1:28–29). In light of such texts, then, and given that, in John's Gospel, "the Jews" are God's "own" people (1:11), it seems possible (if not likely) that in John's Gospel the designation "the Jews" connotes "children of God" (note the association of "the nation" with "the children of God" in 11:51–52). The people to whom Jesus comes and of which he is a part would in this case be, for John, the children of God. This connotation of "the Jews" would then further accentuate the problem of the way "the Jews" and the world as a whole live. In rejecting Jesus, the children of God would be shown (generally speaking) to reject the one who has come into the world so that they (the children of God) might *become* children of God in the way they live (for the idea that one's behavior should align with and reflect one's familial origin and heritage see again John 8:39–42; 1 John 3:10; cf. Lev 11:44–45; 20:7–8). The idea and hope that salvation for the people of God will involve a transformation of the way this people lives in relationship with God is found in various Second Temple texts. In Jub. 1:22–25, for instance, "children of the living God" designates a people who, after returning to God and acknowledging their sin, are given a holy spirit by God and are purified; the children of God will consequently cleave to and do God's commandments (*OTP* 2:54; cf. Jer 31:31–34). In Pss. Sol. 17 it is explained that the children of God will arise with "the Lord Messiah," who will lead this people in righteousness (17:26); the children of God will be those who "have been made holy by the Lord their God" (17:26 [*OTP* 2:667]). Such texts further suggest that, in John's Gospel, to be "children of God" pertains not only to God's election—to an adoptive status—but also to a way of living in relationship with God and others. John's portrayal of Jesus's mission parallels these texts in certain respects: Jesus has come into the world to recreate human beings through the Spirit (3:1–8; 20:22), so that they are born of God (1:13) and live as does the Son of God (1:16–17; 8:34–36; 12:25–26; 14:19; 17:17–19).

[93] On the relationship between the law given through Moses and the "grace and truth" that, for John, has come into existence through Jesus (1:17; cf. 1:3c-4), Bauckham writes, "The law was grace and truth in words. The same grace and truth of God 'became' through Jesus—happened and were seen in his life and death. Jesus spoke the words of God's grace and truth, certainly, but he also enacted God's grace and truth" (*Gospel of Glory*, 52).

[94] For a helpful survey of this verse's history of interpretation see Vellanickal, *Divine Sonship*, 105–16. Vellanickal finds γενέσθαι here in 1:12 to indicate "that John considers the spiritual change in men, not as something static that takes place once for all at a definite moment in history, but as something that gradually takes place, and remains dynamic moving towards a final perfection" (140). On the sense of ἐξουσία here in v. 12 Brown writes, "to make of this a semi-judicial pronouncement whereby the Word gave men the *right* to become God's sons is to introduce an element strange to Johannine thought; sonship is based on divine begetting, not on any claim on man's part" (*John (I-XII)*, 11). Brown thus translates ἔδωκεν αὐτοῖς ἐξουσίαν in v. 12 as "he empowered" (3).

are not simply equated with the "children of God."[95] Rather, believers are described here (v. 12) as being enabled and empowered by Jesus to become children of God (cf. Jesus's later exhortation for his disciples to "become" his disciples in 15:8).[96] The point that, for John, salvation is in various ways a process will be demonstrated further in the chapters that follow.

Conclusion

Perhaps not surprisingly, John's prologue introduces both the way in which Jesus brings about salvation and the predicament from which Jesus saves. "What has come into existence in him," John tells us, "was life, and that life was the light of human beings" (1:3c–4). In and through his coming and going Jesus made life an accomplished fact. He realized in the world and made "flesh" the way of life that is light and knowledge of God, steadfast love and faithfulness. Believers in Jesus, through receiving life from his "fullness," are empowered to live like the Son of God and become what they are already called: children of God (vv. 12–17). Although Jesus, the light, was met in the world by an opposition that would eventually bring about his death, "the darkness" did not overcome the light, for the light continues to shine in the darkness (v. 5). Jesus, as we are told and shown later in John's Gospel, is "the resurrection and the life" (11:25).

Over the course of John's Gospel it becomes clear that "the darkness" cited in the prologue (1:5) designates and attributes to human beings a way or manner of life that is wayward and misguided. Human beings, in John's view of things, have been living in darkness, which is to do evil (3:19–20) and be lost (12:35). It was the predilection of human beings for the darkness that led them (generally speaking) to reject the light upon his advent in the world (3:19). All human beings in fact were living in darkness before Jesus's advent, for Jesus has come into the world, according to John, so that those who believe in him may not "remain" or "continue" in the darkness (12:46). Jesus calls people to live in the darkness *no longer* and, instead, follow him, the light of the world (8:12; 12:35–36).

---

[95] Theodor Zahn makes a related point: "Since it is not said: τέκνα θεοῦ ἐγένοντο or γεγόνασιν, the words at hand therefore should not be understood as if those [ἐγένοντο or γεγόνασιν] stood there" (*Das Evangelium des Johannes*, 5th and 6th eds. [Leipzig: Deichert, 1921], 71).

[96] Dukes, like Vellanickal, finds that in John's Gospel there is "both a realized and a future sense in which a [person] becomes a 'child' of God" ("Salvation," 136). This echoes Cyril of Alexandria, who, while commenting on John 1:12, says the following about God's adoption and ongoing formation of believers:

> We who bore the image of the earthly man could not escape corruption unless the call to sonship placed in us the splendor of the image of the heavenly man. We became participants in him through the Spirit. We were sealed into his likeness, and we ascend to the archetypal form of the image according to which Holy Scripture says we were also made. Once we recover the ancient beauty of our nature in this way and are refashioned in relation to the divine nature, we will be superior to the evils that befell us because of transgression. Therefore, we rise up to an honor above our nature because of Christ. (*In Jo.* 1.9.91; trans. David R. Maxwell, *Commentary on John*, ed. Joel C. Elowsky, vol. 1, Ancient Christian Texts [Downers Grove, IL: IVP Academic, 2013], 60)

The matters of ignorance and knowledge of God in John's Gospel further accentuate the problem of the world's way of life. The ignorance of God that is attributed to human beings—particularly God's "own" people—in the prologue (1:10–11) and in what follows (7:28; 8:19, 55; 15:21; 16:3; 17:25) signifies a failure on the part of human beings to live faithfully to God and do his will. Unlike Jesus, who knows God and keeps God's word (8:55), God's own people and the world as a whole have not known God. John's description of salvation as knowledge of God (17:3) conveys that, like the darkness, the world's ignorance of God preceded and prompted Jesus's advent (cf. 3:17; 12:47). "Ignorance" of God expresses the problem of "the darkness" in different but complementary terms (cf. 12:35).

For John, then, both the human predicament and its "solution" pertain to what human beings *do*, that is, to how human beings live in relationship with God and one another. In and through his coming and going Jesus disregards himself for the sake of God and others (10:17–18; 12:25), out of love for God and others and in faithfulness to God. Jesus sanctifies himself (17:19) in order to realize in himself (i.e., in his "flesh") the way of life that leads to and is eternal life. Jesus is indeed the way and the truth and the life (14:6), in the light of which the extent of the world's darkness and ignorance of God is revealed. And to find John to portray Jesus's mission or soteriological purpose in this fashion raises the question of whether John regards the human predicament to be a reality that, in various ways, persists beyond the emergence of belief, since the way Jesus lives is for John the soteriological basis, pattern, and goal for all those who believe in him. Are believers, for John, instantly and wholly transformed into Jesus's likeness, that is, into "children of God" (1:12–13), "children of light" (12:36), in the moment they come to believe in Jesus (i.e., in the "moment of decision")? We observed above that, in John's Gospel, believers are not simply equated with the "children of God": to those who believe Jesus gives power to *become* children of God (1:12). Might John suggest, then, that the way all human beings were living prior to Jesus's advent is not completely rectified or resolved in the emergence of belief, but instead is a reality that believers must endure and struggle against as they both are and "become" children of God? We will gain further clarity on this matter as our study of the human predicament in John's Gospel continues.

3

Illness, Disability, and Death: The Man with a Disabling Illness at Bethzatha and Jesus's Consequent Monologue

In Chapter 2 we observed that, in the Gospel of John, Jesus's mission to give life to the world is prompted in part by the darkness and ignorance of God in which all human beings were living prior to Jesus's advent. The problem of "the darkness" and of the world's failure to "know" God is introduced in John's prologue and developed over the course of John's narrative. In John 5, while Jesus is in Jerusalem for a festival, other matters of interest come into focus, namely, illness, disability, and death. Our analysis of these matters will demonstrate three main points. First, illness or bodily infirmity, disability (in a qualified sense), and death are interrelated aspects of the human predicament in John's Gospel. This point leads to two additional ones: the human predicament in John's Gospel is wholistic in nature and, also, is not wholly rectified or resolved in the emergence of belief. Salvation, in John's view of things, involves bodily renewal and transformation. The matters of "death" and "disability" in John's Gospel will also be found to accentuate further the problem of what human beings *do*. Our analysis of these matters, consequently, will inform and further substantiate this study's basic claim: the human predicament in the Gospel of John is a way or manner of life. The human predicament is for John not corporeality itself but, rather, *the way* human beings live corporeally. Salvation from this way of life occurs in toto on "the last day," when those who believe and remain in Jesus are raised up in "the resurrection of life" (5:29).

Our analysis of these matters takes its cues from John's narrative. "Illness" is shown to be problematic initially when Jesus learns about and heals an official's son (4:46–54), but the problem of illness comes to the fore when Jesus subsequently meets at Bethzatha, among a "multitude" of people with illnesses and/or disabilities, a man who has been ill for thirty-eight years (5:1–15). Our analysis of this scene will show that the healing Jesus effects for this man involves physical as well as social restoration, for, at a time when the Jerusalem temple is a place of great celebration and activity, Jesus enables the man to leave Bethzatha and go to the temple. Jesus gives "life" to this man in the sense that he cures the man of his disabling illness and, thereby, enables him to participate in the communal and religious life of his society. We will find the scene to suggest therefore that, for John, the human predicament includes illness or bodily infirmity. The scene will be found to suggest in fact that illness is a significant aspect of the human predicament in John's Gospel, for we will observe that illness is here depicted as a condition that can become so debilitating for human beings that certain physical and relational capacities become chronically impaired. That Jesus is shown not only here but on several occasions in John's Gospel to heal people from illness substantiates the point that, for John, illness or bodily infirmity is a significant aspect of the predicament in which human beings find themselves, on account of which Jesus has come into the world. The "miracles" Jesus is either said or shown to do for people who are sick indicate that the quality or condition of human corporeality is a focus of Jesus's mission in John's Gospel. The account of Jesus and the man at Bethzatha consequently bears significance beyond a revelatory or symbolic function.

The point that, for John, the human predicament involves the bodily frailty and decay to which human beings are subject, which the account of Jesus and the man at Bethzatha suggests, will be found to be substantiated also by the discourse that immediately follows this account, a discourse in which Jesus speaks about the Father and Son's unified intention to give life and deliver human beings from death (5:16–29). "Death" in John's Gospel, as we will observe, is both a bodily cessation or end of life that becomes absolute in "the resurrection of condemnation" (v. 29b) and a way or manner of life that has this eschatological condemnation as its ultimate end. Those who believe in Jesus and do good, by contrast, will one day arise from their graves in "the resurrection of life" (v. 29a). This resurrection of believers to eternal life, as Jesus explains elsewhere in John's Gospel, depends on and follows from Jesus's own resurrection (6:57; 10:17; 11:23–26; 14:19), so the resurrection of Jesus is additional confirmation that, for John, the predicament from which Jesus saves human beings consists of bodily infirmity and death.

In John 5 "illness" and "death" are not the only problems that come into focus, though. As Jesus arrives in Jerusalem we are told about a multitude of people there with various forms of what we now understand and refer to as "disability."[1] The question of "disability" in John's Gospel is important theologically. What conclusions should we draw from the fact that, in John's Gospel, Jesus is shown on multiple occasions to heal or deliver a person from a physical impairment? For modern interpreters in particular, an impairment such as congenital blindness, for instance, might be regarded simply as a difference of ability (rather than as a physical "defect") and embraced as an integral aspect of personal identity and distinctiveness. Does the fact that, in John's Gospel, Jesus delivers certain people from their impairments indicate that, for John, all such impairments are to be regarded as problematic? Are we to conclude that, according to John, God views people with disabilities as in some way "defective"?

Such questions make necessary certain definitions and distinctions. A helpful definition of "disability," and one that seems suitable for our analysis of John's Gospel, is formulated by Jeremy Schipper, who examines Isaiah's "Suffering Servant" (Isa 53) in light of disability studies: "disability" may be defined as "*the social experience of*

---

[1] For a biblical theology of disability, see Amos Yong, *The Bible, Disability, and the Church: A New Vision of the People of God* (Grand Rapids, MI: Eerdmans, 2011).

persons with certain impairments."[2] This definition accords with a "cultural" model of disability, which seems to appreciate most aptly both the corporeal and social factors that comprise disability.[3] On the basis of this conception, a distinction may be made to some degree between "impairments," which may be defined as comparatively significant differences of human ability that are either congenital or acquired through various circumstances, and the social experience of persons with impairments, which is again "disability."[4] Additionally, impairments and disability may be distinguished from "illness" in the sense that illness or bodily "infirmity" signifies a condition of poor or weak health.[5]

Informed by these definitions and distinctions, our ensuing exegetical analysis will show that, like illness, "disability" is an aspect of the human predicament in John's Gospel, but in a way that is directly related to illness and, also, in ways that are not. The case of the man whom Jesus encounters at Bethzatha makes clear that physical impairments can be a product of illness. The scene indicates that a physical impairment can be a circumstance of poor or weak health, which, according to John, is a problem Jesus addresses by healing people from illness and, ultimately, raising up on the last day all those who believe and remain in him from their graves (5:28–29; 6:39–40). In the case of the man born blind (John 9), though, the man's physical impairment—congenital blindness—is *not* associated with illness or poor health. The man, prior to receiving sight, is in fact depicted as being quite capable and healthy. Where the two scenes parallel one another, with respect to the matter of "disability," is in John's portrayal of each person's *social experience of impairment*: each person's social experience is shown to have been negative or problematic. In portraying the social experience of people with impairments in this way, John implicitly indicts the social environment in which these people live and of which they are a part. "The world" in

---

[2] Jeremy Schipper, *Disability and Isaiah's Suffering Servant*, Biblical Refigurations (Oxford: Oxford University Press, 2011), 18; italics original.

[3] Schipper explains a "cultural" model of disability by describing its dissimilarity to "medical" and "social" models. A medical model views disability "as an anomalous condition isolated in an individual's body and in need of diagnosis and correction or cure"; a social model views "disability" as designating the "socially created discrimination against people with impairments. … [T]he label of disability does not come from any intrinsic property of the impairment itself. Rather, it comes from the perceived frequency or rarity of the impairment within a particular society" (*Disability*, 16). Schipper goes on to explain that the social model has received criticism "because it defines disability primarily as a social construction. Critics of the social model emphasize that disability is a real, lived social experience that describes how many people with impairments experience the world" (16–17). On the differences between cultural and social models see also Sharon L. Snyder and David T. Mitchell, *Cultural Locations of Disability* (Chicago: University of Chicago Press, 2006), 5–11.

[4] Distinguishing between "impairment" and "disability" is typically a feature of social models. In making this distinction I wish not to deny or neglect the mutually informing nature of impairment and social experience (as seems to happen in social models) but to acknowledge and attribute significance to both aspects. "Environment and bodily variation (particularly those traits experienced as socially stigmatized differences) inevitably impinge upon each other" (Snyder and Mitchell, *Cultural Locations*, 6–7). This is undoubtedly true, yet we can still speak of "environment and bodily variation."

[5] Schipper, while commenting on the medical model of disability, points out that "the focus on a cure and correction … overlooks the fact that, although a disease may result in a disability, a healthy person with a disability is not an oxymoron" (*Disability*, 15).

which Jesus encounters people with disabilities is depicted as one that disadvantages and marginalizes such people. The reality of disability in John's Gospel therefore magnifies the problem of the way human beings treat and relate to one another. Disability is shown to be a problem that involves and pertains to all human beings, not just those with impairments. Additionally, John suggests that disability is problematic at an individual level if a physical impairment is something a person wishes no longer to experience. As a result of the circumstances in which we find people with disabilities in John's Gospel, then, our analysis will suggest it is unwarranted to conclude that John considers "disability" to be an aspect of the human predicament without qualification (i.e., irrespective of social context, cause, and/or personal volition). The point that, for John, the risen and glorified Jesus remains pierced and blemished (20:27) seems in fact to indicate that, in the Gospel of John, God is to be thought of not merely as including in his kingdom, but as affirming, people with what some might consider to be blemishes, defects, or disfigurements.

The Man at Bethzatha, Illness, and Disability

The meeting of Jesus and the man at Bethzatha is prefaced by a description of the scene's setting: after Jesus heals an official's son from illness (4:46–54), it is then said that "there was a festival of the Jews, and Jesus went up to Jerusalem" (5:1). "And in Jerusalem near the Sheep Gate,"[6] John continues, "there is a pool—called Bethzatha in Hebrew— that has five porticoes.[7] In these porticoes would lie (κατέκειτο) a multitude of the sick, blind, crippled, and paralyzed" (vv. 2–3).[8] With respect to our current interests,

---

[6] I understand κολυμβήθρα ("pool") to be nominative and supply the word "gate" (which is absent in the Greek), since (1) the book of Nehemiah refers to such a gate in Jerusalem (3:1, 32; 12:39); and (2) archeological excavations in Jerusalem have discovered the remains of a pool with five porticoes near the approximate location of this "Sheep Gate" (on both points see Urban C. von Wahlde, "Archeology and John's Gospel," in *Jesus and Archeology*, ed. James H. Charlesworth [Grand Rapids, MI: Eerdmans, 2006], 559–66).

[7] The external evidence for the name Βηθζαθά includes א, 33, and all (or the majority of) the Old Latin witnesses, but other names are attested as well (e.g., βηθεσδά; Βηθσαϊδά [see John 1:44]). Bruce Metzger notes that a majority of the UBS editorial committee found Βηθζαθά to be "the least unsatisfactory reading" of the available options (*A Textual Commentary on the Greek New Testament*, 2nd ed. [Stuttgart: Deutsche Bibelgesellschaft/United Bible Societies, 1994], 178).

[8] Concerning the people cited in v. 3, some translators and commentators find ἀσθενούντων ("sick") to function as an umbrella term that covers and generally describes τυφλῶν, χωλῶν, and ξηρῶν (the NRSV, for instance, translates v. 3 in this way: "In these lay many invalids—blind, lame, and paralyzed"). The translation of this verse is important from a disabilities perspective (see below) and multiple factors speak against the line of interpretation just noted. First, to regard ἀσθενούντων as signifying people who are "sick" or "ill" and, then, regard this description as applying to all those who are "blind," "crippled," and "paralyzed," assumes that all of these latter conditions are, in John's view of things, products and forms of "illness." But this assumption lacks basis. In Israel's Scriptures as well as in Second Temple literature there are instances in which "blindness" is described as the product of old age (see, e.g., Gen 27:1; 48:10; 1 Sam 4:15; 1 Kgs 14:4; Josephus, *Ant.* 1.267), and there are several instances in which blindness and lameness are described individually or collectively as products of injury (see, e.g., Exod 21:24–26; Lev 24:19–20; 2 Sam 4:4 [cf. 9:13]; 2 Kgs 25:7; Josephus *Ant.* 7.113; cf. Zech 11:17; Matt 18:8; Mark 9:45). In fact, blindness and lameness are generally categorized in Israel's Scriptures, as well as in Second Temple literature, either as "blemishes"/"defects" (מום; μῶμος) or as products of "mutilation"

this description of the scene's setting is important because it implicitly introduces a juxtaposition of two places: the Jerusalem temple and Bethzatha. The temple is the center of the festival that is or soon will be taking place, and Jesus will soon appear there (v. 14). In fact, whenever Jesus is said in John's Gospel to go to Jerusalem on the occasion of a "festival," Jesus, unless it is the hour of his death and glorification, always ends up at the temple.[9] Given that the festivals are Jewish celebrations (2:13; 5:1; 6:4; 7:2), it is not surprising that "the Jews," "the Pharisees," "people of Jerusalem," as well as "crowds" of people are also said to be at the temple on such occasions.[10] The temple, especially during the festivals, is indeed the place "where all Jews come together" (18:20). That Jesus is said to go up from Galilee to Jerusalem on the occasion of a festival (5:1; cf. 4:54), then, implies that at this juncture the Jewish people are or soon will be gathering, worshipping, and celebrating at the temple.

Importantly, this presentation of the temple as the destination of the Jewish people during the festivals reflects Jewish practice during the Second Temple period. Until its destruction the Second Temple was evidently always central to the social and religious life of the Jewish people living in ancient Palestine, but during the festivals the temple was particularly the center of Jewish life.[11] At such times Jews in Judea and

(λωβάομαι; πηρόω; cf. πήρωσις ["defect" or "disabling"]), not as "illnesses" (see Lev 21:16–23; 24:19–20 [note מום; μῶμος]; Philo, *Spec.* 1.117, 242; *Leg.* 2.97 ["mutilated, whole"]; Josephus, *Ant.* 7.61 [cf. λωβάομαι in *Ant.* 14.366; *Ag. Ap.* 1.233–234] *J.W.* 5.228–229 ["physical disabling"; note also ἄμωμος]; Apocr. Ezek. 1:20; cf. 2 Sam 14:25; Song 4:7; Dan 1:4; 1QSa II, 3–10; 1QM VII, 4–5; Philo, *Agr.* 130; T. Levi 9:10). This point casts serious doubt on the idea that, in John 5:3, ἀσθενούντων categorizes people who are blind, lame, and paralyzed collectively as "sick" or "ill" (for the categorization of blindness, lameness, and other impairments in Israel's Scriptures and, also, in the Qumran literature, see Saul M. Olyan, *Disability in the Hebrew Bible: Interpreting Mental and Physical Differences* [Cambridge: Cambridge University Press, 2008], 26–61, 101–18). It is possible perhaps that ἀσθενούντων (v. 3), rather than signifying people who are "sick" or "ill," signifies people who are "weak" because of injury, old age, illness, and/or something else. It might then be plausible to regard ἀσθενούντων as an umbrella term for τυφλῶν, χωλῶν, and ξηρῶν. This view is likewise problematic, though, because ἀσθενέω then seems far too broad and vague to categorize the particular condition of the man whom Jesus encounters and heals (v. 7; note also ἀσθένεια in v. 5). This point also raises a further problem for either of the views just noted. If ἀσθενούντων (v. 3) signifies a broad category that encompasses various specific impairments, and if John then proceeds to list these impairments with the words τυφλῶν, χωλῶν, and ξηρῶν, then one would expect John to use one of these latter, supposedly more specific terms to describe the man whom Jesus encounters, but John does not. John uses only ἀσθένεια (v. 5) and ἀσθενέω (v. 7) to categorize the man's condition. If ἀσθενούντων functions as an umbrella term, does not one of the more specific terms with which John unpacks ἀσθενούντων apply to the man whom Jesus heals? Why does John use *only* the umbrella category to describe the man's impairment? This interpretive difficulty disappears if ἀσθενούντων, like the terms that follow it, refers to a rather distinct physical condition: "sick." To understand ἀσθενούντων in this way seems to accord with how ἀσθενέω as well as ἀσθένεια are used elsewhere in John's Gospel (see esp. 4:46–53; 11:1–6). It is undoubtedly significant as well, with respect to the matter at hand, that, while the man whom Jesus heals in John 9 is said on (by my count) eleven different occasions in John's Gospel to be or to have been "blind" (τυφλός), the man is not once said to be or to have been "sick" or "weak." All of these points call into question and, collectively, make rather unviable the view that, in John 5:3, ἀσθενούντων functions as an umbrella term that applies to and generally describes τυφλῶν, χωλῶν, and ξηρῶν (translations that align with the one affirmed in this study ["a multitude of the sick, blind, crippled, and paralyzed"] include the CEB, CEV, NASB, and NET).

[9] In addition to 5:1–15, see 2:13–25 and 7:1–8:59; note also 10:22–23. Cf. 6:1–71; 12:1–19:42.
[10] See especially 2:18–20; 7:11–31; 8:12–20; 10:22–39; 11:55–56; cf. 4:45; 12:12, 20.
[11] On the importance of the Jerusalem temple to early Judaism, D. M. Gurtner and N. Perrin write, "For all its diversity, Judaism was unified by three central components: Scripture, Sabbath, and the temple.

its surrounding regions (even the Diaspora) would come to the Jerusalem temple for corporate and personal worship, to observe and offer sacrifices, pray, sing, and hear the recitation of scripture.¹² Philo describes the temple as the destination of great crowds during the festivals; at such times, he says, there was especially an atmosphere of joy, unity, and devotion:

> Countless multitudes from countless cities come, some over land, others over sea, from east and west and north and south at every feast. They take the temple for their port as a general haven and safe refuge from the bustle and great turmoil of life, and there they seek to find calm weather, and, released from the cares whose yoke has been heavy upon them from their earliest years, to enjoy a brief breathing-space in scenes of genial cheerfulness. Thus filled with comfortable hopes they devote the leisure, as is their bounden duty, to holiness and the honoring of God. Friendships are formed between those who hitherto knew not each other, and the sacrifices and libations are the occasion of reciprocity of feeling and constitute the surest pledge that all are of one mind.¹³

Such historical context further suggests that, in John 5, the description of Jesus as journeying from Galilee to Jerusalem on the occasion of a festival (v. 1) implies that at this juncture the Jewish people are or soon will be gathering and celebrating at the temple. As Jesus comes to Jerusalem the temple is especially at this time the center of Jewish life.

While in Jerusalem on this occasion, though, Jesus comes to a place that differs rather markedly from the temple in its atmosphere and appeal. Jesus comes to a place at which little, if any, celebration has been and will be occurring, given the circumstances that lead people here and cause them to stay. Bethzatha (v. 2) is where people with illnesses and/or disabilities lie and wait in hope of obtaining healing and relief, which is evidently thought to be obtained by the first person who enters the pool when its waters are mysteriously "troubled." A "multitude" of people seems in fact to be found at the pool on a consistent basis, as the imperfect verb κατέκειτο (v. 3), in

---

The temple in first-century AD Palestine was central to Jewish life and practice; it was the centerpiece of not only Israelite religious practices, but also societal structures and political conflicts for the environment in which Jesus lived, ministered, and died" ("Temple," *DJG* 939). James C. VanderKam notes that "[o]ne of the important functions served by the temple was as the center for celebration of festivals" (*An Introduction to Early Judaism* [Grand Rapids, MI: Eerdmans, 2001], 204).

¹² For descriptions of such activity at the Jerusalem temple (during the festivals or otherwise) see Sir 50:12–21; *Let. Aris.* 88, 92–95; Philo, *Spec.* 1.167–193; Josephus, *Ag. Ap.* 2.193–198; *Ant.* 3.237–257; Matt 5:23–24; 8:4; Luke 1:10; 2:22–38; 21:1–4; 24:53; John 12:20; Acts 3:1; m. Pesaḥ. 5:5–10; m. Sukkah 5:1–7; m. Tamid 3:8; 4:1–5:1; 5:6–7:4. Cf. Exod 29:38–42; Lev 1–7, 23; Num 10:10; 28–29; 1 Chr 23:4–5, 30–31; 2 Chr 29:20–30:27; Ps 116:17–19 (115:8–10 LXX); Isa 56:7; Neh 7:73–8:8.

¹³ *Spec.* 1.69–70 (Colson and Whitaker, LCL); see also Josephus, *Ant.* 4.203. Although Philo's description is perhaps idealized to a certain extent, it is nevertheless the testimony of one who (per Philo) journeyed to the Jerusalem temple on at least one occasion (*Prov.* 2.64). Philo says he journeyed to the temple "for the purpose of offering prayers and sacrifices" (*Prov.* 2.64). E. P. Sanders offers an estimate of the average number that would attend the festivals in Jerusalem: "While we can never know how many people were present at one time, it seems to me reasonable to think of 300,000 to 500,000 people attending the festivals in Jerusalem, especially Passover" (*Judaism: Practice and Belief, 63 BCE–66 CE* [London: SCM Press; Philadelphia, PA: Trinity Press International, 1992], 128).

accordance with the introductory description of Bethzatha (v. 2), seems to signify what was commonly or regularly transpiring at the pool: a multitude of people with illnesses and/or disabilities "would regularly lie" (κατέκειτο) at Bethzatha.[14] That people would "lie" there also conveys that people would remain at Bethzatha for some time. This point is made explicit, according to certain ancient manuscripts and witnesses, by the statement that people would lie at Bethzatha "waiting for the movement of the water" (ἐκδεχομένων τὴν τοῦ ὕδατος κίνησιν).[15] Other ancient manuscripts and witnesses suggest that this mysterious "movement" occurred infrequently (κατὰ καιρόν [v. 4]), and that only the first person who entered the pool at this time would be healed.[16] This infrequency of the water's mysterious movement agrees with the point that a multitude of people are regularly found at Bethzatha: the water's troubling rarely (perhaps never) occurs often enough to reduce by any significant amount the number of people lying at the pool. That only one person gains healing on each mysterious occasion agrees with the testimony of the particular man whom Jesus meets: the man speaks of a single person (ἄλλος) reaching the pool at the opportune time (v. 7). Afterward the rest of the multitude apparently returns, by and large, to lying and waiting. Bethzatha is therefore depicted as a place of misery and frustration. It is the destination for those who are physically debilitated and/or socially disadvantaged (given their impairments), and out of all the people that lie and wait at Bethzatha it seems that only a few ever leave in any way satisfied or content.

The juxtaposition of the temple, on the one hand, which is where the Jewish people are or soon will be congregating during the festival, and Bethzatha, on the other, which is where people with illnesses and/or disabilities congregate, comes to the fore as the scene unfolds. So too does the degree to which Bethzatha is a place of discontent and misery, for among the many people lying at Bethzatha Jesus encounters a man who has been ill for "thirty-eight years" (v. 5). The man's chronic illness (ἀσθενείᾳ [v. 5]) as well as his presence "there" (ἐκεῖ [v. 5]) identify him as one of the "multitude" just mentioned (v. 3), as does the detail that Jesus sees him "lying" there (κατακείμενον [v. 6]), waiting for the stirring of the water (v. 7). That the man's situation is and has been dire is indicated by the duration of the man's illness (v. 5), by the man's impaired mobility (vv. 7–8), by the man's lack of a person or people to enable his mobility (v. 7), and by the amount of time the man has spent at Bethzatha, which seems to constitute a large portion, if not the entirety, of the time the man has been ill. When Jesus is said to see the man lying at Bethzatha (v. 6), Jesus is then said to know that the man

---

[14] The verb κατέκειτο in v. 3 seems to be a "customary" imperfect (see Wallace, *Greek Grammar*, 548). Michaels explains the significance of the verb and its local cotext in this way: "The scene unfolds, not merely as something that met Jesus' eyes when he arrived in Jerusalem, but as what went on at the pool on a regular basis, whether at the Jewish festivals or all the time. It is a customary or repeated scene that the reader is invited to visualize, not a one-time event" (*John*, 289–90).

[15] Although v. 3, in its earliest form, perhaps did not conclude with these words (their attestation includes A^c, C^3, D, K, W^s, Γ, Δ, 078, $f^{1.13}$, 33, 892, 𝔐, the Vulgate and part of the Old Latin, the Syriac *Peshitta* and *Harklensis*, and some Bohairic witnesses), these words may nevertheless serve as an interpretive aid since, if they are not "original," they therefore represent an ancient interpretive gloss. Brown thinks these words in fact "may be original" (*John (I–XII)*, 207).

[16] The external evidence for v. 4 includes A, C^3, K, L, Γ, Δ, $f^{1.13}$, 𝔐, the Old Latin (with minor differences), the Syriac *Peshitta* and *Harklensis*, and some Bohairic witnesses.

"already has a long time" (πολὺν ἤδη χρόνον ἔχει [v. 6]). It is possible that this "long time," rather than representing both the duration of the man's illness and that of the man's stay at Bethzatha as a single period of time, or rather than signifying only the duration of the man's stay, instead signifies only the duration of the man's illness (v. 5), but multiple factors make this interpretation less favorable.

First, the sequence and structure of the indirect discourse in which the words πολὺν ἤδη χρόνον ἔχει occur (v. 6) shape the meaning of these words. Jesus is said to know that the man "has a long time" *immediately after* Jesus is said to see the man "lying" (κατακείμενον) at Bethzatha, which suggests that "a long time" refers to the amount of time the man has been doing this, that is, "lying" in Bethzatha's porticoes.[17] The structure of this indirect discourse is significant in the sense that what Jesus "sees" (i.e., the man "lying" at Bethzatha) parallels or corresponds to what Jesus "knows" (i.e., that the man "has a long time"), since both constitute the object of Jesus's perception or thinking. This correspondence further suggests that "a long time" pertains to how long the man has been lying at Bethzatha.

Additionally, the man's testimony (v. 7) implies that the length of his stay at Bethzatha has been great. In response to Jesus's question, "Do you wish to be well?" (v. 6), the man explains that he attempts to enter the pool when its water is troubled (ἐν ᾧ δὲ ἔρχομαι ἐγώ [v. 7]). Because illness has impaired his physical mobility, though, and because the man has no one to assist him, "another goes down (καταβαίνει) ahead of me," the man says (v. 7). The present tense verbs here (ἔρχομαι, καταβαίνει) signify iterative or customary action, indicating that, given the infrequency of the water's troubling (vv. 3–4), the man has been at Bethzatha for a considerable length of time. The man's lack of assistance further suggests this. The man tells Jesus that he does not have anyone (ἄνθρωπον οὐκ ἔχω) who, when the water is troubled, might "put" him (βάλῃ με) in the pool (v. 7). This implies that, with respect to the matter of the man's mobility, the man does not have anyone *at all*, and thus that the man is and has been unable to leave Bethzatha. The man is depicted as being stranded there. The man's immobility is further emphasized when Jesus says to the man, "Rise, pick up your mat, and walk" (v. 8), which the man immediately does (v. 9). Prior to this the man was apparently unable to "walk" and, thus, leave Bethzatha, given that the man did not have anyone to enable his mobility.[18]

---

[17] As noted above, "a long time" may likewise signify the duration of the man's illness (thirty-eight years [v. 5]) if this and the man's time at Bethzatha are one and the same.

[18] In v. 8, the man's impaired mobility is highlighted not only by the imperative verbs ἔγειρε ("rise") and περιπάτει ("walk") but also by the noun κράβαττος ("mat" or "stretcher"). When κράβαττος occurs in the NT (I find no occurrences in the LXX and in the works of Philo and Josephus), the word designates either (a) that on which people carry (or carried) a person with an illness and/or disability (Mark 2:3–12; 6:55–56); or (b) that on which a person with a disabling illness lies or lay previously (John 5:3–12; Acts 5:15; 9:33–35). In all of these instances, it is only after being healed that one said to lie on such a "mat" is depicted as carrying it; prior to such healing, the person in question is carried on the "mat" or "stretcher" and brought to his or her healer (cf. also κλίνη ["bed," "stretcher"] in Matt 9:2–7; Luke 5:17–19; κλινίδιον ["bed," "stretcher"] in Luke 5:17–19, 24; κλινάριον ["bed," "stretcher"] in Acts 5:15). "In a number of contexts the terms κλινίδιον, κλινάριον, and κράβαττος refer to cots or stretchers on which sick or convalescent persons might be resting or on which they could be transported" (L&N, 1:67 [6.107]). With respect to John 5, this usage suggests that, when Jesus commands the man to pick up his "mat" and "walk" (v. 8), κράβαττος further indicates that the man is one who heretofore has required the assistance of others for transportation.

For these reasons it seems preferable to understand "a long time" (v. 6) as referring to the length of the man's stay at Bethzatha.[19] The man is depicted, then, as having been ill for thirty-eight years (v. 5) and as having been at Bethzatha—among the "multitude" of people regularly found there—for much if not all of this time, waiting and hoping to obtain healing and relief. A reality of some complexity is therefore shown to grip the man. The man's illness, which he has had for thirty-eight years, is a disabling one in the sense that it has caused the man's physical mobility to be severely impaired. Importantly, though, the man's dilemma has consisted of more than his physical debilitation, for the man has been stranded at Bethzatha for a considerable portion, if not for the entirety, of the time he has been ill. The man is and has been unable to participate in the religious and communal life of his people, for he has been languishing in Bethzatha's porticoes without assistance (at least with respect to his mobility) for "a long time" (v. 6). The setting of a "festival" (v. 1) highlights the man's social dissociation. At a time of festal celebration, when the Jerusalem temple is in particular the place at which the Jewish people are or soon will be gathering and worshipping, the man whom Jesus encounters at Bethzatha is and will be unable to join his fellow "Jews" as they commune at the temple, for the man is immobile and has no one to assist him with his mobility.[20] The man has been, is, and will be unable to go to the place "where all Jews come together" (18:20). The man is consequently depicted as physically debilitated and, also, socially dissociated. That Jesus cures the man of his debilitated health and physical impairment, enabling the man to pick up his mat and walk (v. 8), confirms that the physical condition the man has endured is indeed considered to be problematic. That Jesus then finds the man *in the temple* (ἐν τῷ ἱερῷ [v. 14]) and here declares to the man, "Behold! You have been made well!" (v. 14), confirms that the social dissociation the man has endured is likewise considered to be problematic. In curing the man of his illness Jesus enables the man to leave Bethzatha and go to the place where the Jewish people are gathering, worshipping, and celebrating. That Jesus pronounces the man "well" when Jesus finds him in the temple (v. 14) indicates that the healing Jesus brings about for the man involves the man's physical health (cf. vv. 8–13) *as well as* the man's inclusion and participation in the religious and communal life of his society. The life Jesus has given to the man (cf. vv. 17, 21), so as to make him "well," pertains to the man's physical and, also, social well-being.[21]

---

[19] Translations that interpret πολὺν ἤδη χρόνον ἔχει as referring to the man's time at Bethzatha include the CEB, ESV, ISV, RSV, and NRSV; commentators include Rudolf Schnackenburg (*The Gospel according to St. John: Commentary on Chapters 5–12*, trans. Cecily Hastings, Francis McDonagh, David Smith, and Richard Foley [New York: Crossroad, 1990], 92), Ernst Haenchen (*John: A Commentary on the Gospel of John, Chapters 1–6*, ed. Robert W. Funk and Ulrich Busse, trans. Robert W. Funk, Hermeneia [Philadelphia, PA: Fortress, 1984], 242, 245), and Thompson (*John*, 119). Commentators who understand the man to have been at Bethzatha for thirty-eight years include Bultmann (*John*, 241–2) and Brunner (*John*, 296–7).

[20] That the man with a disabling illness is a "Jew" becomes clear when, after he is healed, "the Jews" rebuke him for carrying his mat on a sabbath day: "It is the sabbath; it is not lawful for you (οὐκ ἔξεστίν σοι) to carry your mat," they tell him (5:10).

[21] Bennema describes the man's illness as a form of "physical oppression" that prevented the man from participating "in various social and religious activities. The ill man at the pool of Bethesda had not been able to take part in the social-religious life of his day for thirty-eight years"; as such, Jesus's healing of the man "was not only a physical liberation but also a social-religious one—he could enter

Given that Jesus attends to the man and delivers him from these circumstances, it seems important to consider what is said or shown to have caused these circumstances. The man's debilitated health, as we have observed, is categorized as an "illness" (vv. 5, 7; cf. v. 3), and it was undoubtedly this illness that caused the man's physical mobility to be severely impaired.[22] "Illness" seems in fact to be a major aspect of the human predicament in John's Gospel, for the condition of the man whom Jesus meets at Bethzatha makes clear that illness is detrimental to the physical and relational capacities of human beings, and that illness can be chronically disabling. But what about the man's social dissociation? Is the man's isolation and exclusion from the communal life of his people to be attributed wholly to the man's illness? John suggests otherwise.

As we observed above, John describes the man as having been at Bethzatha for much if not all of the duration of the man's illness. The man was there "a long time" (v. 6), which, if not being equal to thirty-eight years (v. 5), undoubtedly represents a substantial portion of this time frame. The man's report about his experience at Bethzatha (v. 7) also indicates a stay of considerable length. The man's statement that, over the course of his many attempts to enter the pool at the water's stirring (which occurred infrequently), he did not have someone to set him in the pool (ἄνθρωπον οὐκ ἔχω [v. 7]) implies that, at least with respect to the matter of the man's mobility, the man did not have anyone *at all*, and thus that the man was unable to leave Bethzatha. The man, as one who was unable to "walk" (v. 8), always lacked a person or people to accommodate his impaired mobility. The man is consequently depicted as being stranded at Bethzatha for "a long time." John seems to show, then, that the man was dissociated from the communal life of his society because the man was at Bethzatha for a considerable portion, if not for the entirety, of the thirty-eight years the man was ill. But, importantly, John indicates that the man was at Bethzatha for such a great amount of time, not only because the man's mobility was impaired but also because the man did not have anyone to enable his mobility. It was the man's disabling illness, coupled with his lack of assistance, that left the man stranded at Bethzatha for the long time the man was there. John's description of the man's social experience of his impairment therefore seems implicitly to indict the man's society. The fact that the

---

the temple again (5:14)" ("The Sword of the Messiah," 51, 53). It is not merely the man's illness that prevented the man from participating in the religious and social life of his community, however.

[22] Interestingly, Jaime Clark-Soles, in her reading of John 5:1–18 from a disabilities perspective, finds that "no specific details are given about [the man's] impairment or how he became impaired" ("John, First-Third John, and Revelation," in *The Bible and Disability: A Commentary*, ed. Sarah J. Melcher, Mikeal C. Parsons, and Amos Yong, Studies in Religion, Theology, and Disability [Waco, TX: Baylor University Press, 2017], 342). What leads Clark-Soles to this conclusion is rather unclear. Clark-Soles says that "a chronic impairment is vastly different from an illness" (336), but she then proceeds to describe the man at Bethzatha repeatedly as "ill" and as having an "illness" (340–1), and she implies that, unlike the man born blind, the man at Bethzatha has an acquired disability (346). Some of her comments consequently suggest that Clark-Soles regards the man's impairment and disability to be the product of illness. Unfortunately, Clark-Soles does not define "illness" or say how, in John's Gospel, "illness" should be understood with respect to "impairment" and "disability." I am therefore left to surmise that, because Clark-Soles regards ἀσθενούντων in John 5:3 as "a generic term covering a variety of impairments" (340), Clark-Soles finds the man at Bethzatha to be "ill" in the sense that the man has an impairment. Clark-Soles apparently assumes that, in John's Gospel, to have a disability is to have an "illness." For the various problems such an interpretation presents (which I find to make such an interpretation rather unviable) see above, in connection with John 5:3.

man's well-being is shown to involve not only his physical health but also his inclusion in his society's communal and religious life (v. 14; cf. v. 1) seems to incriminate the man's social environment, for the man's inclusion in this communal life is something that, presumably, his society could have enabled or fostered, at least to an extent greater than what John suggests.[23] In restoring the man physically and socially, Jesus delivers the man from his disabling illness as well as from his social dissociation, both of which the man endured for a long time.

Two additional features of the story require comment. First, note that the man at Bethzatha desired to be healed. The man's regular attempts to enter the pool at the water's stirring seem to make this clear. The man recounts his attempts in response to the question Jesus poses to him (v. 6): "Do you wish to be well?" Second, although Jesus attributes to the man a preceding life of "sin" when Jesus exhorts him to "sin no longer" (v. 14), and although Jesus then follows this exhortation with a warning about something "worse" (than the man's former situation) that will befall the man if he does not in some sense change his ways (v. 14), it is not necessarily the case that the man's illness should be viewed as a consequence of his sin.[24] Because of Jesus's concern for the man's well-being, Jesus may compare the outcome awaiting the man (if he does not change his ways) with his former condition in order to seize the man's attention and convict him of his wrongdoing. Jesus's exhortation and declaration about what is "worse" may simply serve to make clear to the man that, while he has been "made well," nevertheless *all is not well* for the man.

---

[23] Thompson, while dismissing the idea (rightly) that the man is depicted as lacking genuine interest in being healed, reaches a similar conclusion with respect to the man's situation: "The fact that for thirty-eight years the man has languished, without assistance, indicts his society, not him" (*John*, 121). Some scholars seem to assume, evidently on the basis of Lev 21:16–23 and 2 Sam 5:8, that in the first-century CE people with physical impairments were not permitted in the Jerusalem temple. I find no grounds for such an assumption, however. In Lev 21:16–23, what is under consideration is the vocation of serving in the sanctuary as "priests": people with physical impairments or "defects" are to be excluded from officiating the sacrifices. Concerning 2 Sam 5:8 ("Therefore it is said, the blind and the lame shall not come into the house"), there is debate about how this statement should be interpreted. Some have argued (quite persuasively, I think) that the statement's purpose is narrative irony (i.e., to develop an ironic parallel between David and Saul and their respective ancestral lines) rather than to explain or justify any actual proscription (see Anthony R. Ceresko, "The Identity of 'the Blind and the Lame' (*'iwwēr ûpissēaḥḥ*) in 2 Samuel 5:8b," *CBQ* 63 [2001]: 23–30; Jeremy Schipper, "Reconsidering the Imagery of Disability in 2 Samuel 5:8b," *CBQ* 67 [2005]: 422–34). If the statement does reflect an actual proscription, questions arise as to whether this proscription was in effect in the first century and, if so, to what extent. A scene in the Gospel of Matthew suggests that such a proscription was *not* in effect: after Jesus comes to the Jerusalem temple and there drives out those who were selling and buying, we are told, "And the blind and the lame came to him in the temple (καὶ προσῆλθον αὐτῷ τυφλοὶ καὶ χωλοὶ ἐν τῷ ἱερῷ), and he healed them" (21:12–14). Jesus is then praised in the temple by the children there (21:15; cf. v. 9). There is no hint in this passage of "the blind and the lame" being censured or reprimanded in any way for entering the temple, or even of "the blind and the lame" doing something out of the ordinary here. This text therefore contradicts the idea that people with physical impairments or disabilities were not allowed in the first century to enter the Jerusalem temple and attend its various events.

[24] So also Barrett: "It is neither said nor implied that the man's illness was the consequence of sin" (*St. John*, 255). The fact that "sin" is not mentioned in connection with the respective illnesses of the official's son (4:46–54) and Lazarus (11:1–44) should give one pause about assuming for John any direct correlation between a person's illness and sin (note also that sin is not mentioned in connection with "the sick" in 6:2).

To sum up our conclusions thus far, then, we have found John's account of Jesus and the man at Bethzatha to suggest two main points with respect to John's portrayal of the human predicament. The account suggests, first, that "illness" is a significant aspect of the human predicament, for the condition of the man whom Jesus meets at Bethzatha makes clear that illness debilitates the physical and relational capacities of human beings and can be chronically disabling. Jesus makes the man "well" in the sense that Jesus restores the man both physically and socially. The account suggests, second, that the manner or character of "the world" in which Jesus encounters the man at Bethzatha is also a significant aspect of the human predicament, for the man's "disability," that is, the man's social experience of his impairment, is shown to have been characterized by the man's isolation and exclusion from the communal and religious life of his society. The man's social environment is depicted as being unaccommodating and callous toward people with disabilities, for it is depicted as allowing the man to languish in Bethzatha's porticoes for a significant portion, if not for the entirety, of the thirty-eight years the man was ill. The fact that Jesus pronounces the man "well" when Jesus finds him in the temple (v. 14), on the one hand, highlights the importance for the man's well-being of his inclusion and participation in his society's religious and communal activities and events. On the other hand, though, Jesus's pronouncement implicitly indicts the way the man's society treated him over the course of his illness, for during this time the man was excluded from his society's religious and communal life. The scene indicates that "disability" is problematic, furthermore, insofar as it is a product of illness.

Illness and Disability in the Wider Narrative of John's Gospel

The point that, for John, "illness" as well as "disability" (understood as the social experience of people with impairments) are aspects of the human predicament is substantiated further by the fact that illness and disability are respectively shown on more than one occasion in John's Gospel to be a problem Jesus addresses. The reality of "disability" is encountered again when, in John 9, Jesus meets a man "blind from birth" (τυφλὸν ἐκ γενετῆς [v. 1]). John portrays the man's social experience of his blindness as a problem in two respects: the man, because of his blindness, has been socially marginalized as well as disadvantaged.[25] The man has been socially marginalized in the sense that his blindness has led others to attribute "sin" both to him and his family (vv. 2, 34). Jesus declares that to judge and treat the man and his family in this way is wrong (v. 3). The man has been socially disadvantaged in the sense that, because of his blindness, the man has been a "beggar" (v. 8a). The man is known within his community as "the one who sits and begs" (v. 8b). According to Ben Sira it is better to die than to beg (Sir 40:28–30), and in the Gospel of Luke "begging" is considered by the parabolic manager to be shameful (Luke 16:3).[26] That John likewise finds begging to be problematic is indicated by the fact that the man born blind no longer sits and

---

[25] I use and understand the word "marginalized" to mean the following: considered by others to have a marginal social position or status and treated accordingly.

[26] Cf. Job 27:14 LXX; Ps 109:10; Mark 10:46–52; Luke 18:35–43.

begs once he receives sight. Following the man's reception of sight, his neighbors and acquaintances, who knew him formerly as a beggar (v. 8a), become uncertain about who he is (vv. 8–9), which conveys that the man is dramatically different and, thus, unfamiliar to his community. However, the uncertainty on the part of the man's community pertains initially to the man's social position or standing as a beggar: the man's neighbors and acquaintances wonder *not* whether he is the man born blind but whether he is "the one who sits and begs" (v. 8b). The implication here is that the man is found to be different and unfamiliar, at least initially, because he is not a beggar. It is difficult to interpret the initial uncertainty on the part of the man's community as meaning otherwise. John consequently portrays the man born blind as one who was a beggar previously but, because of receiving sight, is a beggar no longer. The man's acquired ability to see enables him to leave behind the life of begging that previously defined him.

From this last point it then follows that, in giving sight to the man born blind, Jesus delivers the man from begging. The man is no longer socially disadvantaged and marginalized as a "beggar" because the man is no longer blind. The importance of this change in the man's socioeconomic position or standing is evinced by the fact that John refers to this change immediately after the man receives sight. When the man is said to come back from Siloam "seeing" (v. 7), the man's new condition is then juxtaposed with the man's former one (τὸ πρότερον ["formerly"; v. 8a]), but this former condition, as was noted above, is defined here not as one of blindness but as one of begging. This juxtaposition is undoubtedly significant. Evidently, then, John portrays the man's social experience of his blindness as a problem that Jesus addresses, at least to a certain extent (note that the man's fellow "Jews" continue to attribute sin to the man and his family [v. 34]). To be sure, the man's social experience of his impairment seems to be neither the *only* problem that Jesus addresses here nor the main one, given that it is the emergence of faith on the part of the man that John emphasizes above all else. Unlike the man at Bethzatha, the man born blind comes to believe in Jesus (vv. 35–38; cf. vv. 17, 22, 27–33). Important as well is the point that the man born blind desires the ability to see. Given the opportunity presented him (vv. 6-7a), the man heeds Jesus's instructions and does his part to bring to fruition what Jesus offers: the man goes and washes in the pool of Siloam, just as Jesus had instructed him (vv. 7b, 11, 15). The man seems delighted to have the ability to see (vv. 11, 15, 17, 27, 30–33). Nevertheless, what Jesus delivers the man from through giving the man sight is, in part, the man's life as a beggar. This is thus another instance in which "disability," that is, the social experience of people with impairments, is shown to be a problem that Jesus addresses.

The problem of "illness" is encountered again when, in John 11, illness (ἀσθένεια) is shown to cause the death of Lazarus.[27] Lazarus is of course the one who dies, but his death deeply affects his family and community: Mary and Martha (Lazarus's sisters)

---

[27] Clement of Alexandria cites John 11:43 (and seems to draw on John's Gospel more broadly) in support of his contention that salvation addresses physical debilitation and decay: "But the good Instructor, the Wisdom, the Word of the Father, who made humanity, cares for the whole nature of His creature; the all-sufficient Physician of humanity, the Savior, heals both body and soul. 'Rise up,' He said to the paralytic [Mark 2:11]. ... And to the dead he said, 'Lazarus, go forth'" (*Paed.* 1.2 [SC 70:118; *ANF* 2:210; trans. modified]).

mourn the loss of their brother, and Mary weeps (vv. 19, 33); many fellow "Jews" come to console Mary and Martha (vv. 19, 31), and they weep (v. 33); and Jesus is said to experience indignation when he sees this great sadness over Lazarus's death (Ἰησοῦς ... ἐνεβριμήσατο τῷ πνεύματι [v. 33]). Jesus becomes "greatly distressed" (ἐτάραξεν ἑαυτόν) and he too weeps (vv. 33–35). Jesus is then said again to become indignant when he comes to Lazarus's tomb (v. 38). In John 4 it is likewise "illness" that so debilitates the son of a royal official that the boy's death is thought to be imminent (vv. 46–54). The official is so distressed that he leaves his son at Capernaum and travels to Cana to meet with Jesus and request that he "come down" before his child dies (vv. 47, 49).

That Jesus repeatedly heals people of their illnesses and, in some cases, does so voluntarily conveys that illness is a focus of Jesus's mission in John's Gospel. Jesus heals the man with a disabling illness at Bethzatha without solicitation (5:5–9). In raising Lazarus Jesus does what is unthinkable for Lazarus's family and community (11:23–26, 39–40), and so again Jesus heals and imparts life voluntarily (cf. 5:21, 25–26).[28] Jesus is described in fact as attracting great crowds because "they saw the miracles he was continuously doing (ἐποίει) for the sick" (6:2). It is true that in the case of the official's son (4:46–54) Jesus's initial response to the official's request is rather negative: "Unless you see signs and wonders, you will not believe" (v. 48). But this rebuke seems due to the official's stipulations about how the healing should occur, rather than to the healing itself.[29] Delivering people from illness seems to follow quite simply from Jesus's intention for people to have "life to the fullest" (10:10).[30] John's presentation of Jesus as the incarnate Word and divine Son whom the Father has sent into the world to heal and impart life evokes portrayals of God as healer in Israel's Scriptures: "I am the Lord who heals you," God declares to Israel (Exod 15:25). "I will restore health to you and I will heal you from your wounds, the Lord says" (Jer 30:17).[31] John's presentation of Jesus as God's agent of healing and life also evokes portrayals of the inbreaking of God's reign and rule in and through Jesus found elsewhere in the NT.[32]

---

[28] Although Martha's statement in 11:22 ("Even now I know that whatever you ask from God, God will give you") seems to affirm Jesus's authority and ability to provide help or relief, it is nevertheless quite vague. It may in fact be ironic in its unwitting prescience. Martha's ensuing statement that Lazarus will rise "in the resurrection at the last day" (v. 24), together with her reluctance to have the stone removed from Lazarus's tomb at Jesus's request (vv. 39–40), implies that the idea of Jesus restoring Lazarus to life, four days after his death, is an idea unavailable to Martha.

[29] The official repeatedly asks Jesus to "come down" to Capernaum to heal his son (vv. 47, 49), suggesting perhaps that the official expects a wondrous exhibition and visual display (σημεῖα καὶ τέρατα [v. 48]) characteristic of wonder-workers (cf. Matt 24:24; Mark 13:22; Josephus, *Ant.* 20.167–168; see also Philo, *Mos.* 1.90–91, 95). Jesus will heal the boy simply with a word (v. 50), from afar (but cf. 9:6–7).

[30] "Jesus' healings ... belong to a cluster of events associated with the Gospel's transformative and imperial contesting vision and experience of 'eternal life' or 'life of the age' (*zōē aiōnios*)" (Warren Carter, "'The blind, lame and paralyzed' (John 5:3): John's Gospel, Disability Studies, and Postcolonial Perspectives," in *Disability Studies and Biblical Literature*, ed. Candida R. Moss and Jeremy Schipper [New York: Palgrave Macmillan, 2011], 144).

[31] See also, e.g., 2 Kgs 20:5; 2 Chr 30:20; Pss 6:2; 30:2; 103:2–3; 107:17–20; Isa 6:10; 19:22; 30:26; 57:18–19; Jer 3:22; 17:14; 33:6; Hos 6:1; 14:4; Wis 16:10–12; Sir 34:20; 38:9. Cf. Deut 28:27; 32:39; Job 5:18.

[32] See, e.g., Matt 4:23–24; 8:16; 9:35; 10:1, 7–8; 11:1–6; 14:14; Mark 1:34; 3:10; 6:13; Luke 5:15; 6:18–19; 7:18–23; 8:43–48; 9:1–2, 6, 11; 10:9; Acts 4:30; 5:12–16; 9:32–35; 10:38; 28:8–9. Cf. 1 Cor 12:9, 28; Jas 5:16.

Summary and Implications

The wider narrative of John's Gospel confirms what we have found Jesus's encounter with the man at Bethzatha to suggest. For John, "illness" as well as "disability" (as defined above) are significant aspects of the predicament in which human beings find themselves, on account of which Jesus has come into the world. People with illnesses and/or disabilities are shown to be a focus of Jesus's mission. Consequently, the human predicament, according to John's delineation of it, involves physical debilitation and decay. It is wholistic and comprehensive in scope. John's portrayal of the social experience of people with impairments also magnifies the problem of the way human beings treat and relate to one another, that is, the problem of human conduct.

Illness and disability converge in the case of the man at Bethzatha and are respectively shown to be problematic elsewhere in John's Gospel. The problem of illness is introduced in the account of Jesus and the official's son (4:46–54), which immediately precedes the account of Jesus and the man at Bethzatha, and illness again comes to the fore in the case of Lazarus (11:1–44). Jesus is described in fact as doing many miracles for the sick (6:2). Following the scene at Bethzatha, the problem of disability is encountered again when Jesus meets a man blind from birth (John 9). This scene parallels the one with Jesus and the man at Bethzatha in the sense that, in each case, the social environment in which Jesus encounters a person with an impairment is implicitly shown to be unaccommodating and callous toward such people. And yet, with respect to the matters of illness and disability, there is an important sense in which these scenes differ: whereas in the case of the man at Bethzatha the man's impairment is an aspect of his illness or debilitated health, the health of the man born blind is not once described as debilitated, poor, or weak. In fact, the man born blind is depicted, prior to receiving sight, as being quite healthy and capable, for it is while being blind that the man carries out Jesus's instructions to go and wash in the pool of Siloam (vv. 7, 11, 15). John indicates neither that the man required assistance to do this nor that he received assistance.[33] The man's physical impairment seems to be a problem, according to John, not because it is a condition of poor or weak health but because of how the man's community as well as the man himself responded to it. Within the man's social environment, his congenital blindness was deemed to be a result of "sin" and relegated the man to a life of begging. Perhaps in reaction to this in some ways, but perhaps in other ways not, the man wanted to "see," both literally (v. 7) and figuratively (v. 36). These circumstances were an opportunity for the work of God (v. 3).

"Disability" is therefore shown in John's Gospel to be problematic in the following ways: (1) "the world" in which people with disabilities live and of which they are a part is an environment that disadvantages and marginalizes such people; (2) disability can be a product of illness; and (3) a physical impairment, as a comparatively significant difference of human ability, can be something a person wishes no longer to experience. Accordingly, it seems unwarranted to conclude that the Gospel of John considers

---

[33] This point calls into question the claim of Louise J. Lawrence that the man born blind is portrayed as "dependent," "childlike," and "passive" (*Sense and Stigma in the Gospels: Depictions of Sensory-Disabled Characters*, Biblical Refigurations [Oxford: Oxford University Press, 2013], 40).

"disability" to be an aspect of the human predicament without qualification (i.e., irrespective of social context, cause, and/or personal volition).

These conclusions bring to light a further point. The problems of illness and disability indicate that, for John, the human predicament is a complex reality that in various ways persists for human beings subsequent to the emergence of belief in Jesus. Although people with illnesses and/or disabilities are shown in John's Gospel to be a focus of Jesus's mission, John does not suggest that the problems of illness and disability are resolved either during Jesus's advent or even once Jesus returns to the Father. That, for John, "death" continues to be a reality even for those who come to believe in Jesus (more will be said about this shortly) implies in fact that illness—as that which can lead to and cause death—likewise continues to be a reality that believers must endure until "the last day."[34] The persistence of illness has implications for the problem of disability (given that illness can result in disability), as does the point that "the world" will evidently continue for John—following Jesus's departure to the Father—to be a context in which persist hate (15:18–20), injustice (16:2–3, 8–11, 33), and evil (17:15). The reality of disability, as we have observed, is shaped to a great extent by the social environment in which people with disabilities live.

Importantly, though, John does not seem to envision "the world" continuing on into perpetuity in the wayward condition John ascribes to it, for in and through the advent of Jesus the world and its ruler have been judged and overcome (12:31; 16:33), and on "the last day" those who do evil will have as their end "the resurrection of condemnation" (5:29; cf. 12:48). The waywardness of the world, according to John, gives way to the "kingdom of God" (3:3–5; cf. 1:49; 12:13–15; 18:36) and to a people that follows Jesus's example and shares in his life—the children of God, a community that will on the last day experience the "resurrection of life" (5:29; see also 6:39–40, 44, 54). This resurrection undoubtedly spells the end of illness as well as of disability as a problematic social experience. To be sure, John does not say how people with disabilities should and will be treated within this community of God, but given that it is to be defined by selfless and other-oriented love (12:25–26; 13:34–35; 15:12–13), following from the love and life of the Father and Son (15:9–10; 17:21–23), one may presume that John envisions this community as being attentive to the needs and abilities of all those that comprise it, and as concerning itself until the last day with people of differing and various abilities who have not yet joined its fold, as Jesus did.[35] Such an interpretation of course requires that, for John, God does not view people with disabilities as necessarily in need of correction or cure, but instead welcomes into his kingdom people with what some might consider to be human "defects." But this is in fact what John suggests. The one who ascends and returns to the Father in glory is pierced and blemished (20:27; cf. v. 25).[36] The wounds Jesus acquires through his self-offering unto death are not erased in his resurrection and exaltation, but remain

---

[34] For this "last day" in John's Gospel see 6:39–40, 44, 54; 11:24; 12:48; cf. 5:28–29.

[35] Gorman speaks of the other-oriented character of the community of faith in John's Gospel as a "missional spirituality" that may also be termed "missional theosis" (*Abide and Go*, passim).

[36] Nancy L. Eiesland, in her book *The Disabled God: Toward a Liberatory Theology of Disability* (Nashville, TN: Abingdon, 1994), develops from a disabilities perspective the theological significance of the point that, in Luke and John, the risen Jesus remains pierced and blemished (98–105).

as scars.[37] According to John, then, the Son of the Father, whom the Father eternally glorifies and receives into his very "bosom" (1:18), is and evidently always will be marred. This suggests that, for John, God is to be thought of not merely as including in his kingdom, but as affirming, people with what some might consider to be blemishes, defects, or disfigurements.

To Pass from Death into Life

It is a time of festal celebration when Jesus comes to Bethzatha and heals a man who has been ill for thirty-eight years, but it is also a sabbath day (vv. 9–10), which causes Jesus's fellow "Jews" to regard the healing as a violation of the sabbath and to become hostile toward Jesus, whom they deem to be a lawbreaker (v. 16; cf. v. 18; 7:21–24). In response, Jesus defends his action by explaining that, just as his Father is still working, so also he is working (v. 17). The healing of the man at Bethzatha indicates that the "work" Jesus speaks of here, as that which encompasses this healing at the very least, involves delivering people from the physical debilitation and decay to which they are subject. This aspect of Jesus's mission then comes to the fore as Jesus proceeds to speak about the unified intention of the Father and Son to give life and deliver people from death (5:21–29). Like the matters of "illness" and "disability" in John's Gospel, the matter of "death" will be found to indicate that John in no way considers human corporeality to be soteriologically irrelevant. On the contrary, what is said about death here and elsewhere in John's Gospel further conveys that, for John, it is not corporeality itself that is problematic but, rather, *the way* people live corporeally. "Death" in John's Gospel, like disability, will also be found to accentuate further the problem of what people *do*.

Death as a Bodily and Relative Reality

After the Father and Son's own people, "the Jews" (v. 18; cf. 1:11), take offense at the equality with God Jesus attributes to himself by associating his "work" with that of the Father (vv. 17–18), Jesus explains that he does nothing by himself, but acts in complete dependence on and in total conformity with the will and work of the Father (vv. 19–20; cf. v. 30).[38] Jesus then elaborates on this unified intention and activity of the Father and Son when he says the following: "For just as the Father raises the dead and gives them life, so also the Son gives life to whomever he wishes" (v. 21). This work of the Father and Son to give life (lit., to "make alive" [ζῳοποιέω]) undoubtedly encompasses the raising of Lazarus (11:38–44) as well as Jesus's other miracles of healing, given that Jesus has just been shown to heal both a boy on the verge of death (4:46–54) and,

---

[37] Candida R. Moss argues that the marks in the risen Jesus's hands (John 20:25–27) should indeed be understood as "scars" rather than as open wounds ("The Marks of the Nails: Scars, Wounds, and the Resurrection of Jesus in John," *Early Christianity* 8 [2017]: 48–68).

[38] On Jesus's alignment with, obedience to, and realization of the will of the Father see also 4:34; 6:38; 7:16–18; 8:29, 55; 10:30; 14:31; 15:10; 17:4; 19:30.

then, a man with a disabling illness (5:1–15; note that "illness" is what causes Lazarus to die). The description of the Father as raising and giving life to "the dead" seems to refer in particular, however, to the events of "the last day" (6:39–59; 11:24; 12:48), for it is this day that Jesus proceeds to speak about: the hour is coming (and is clearly not "now" [cf. v. 25]) when "all those who are in the graves" will arise either to new life or condemnation (vv. 28–29; cf. 15:6). The scene described here is the eschaton, and the image of people arising to new life from their "graves" (τοῖς μνημείοις) conveys that, for believers, eternal life involves bodily renewal and transformation. Physical debilitation and decay, rather than being dismissed as inconsequential to the human predicament, is here described as a problem that salvation addresses. The resurrection of Jesus from *his* "grave" (μνημεῖον [9x in 19:41-20:8]) further underscores this point, for Jesus's resurrection is described elsewhere in John's Gospel as the basis of the resurrection of all those who believe and live in him (11:25–26; 14:19).[39] Jesus's statement about the Father and Son's mutual work to raise the dead and give life (v. 21) therefore conveys that a major focus of the Father and Son's soteriological purpose is to deliver human beings from "death" as the bodily cessation or end of life. "The dead" (τοὺς νεκρούς [v. 21]) designates in particular all those believers who, upon the arrival in the world of "the last day," are no longer alive in the world, for they have been buried and on this day will arise from their graves—by the will and work of the Father and Son—to life everlasting.

Importantly, though, there seems to be a sense in which "death" is relative for John. As just observed, the statement that the Father will raise the dead and give them life (v. 21) indicates that human beings do not become invulnerable to death through coming to believe in Jesus. The Fourth Gospel is well aware that believers still die (5:28–29; 16:2; 21:19, 22–23), and that the emergence of faith on the part of human beings does not in and of itself resolve the problem of death. Jesus makes this point clear when, after Lazarus has died (11:13–14), he says the following to Martha: "The person who believes in me, even if she or he dies (κἂν ἀποθάνῃ), will live" (11:25). However, Jesus immediately qualifies this statement by declaring that every person "who lives and believes in me will never die" (11:26).[40] Taken together, these statements suggest that, for John, while those who live and believe in Jesus may die in (or with respect to) "the world," they never die with respect to God.[41] Believers who die, in John's view of things, evidently continue living to God (despite having died in the world) by the will and power of God, who raises up believers in "the resurrection of life" on the last day.[42] Jesus provides the basis for this new life, for he is himself "the resurrection and

---

[39] On this point see Chapter 2. Maximus the Confessor finds that, in John 11:26, Jesus speaks of believers receiving life in the resurrection through their "participation" in him (*Amb.* 7 [PG 91:1100b-c]).

[40] πᾶς ὁ ζῶν καὶ πιστεύων εἰς ἐμὲ οὐ μὴ ἀποθάνῃ εἰς τὸν αἰῶνα.

[41] Cf. Matt 22:31–32; Mark 12:26–27; Luke 20:37–38 ("for all are living to God" [πάντες γὰρ αὐτῷ ζῶσιν]).

[42] Concerning the question of an "intermediate state," Joel Green helpfully substantiates from the biblical witness a perspective put forward by, among others, F. F. Bruce, who writes: "The tension created by the postulated interval between death and resurrection might be relieved today if it were suggested that in the consciousness of the departed believer there is no interval between dissolution and investiture, however long an interval might be measured by the calendar of earth-bound human history" (*Paul: Apostle of the Heart Set Free* [Grand Rapids, MI: Eerdmans, 1977], 312 n.40; cited in Green, *Body, Soul, and Human Life*, 152).

the life" (11:25; cf. 10:17–18; 12:25–26). Jesus, "the bread of life" (6:35), has come into the world in order that (ἵνα) human beings may receive life from him and not die (6:50–51). "If someone keeps my word," Jesus says, "this person will never see death" (8:51). For John, then, it seems that "death," understood as the bodily cessation or end of life, can be absolute (in the sense of eschatological condemnation) as well as relative, in accordance with God's will and power. The relativity of death, that is, the point that a person who lives and believes in Jesus, though she or he might die (in the world), never dies (with respect to God), points forward to the day when God will raise up his people in the resurrection of life (5:21, 28–29; 6:39–59; 11:25).

Death as a Way of Life

Our assessment so far of "death" in John's Gospel might give one pause: is not salvation from death realized for John in the moment one believes?[43] Yes and no. In the course of his discourse on the unified intention of the Father and Son to give life, the Son says the following: "the person who hears my word and believes in the one who sent me has eternal life and does not come into condemnation, but has passed from death into life" (v. 24). Given that, for John, human beings do not become invulnerable to death in the moment they come to believe in Jesus (note again vv. 21, 28–29; 11:25; 16:2; 21:19, 22–23), the "death" Jesus speaks of here is undoubtedly the cessation or end of life that is absolute or eschatological (i.e., that occurs on "the last day"). That Jesus connects this death with "condemnation" (v. 24; cf. vv. 28–29; 8:51; 12:48) confirms this. But how can salvation from the death that is absolute or eschatological be realized for those who have not yet died? How can one pass from death into life if one is not yet dead? The answer of course is that, for John, human beings are not actually alive or living until they come to believe in Jesus. The way or manner in which human beings live, prior to living and believing in Jesus, is in fact not life at all, but death. Jesus's ensuing statement makes this point clear: "the hour is coming and is here" (καὶ νῦν ἐστιν; cf. v. 28), Jesus says, "when the dead (οἱ νεκροί) will hear the voice of the Son of God, and those who hear (οἱ ἀκούσαντες) will live" (v. 25). The plurals οἱ νεκροί and οἱ ἀκούσαντες indicate that the raising of Lazarus is not what Jesus is referring to here. Jesus's words about the possibility of passing "from death into life" *in the course of one's life in the world* (v. 24), and about "the dead" coming to life during the Son's advent through hearing and believing in the Son (v. 25), therefore convey that "death" is for John not only a bodily cessation of life that becomes absolute in "the resurrection of condemnation" (vv. 28–29; cf. 8:51; 12:48; 15:6) but also a way or manner of life that has this eschatological "death" as its ultimate end.[44] In the Gospel of John "death"

---

[43] Recall, for instance, the interpretation of Forestell (cited in Chapter 1): for John "eternal life or salvation does not lie in the future. It is the present possession of all those who believe in Christ" (*Word of the Cross*, 119). "The Easter Message in John is primarily a message of life with God beyond the grave and not one of bodily resurrection"; in John's view of things "physical death and resurrection become of incidental importance" (96, 204).

[44] About "death" and its relationship to "sin" in John's Gospel, Koester writes:

> In John's Gospel, death is a process. If true life is lived in relationship with God, then those who are hostile to God separate themselves from the source of life. Their relationship with

comprises a certain trajectory, course, or path of life that leads to "death" as an absolute end of life.[45] This way of life ends in death because it is defined by evil works (οἱ δὲ τὰ φαῦλα πράξαντες ... [5:29]). And evidently John considers *all* human beings, prior to Jesus's advent, as having been "dead," for the ones who come to believe in Jesus pass "from death into life." For John, Jesus becomes flesh in order to give life to a world that was and is "dead."

This fuller understanding of "death" in John's Gospel illumines the sense in which salvation from death is realized for John in the emergence of belief. In the moment a person comes to believe in Jesus, the direction and orientation of this person's life, and thus this person's ultimate end, immediately change. The believer is no longer "dead," for she is now following and living in Jesus, "the way and the truth and the life" (14:6). In coming to believe in Jesus people receive and enter into communion with the one who has realized salvation on their behalf (11:25-26; 12:25-26; 17:19).[46] The children of God live because and by means of the Son of God: "Because I live," Jesus tells his disciples, "you will live also" (14:19; see also 6:57). For John, then, the one who receives and believes in Jesus has "passed" from death into life insofar as the ultimate outcome awaiting this person (the resurrection of life), and the course of life leading thereto, has changed. Yet, because believers still die, and because the possibility remains for believers—while in the world—to be swayed by evil and, ultimately, to turn away from the Father and Son (6:60-66; 15:2-6; 16:1; 17:11-15), it seems that, for John, "death" as a bodily cessation and way of life will continue to affect believers until their resurrection on "the last day."[47] That, for John, liberation from "sin" is not realized in

> God dies, even while their bodies are still functioning. As this separation continues, it can eventually become permanent; so that sin culminates in the death that is final separation from God (8:21, 24). (*Word of Life*, 66)

[45] The Fourth Evangelist is not alone in portraying "death" in this way. Death is likewise described as a way or manner of life in 1 John: "We know that we have passed from death into life (μεταβεβήκαμεν ἐκ τοῦ θανάτου εἰς τὴν ζωήν) because we love one another; the one who does not love remains in death" (3:14; cf. John 5:24). Note also Paul's words in Rom 8:6: "The direction of the mind oriented by selfish desire is death (θάνατος), but the direction of the mind oriented by the Spirit is life (ζωή) and peace." See further Matt 8:22; Luke 15:24, 32; Rom 7:9-10; 8:10; 1 Cor 1:18; 2 Cor 4:3; Eph 2:1-5; Col 2:13; Jas 1:15; Rev 3:1. In Israel's Scriptures see, e.g., Deut 30:15-20; Prov 2:16-19; 8:35-36; Jer 21:8-10; Ezek 18:30-32; 33:10-11. See also Sir 15:15-17; 2 Esd 7:48; Sib. Or. 8:399-401; 13:4. Cf., though, Num 23:10; Ps 116:15; Isa 53:10-12.

[46] Athanasius, in the course of offering in his *De incarnatione* an account of the predicament in which human beings find themselves, echoes the Gospel of John (particularly the prologue, 12:45, and 14:7-9) in describing the mission of Jesus:

> So the Word of God came himself, in order that he being the image of the Father, the human being "in the image" might be recreated. It could not, again, have been done in any other way, without death and corruption being utterly destroyed. So he rightly took a mortal body, that in it death might henceforth be destroyed utterly and human beings be renewed again according to the image. For this purpose, then, there was need of none other than the Image of the Father. (*Inc.* 13; trans. John Behr, *On the Incarnation*, Popular Patristics Series 44A [Yonkers, NY: St. Vladimir's Seminary Press, 2011], 79)

[47] On the eschatology in John 5:16-29 as consisting more or less harmoniously of both realized and future aspects see, e.g., Brown, *John (I-XII)*, 218-21; Beasley-Murray, *John*, 76-7; Lincoln, *Saint John*, 204-5; Michaels, *John*, 320-1; Thompson, *John*, 129-30. On the specific matter of "death" in John's Gospel recall the comments of Frey (cited in Chapter 1): "since the possession of eternal life cannot mean physical immortality, the reality of physical death remains a problem for the disciples." "It is

the moment one comes to believe in Jesus, but is still awaited as a future event (which, as we will see below, is conveyed in John 8), suggests this further.

The problem of "death" in John's Gospel is therefore multifaceted. Death is both a bodily cessation or end of life that becomes absolute in "the resurrection of condemnation" (5:29; cf. 8:51; 12:48; 15:6) and a way or manner of life that has this eschatological "death" as its ultimate end (5:24–25). Put differently, "death" is the path of those who "walk in the darkness" (8:12) and do not know God (17:25). And, for John, *all* human beings were gripped by "death" prior to Jesus's advent, for the ones who come to believe in Jesus pass "from death into life" (5:24–25). Before Jesus's advent "the world" was dead, but Jesus has come into the world in order that people may pass from death into life and not die (6:50–51; 8:51; 11:26). Because Jesus is himself "the resurrection and the life" (11:25), all those who come to believe in him enter into communion with the one who has realized salvation on their behalf, and so live because and by means of him (6:35–58; 14:19; 17:19).

Conclusion

Much may be gleaned from Jesus's encounter with the man at Bethzatha (5:1–15) and from the discourse that ensues (5:16–29). With respect to the matter of the human predicament in John's Gospel, a number of important points come into focus. First, illness or bodily infirmity (which can lead to disability) and death (to which illness can also lead) are aspects of the human predicament in John's Gospel. The healing Jesus brings about for the man at Bethzatha is one of many healings Jesus is said to do for people suffering from illness or physical debilitation. Jesus's subsequent words about the Father and Son's mutual work to deliver people from death by means of bodily resurrection (5:21, 28–29), together with the resurrection of the Son himself (20:1–29; cf. 6:35–58; 14:19), further convey that the plight from which Jesus saves human beings, according to John, consists of (among other things) physical debilitation and death. The human predicament is therefore wholistic for John—it involves the quality or condition of human corporeality. It is *the way* human beings live corporeally. Salvation for John involves bodily renewal and transformation.

This brings to light another important point: for John, the human predicament is a reality that in various ways persists for human beings subsequent to the emergence of belief in Jesus. Although people with illnesses and/or disabilities are shown to be a focus of Jesus's mission, John does not suggest that the interrelated problems of illness, disability, and death are resolved either during Jesus's advent or even once Jesus returns to the Father. On the contrary, John makes clear that believers, until the arrival in the world of "the last day," still die (5:21, 28–29; 11:25), which implies that believers remain susceptible until this last day to illness (which can cause death) and its potential to be disabling. Additionally, although Jesus is said to overcome the world

---

hard to understand how exegetes can claim that [for John] 'death' has become totally irrelevant. ... In my view, this demonstrates a serious disregard of the bodily reality of life, a reality which was shared by the Johannine community as well" ("Eschatology," 80 n.102).

and its ruler (12:31; 16:33), the world is nevertheless described as an environment that will continue, following Jesus's return to the Father, to be gripped by the way of life that leads to and ends in "death" on the last day. This enduring waywardness of the world has implications for (among other things) disability, given that the experience of disability is shaped to a great extent by the social environment in which people with disabilities live. John's portrayal of the social experience of people with impairments magnifies the problem of the way human beings treat and relate to one another, for people with impairments are depicted as socially marginalized and disadvantaged. That Jesus delivers people from such circumstances makes clear that such circumstances are indeed considered to be problematic. Disability is consequently shown to be a problem that involves not just people with impairments but "the world" as a whole.

One other point is worth highlighting here. In John's view of things all human beings, prior to Jesus's advent, were "dead" in the sense that human beings were living in a way that is contrary to the way of life that is true and everlasting, which Jesus realizes in and offers to the world. Before Jesus's advent "the world" was dead, but Jesus has come into the world in order that human beings may pass from death into life and not die. The reception of life by those who believe and live in Jesus notwithstanding, the point that, for John, this preexisting condition of human beings is not wholly resolved in the emergence of belief, but in various and significant ways persists for believers as they both are and "become" children of God (1:12), will be demonstrated further in the chapter that follows. There, in Chapter 4, we will turn our attention to the matter of "sin" in John's Gospel. Our conclusions there will further evince what we have found John's account of the human predicament to indicate thus far: for John, salvation is a process that involves the transformation of the way human beings live in relationship with God and one another. Salvation for John consists of far more than the emergence of belief in a moment of decision.

4

Sin and Its Effects: The Case of "the Jews" Who Believe and Fall Away

Thus far we have observed that, in the Gospel of John, the plight or predicament from which Jesus saves human beings is described as, among other things, "the darkness," a lack of knowledge of God, and "death." With respect to Johannine scholarship, these observations are not controversial. It is in fact quite common for scholars, when considering John's soteriology and theology in particular, to note that John describes the human predicament in these and related ways. Primarily at issue in the present study, though, is not what terms and themes define the human predicament in John's Gospel. What we are primarily disputing is the way these terms and themes are generally understood, for we have found John's presentation of "the darkness" and "death," to name but two pertinent matters, to call into question certain lines of interpretation that are commonly advanced in scholarship. We have observed, for example, that the human predicament is ultimately not a product or result of Jesus's advent, but rather its cause, for Jesus has come into the world in order to save human beings from "the darkness" (12:46–47). Jesus has come into the world so that human beings may pass from death into life (5:24–29). Consequently, the human predicament is ultimately a reality that, for John, *preceded* Jesus's advent. This point is undoubtedly significant for the interpretation of "sin" in John's Gospel, which is often defined as a disposition ("unbelief") that arises in response to Jesus. We have observed as well that the human predicament is a reality that, prior to Jesus's advent, gripped *all* human beings and not merely those who would go on to reject Jesus, for the ones who come to believe in Jesus are no longer "dead," but have passed from death into life. Irrespective of whether some people were "children of God" (in their elected status) before Jesus's advent, all human beings needed to be "born of God" and "become" children of God (1:12–13; 3:1–8). Additionally, we have found that the human predicament for John pertains to what human beings *do*, that is, to how human beings live in relationship with God and others. "The darkness" is characterized by "evil works" (3:19–20); ignorance of God is identified with, among other things, lacking love for God and others (5:37–42) and not keeping the law (7:14–28); and death comprises a course or way of life that is defined by "doing evil" (5:29). John's portrayal of the social experience of people with impairments (i.e., of "disability") further underscores the problem of the way human beings treat and relate to one another. The problem of the way human beings live is highlighted above all by John's portrayal of Jesus, who brings true and everlasting life into existence where it did not exist formerly. Finally, we have observed that, for John, the human predicament is wholistic in nature and persists in various ways for human beings subsequent to the emergence of belief. The problem of death (which involves "illness" or bodily infirmity), for instance, is not wholly resolved when one responds positively in a moment of "decision." The way Jesus lives in relationship with God and others, to which Jesus calls the world (see, e.g., 12:25–26), perhaps most clearly reveals the plight as a reality that is not wholly rectified in the emergence of belief. All of this undoubtedly bears on the matter of "sin" in John's Gospel, to which we will now turn our attention.

After many of Jesus's disciples are said to abandon him as a result of his words about his "flesh" and "blood" (6:52–71), we are then told that the time arrived for the celebration of Tabernacles (7:2), and that Jesus (eventually) journeyed to Jerusalem and taught in the temple (7:10–14). His teaching there produces mixed results: some of the people "believe" while others seek his arrest (7:30–31). Differing judgments about Jesus continue to arise among the people as the festival draws to a close (7:40–44). After Jesus declares himself to be "the light of the world" (8:12), a dispute ensues between Jesus and "the Jews" over the truth of his testimony, and as this dispute unfolds the problem of "sin" comes to the fore.[1] The dialogue takes a positive turn when, as Jesus continues to speak about his commission from and relationship with the Father, many of "the Jews" are said to "believe" in him (8:30). But after Jesus speaks about the nature of discipleship and, also, says more about sin (8:31–36), Jesus discloses that the faith of these believers does not endure (8:37). They will fall away, as their subsequent denunciation of Jesus (8:48, 52) and attempt to stone him (8:59) make clear.

Earlier in John's Gospel sin is attributed to "the world" (1:29) and to the man healed of a disabling illness (5:14), but it is here in John 8 that "sin" is for the first time the subject of an extended discussion. Our analysis of this scene, which will include consideration of how sin is described elsewhere in John's Gospel, will demonstrate the following points. First, in John's Gospel the noun ἁμαρτία is polysemous in the sense that it can denote either (A) "sin" or "wrongdoing," in reference to either an individual act or an enduring pattern of behavior, a way of life (cf. ἁμαρτάνω, ἁμαρτωλός); or (B) "guilt," which is a result of such behavior.[2] "Guilt" seems implied when ἁμαρτία denotes "sin" and, conversely, "sin" or wrongdoing seems implied when ἁμαρτία denotes "guilt." Both nuances of "sin" (i.e., an individual act or a pattern of behavior) are found in 8:21–59. Second, and following from this semantic range, the reality of "sin" for John consists of both a way of life epitomized by certain wayward acts and "guilt," which results from such behavior. Third, for John, "sin" as a way or manner of life continues to influence human beings following the emergence of belief, inclining believers toward ensuing behavior and thinking that is akin to that which has preceded. To the question of whether "sin" is destroyed in the moment one believes, then, John's answer is both "yes" and "no." The "guilt" that people accrue as a result of wrongdoing

---

[1] For scholarship on "sin" in John's Gospel see Chapter 1.
[2] In John's Gospel the noun ἁμαρτία occurs seventeen times, while the verb ἁμαρτάνω and the adjective ἁμαρτωλός each occur a total of four times. The verb σκανδαλίζω occurs twice and the noun ἀναμάρτητος occurs only once, in 8:7.

is removed or cleansed when one comes to believe in Jesus; however, liberation from the wrongdoing—the way of life—that has defined human beings heretofore is not realized in this moment, but is still awaited as a future event. Liberation from sin comes about through living and remaining in Jesus and his word. Believers in Jesus struggle against and resist the enduring influence of sin as they both are and become children of God.

Sin and the Believers Who Fall Away

In the course of the lengthy dialogue between Jesus and "the Jews" that unfolds during Tabernacles (8:12-59), the noun ἁμαρτία first occurs in Jesus's statement about his departure (v. 21): "I am going away, and you will seek me and you will die in your sin (ἐν τῇ ἁμαρτίᾳ ὑμῶν); where I am going you cannot come." With this statement Jesus reiterates a previous one spoken to "the Jews" while teaching in the temple (7:33-34): "I am with you a little while longer and (then) I am going to the one who sent me. You will seek me and you will not find me,[3] and where I am you cannot come." That "the Jews" here repeat his words (specifically v. 34: "You will seek me") as they attempt to understand their meaning (vv. 35-36) implies that Jesus's statement in 7:34 is significant (as does its restatement in 8:21; cf. 13:33). In both statements (i.e., 7:34 and 8:21) Jesus's words about a "seeking" on the part of "the Jews" are identical—"you will seek me" (ζητήσετέ με), Jesus says, and although what immediately follows in each case differs (in 7:34 Jesus says his addressees will not find him, whereas in 8:21 Jesus says his addressees will die in their sin), these respective clauses seem to be mutually explanatory: not to "find" Jesus is to die in sin.[4] But here a question arises: when, and in what sense, will these people "seek" Jesus and not find him?

To this question John's interpreters have offered various answers. Some suggest that Jesus here refers to the future judgment that will occur on the "last day," at which time "the Jews" will realize their error in rejecting Jesus and seek his help, only to find that it is too late.[5] Jesus's contention that his fellow "Jews" will seek him and not find him (7:34), and die in their sin (8:21), refers to the future eschatological event

---

[3] The second instance of με in v. 34 is absent in some witnesses (e.g., p⁶⁶, ℵ, D, and W) and present in others (e.g., p⁷⁵, B, N, and T).

[4] Recall here the point that, for John, human beings, while technically alive, are simultaneously "dead" and approaching "death" (particularly that which will occur on "the last day") if not living in Jesus (5:24-25, 28-29).

[5] Barrett, for instance, says the following while commenting on 7:34: "Now ['the Jews'] were seeking to arrest him; there would be a time (the final judgment rather than a time of national necessity is meant) when, too late, they would seek his aid" (*St. John*, 325). See also Herman N. Ridderbos, *The Gospel according to John: A Theological Commentary*, trans. John Vriend (Grand Rapids, MI: Eerdmans: 1997), 271, 299. Beasley-Murray likewise explains that the "seeking" of "the Jews" described in 7:34 will take place during the judgment (*John*, 112), but Beasley-Murray then goes on to interpret 8:21 rather differently: in this case the seeking of Jesus's addressees "may be meant ironically: they will seek what [Jesus] proclaimed as God's gift through him, but in vain, for they will die in their sin, i.e., the sin of unbelief" (130; here cf. Bultmann [see below]).

that awaits "the Jews," the nature of which is apparently determined according to their present "decision."[6] This decision is their "sin," and because of it they will die. Other interpreters maintain that Jesus speaks of a "seeking" that will commence on the part of "the Jews" as soon as he departs (i.e., to the Father); "the Jews" will not find him, though, because their opportunity to believe will have come and gone.[7] Their "sin," again, is their rejection of Jesus in the moment of "decision," which occurs during Jesus's advent. After Jesus departs, it is "too late."[8]

A rather different possibility presents itself when one recalls Jesus's statement to "the Jews" in 5:39–40, in which Jesus says that his addressees "continually search" (ἐραυνᾶτε) the Scriptures because they suppose in them to have eternal life, yet refuse to come to the one to whom the Scriptures bear witness, the one in whom is found life. An implication here is that Jesus's fellow "Jews" seek "eternal life" (see also 6:33–34), which they think they secure for themselves through searching the Scriptures. The problem, it seems, is that the nature of their "searching" is flawed and, in fact, wayward, for their searching of the Scriptures should lead them to the one to whom the Scriptures bear

---

[6] Ridderbos explains that the implication of Jesus's statement in 8:21 "is that when he has gone it will be too late for ['the Jews'] to invoke his help and to be saved by him. His announcement that he is going away is intended to press them toward a decision" (*John*, 299).

[7] Bultmann, for instance, finds that the time when "the Jews" will seek Jesus is not that of the judgment on the last day, but the time that follows their opportunity to "decide" and respond positively to God's revelation in Jesus. "The Jews" will seek Jesus as soon as he departs, for they will in some sense long for the revelation they have just rejected. When Jesus departs from them,

> the time of the revelation is past. Then "they will seek him," they will long for the revelation, but in vain; for then it will be too late; he will no longer be accessible to them. Thus it is *the historical contingency of the revelation* which throws this terrible weight of responsibility on the hearer of the word. For the revelation is not generally available, but presents itself to man only at a certain limited time of its own choosing. (*John*, 307; italics original)

Brown seems to follow Bultmann on this point. Commenting on 7:34, Brown explains that Jesus's return to the Father "will take away from his hearers their opportunity to believe in him. As he stands before them, he is seeking them out; but when he is gone, they will do the seeking, and they will not find" (*John (I-XII)*, 318; see also 350). Leon Morris suggests, with regard to 8:21, that Jesus "may mean that their moment of insight will come too late. Only after they have crucified Him will they realize who He is. Then their seeking of him will be in vain" (*The Gospel according to John: The English Text with Introduction, Exposition, and Notes*, NICNT [Grand Rapids, MI: Eerdmans, 1971], 445–6).

[8] The idea that a negative "decision" on the part of Jesus's fellow "Jews" becomes irrevocable once Jesus departs, so that a change of heart thereafter is meaningless and "too late," appears to be asserted at least partially on the basis of a particular portrayal of personified Wisdom (Prov 1:20-33), in which it is said that those who reject Wisdom when she "calls" will later on, when trouble arises, not be able to find her, because at this point Wisdom will not answer. With respect to this description of Wisdom in Proverbs, though, it is perhaps important to note that to pursue Wisdom after one has denied her and, thus, after one has lived according to folly seems to be considered futile and "too late" because Wisdom's utility is seen in her ability to prevent disaster from developing in the first place: one follows her so as to keep trouble from arising ("The one who listens to me will live in security and will be undisturbed by the dread of evil" [v. 33]). If one denies her, the repercussions of foolishness necessarily follow ("they will eat the fruit of their way" [vv. 31–32]), and when they do a sudden espousal of wisdom is of no help, because such a person has already made his or her proverbial bed. This understanding may give one pause about the degree to which John's portrayal of Jesus corresponds to the portrayal of Wisdom in Proverbs 1. Does John indicate that there is a point in the life of Jesus's addressees, prior to the eschatological judgment (5:28–29; 12:48), at which time Jesus becomes *unable* to help them (should they seek his help) because they have denied him heretofore? Once Jesus departs, is it indeed "too late" for Jesus to save those who thus far have rejected him?

witness, but it does not.⁹ The Scriptures testify to the one in and through whom "life" is found, but the searching of "the Jews" evidently obscures this fact and, thus, results in a tragic irony: they reject the one they seek, for Jesus is life (6:48; 11:25; 14:6). This rejection of life seems to be both intentional, since Jesus's fellow "Jews" "refuse" (οὐ θέλετε) to come to him (v. 40; cf. vv. 42–47; 8:44),¹⁰ and yet also unintentional, since Jesus's fellow "Jews" do not know and embrace the very thing they seek (i.e., life) when they encounter it. They willfully reject life when it meets and stands before them, yet appear to be oblivious about the direction their current path or course of life is headed.¹¹ This suggests that even their desire for and presumptions about life are flawed, because they do not identify life *qua* life. In light of these preceding words of Jesus to "the Jews" (5:39–40), then, Jesus's statements that "the Jews" will seek him and not find him (7:34), and die in their sin (8:21), seem to refer to the ongoing desire and search of "the Jews" for "life." In rejecting Jesus they reject what they have been searching for all along. Unless they believe (8:24), they will not find the way to the Father (cf. 13:36–14:6). They will continue on a path that leads *not* to life but to death (cf. 5:24–25).

This ongoing, misguided search for life that Jesus attributes to his fellow "Jews" (5:39–40) is important, with respect to our current interests, because it indicates the scope of ἁμαρτία in 8:21. "Sin" here designates not a single, isolated act that occurs in a moment of decision, but an enduring manner or way of life that will continue to define Jesus's fellow "Jews" (unless they believe) unto death, for they will continue to seek and search for life (i.e., Jesus) in a manner that is wayward and disobedient (3:36). It is not merely a solitary decision on the part of these people that will result for them in death, but their continuing disobedience to the very end.¹² Jesus's ensuing

---

⁹ Jesus says here that his fellow "Jews," God's own people (1:11), do not have "the love of God" in them (v. 42; cf. Deut 6:5; Lev 19:18), that they do not seek the glory that comes from God (but receive glory from one another [v. 44]), and that it is Moses who accuses them, for they do not believe his testimony (vv. 45–47).

¹⁰ Brown:

> The refusal is deliberate. ... Disbelief in the face of these witnesses [e.g., John the Baptist and the Scriptures] must be motivated by pride; it is a deliberate disbelief. Jesus is now portrayed as attacking the roots of this disbelief with vigor. If it were an intellectual problem, it could be met by explanation; but it is really a problem of the moral orientation of life and of the love of God. (*John (I-XII)*, 225–8)

¹¹ It seems relevant here that in Prov 1–9 Woman Wisdom is juxtaposed with a "strange woman" (Woman Folly) who "forsakes the friend of her youth and forgets the covenant of her God" (2:16–18); this woman offers sacrifices and pays her vows, but then aspires to lure the weak-minded into adultery (7:14–19). What is most significant here, though, with respect to our current interests, is that, after we are told that this strange woman does not observe "the path of life," it is said that "her ways wander, and she does not know it" (5:6). Evidently, the strange woman intentionally rejects "life" while, at the same time, she is oblivious about the fact that her waywardness leads not to life, but to death (on this reading of Prov 5:6 see Michael V. Fox, *Proverbs 1–9: A New Translation with Introduction and Commentary*, AB 18A [New York: Doubleday, 2000], 189, 192–4). The amalgam of willful disobedience and obliviousness attributed to "the Jews" in John 5:37–47 resembles that of the "strange woman" and those who follow her in Prov 1–9.

¹² Hasitschka, on the basis of his analysis of the Tabernacles discourses, finds that "sin" signifies for John "not only a single act ... but also a sphere of power, which enslaves human beings and in whose sphere of influence human beings hopelessly approach death" (*Befreiung*, 174). Interestingly, Hasitschka suggests that Jesus's words about "the Jews" seeking him (7:34; 8:21) refer to a "seeking" that will commence when Jesus departs (as does, e.g., Bultmann), but that will be new and "positive," for they will have gained a new disposition toward Jesus (as a result of his death) that will in some

statement (v. 24) supports this point: "If you do not believe that I am he," Jesus warns, "you will die in your sins" (ταῖς ἁμαρτίαις). The plural ἁμαρτίαις (2x in v. 24) makes clear that the "sin" (v. 21) of Jesus's addressees consists of multiple acts of wrongdoing, suggesting that Jesus here attributes to them a sinful behavioral pattern and way of life (cf. the evil "deeds" [τὰ ἔργα] spoken of [2x] in 3:19–20).[13] Additionally, the fact that Jesus's addressees do not yet believe in him while he speaks these words (they belong to "the world" [v. 23]) indicates that they are among those who "walk in the darkness," to whom Jesus alluded earlier (v. 12). They are among "the dead" who have not yet heard the voice of the Son of God (5:25). Given that "the darkness" and "death" are in part what prompted Jesus's advent (see, e.g., 6:50; 12:46–47), the "sin" that Jesus here attributes to his fellow "Jews" (8:21, 24) undoubtedly refers not merely to their rejection of Jesus thus far (i.e., in the moment of "decision") but to a waywardness that characterized them *before* Jesus's advent and *continues* to do so now, in the course of his advent. The way in which "the Jews," that is, God's own people (1:11), were living prior to Jesus's advent is evidently an important reason why Jesus has "much to condemn" with respect to them (v. 26). Jesus therefore continues to announce and reveal here that his fellow "Jews," despite the gift of the law (cf. 1:17), have in fact been living in darkness (vv. 12–20), in sin (vv. 21–24), and that they need to receive and follow "the light" if they wish to have life (v. 12). The life of sin that grips them will bring about their "death" (in the sense of eschatological condemnation [cf. 5:28–29; 8:51; 12:48]) if it is not abandoned through believing and living in Jesus, who is the way to the Father (14:6). The wider narrative portrayal of the contrast between Jesus, on the

---

sense better allow for the possibility of belief (199). "The Jews," following Jesus's departure, "will truly seek <u>him</u> for the first time" (199; emphasis original). The problem with this view, it seems to me, is that here (following Jesus's departure) Jesus's addressees will have a change of attitude and seek him in a "positive" way while, at the same time, they still do not believe in him, for Jesus says they will seek him *and* not find him (7:34), and die in their sin (8:21). Hasitschka says Jesus's statements here about "the Jews" not finding him and dying in sin refer to the "futility" of their seeking and finding him by means of their own human abilities and power (200). Irrespective of whether this view is cogent, though, it seems Hasitschka follows Bultmann with regard to Jesus's words about a "seeking" on the part of "the Jews" but modifies Bultmann's view by asserting that, following Jesus's departure, it is *not* too late for "the Jews" to believe. "Sin" is here a power that will continue to exhibit itself in and through Jesus's addressees to the very end, *unless* they believe.

[13] Hasitschka finds the singular ἁμαρτία in 8:21 to designate a "basic attitude," a "fundamental offense" against God (which is also a coercive power) that is the source of all sinful actions; the plural forms of ἁμαρτία in 8:24 then designate the "totality" of sin (*Befreiung*, 202). "In all individual offenses a basic offense manifests itself; all individual sins are rooted in <u>the</u> sin. <u>The</u> sin is neither a definite single sin nor simply the sum of different sins, nor is it a reality beside them, but a uniform basic attitude, which exhibits itself <u>in</u> and shapes the multiplicity of concrete individual acts" (202; emphasis original). In some contrast to this, Metzner argues against the view that ταῖς ἁμαρτίαις in 8:24 designates multiple transgressions and asks, "Which 'other sins' [besides unbelief] can be meant?" (*Sünde*, 163). Metzner contends that there are "no specific accusations" made against Jesus's fellow "Jews," and although Metzner observes that, for John, "unbelief will be visible in individual offenses and 'evil works' (3:19–21)," it is nevertheless the case that "the individual offenses have as such still no 'sinful' quality in a specific sense" (163–4). In drawing these conclusions, however, Metzner does not seem to consider adequately the wider narrative portrayal of "the Jews," in the course of which it is asserted, for example, that God's own people lack love for God and others (5:42), seek personal glory (5:44), and are "liars" (8:55). It is unclear, furthermore, what justifies Metzner's contention that, for John, "unbelief" occurs in "individual offenses" that, as such, do not offend or transgress in a specific sense.

one hand, and those who deny and oppose him, on the other, evinces what this life of sin comprises: it is characterized by love of self to the detriment of others,[14] and by pursuit of self-glory."[15] "Sin," as that which defines Jesus's adversaries and their deeds, is to affirm and seek to do violence against others,[16] to "lie,"[17] and to have not "the love of God" within oneself.[18] It seems an understatement to say that, for those who have received the law, lacking love for God and others is a serious matter.[19] With respect to the behavior that epitomizes "sin" for John, Forestell is more or less correct: "Murder, hatred, lying, and self-glorification are the trademarks of this life of sin."[20]

This conception of "sin" as a way of life comes to the fore as Jesus continues to speak in the temple (vv. 31–59). After Jesus further elaborates on his fidelity to and reliance on the Father (in response to the question, "Who are you?" [vv. 25–29]), we are told that, while he was explaining these things, "many believed in him" (πολλοὶ ἐπίστευσαν εἰς αὐτόν [v. 30]). To these "Jews," who are described further as those "who have believed in him" (τοὺς πεπιστευκότας αὐτῷ Ἰουδαίους),[21] Jesus then speaks directly and emphasizes the need for their belief to continue and endure: only those

---

[14] 12:25–26; cf. 5:10–15 (the man who had languished at Bethzatha, now healed, seeks to safeguard his own well-being at the expense of his healer); 12:4–6 (Judas Iscariot is a thief and evidently cares more about himself than the poor [here cf. 10:10]); 19:8–16 (Pilate, although he repeatedly finds Jesus to be innocent [18:38; 19:4, 6, 12], nevertheless has Jesus crucified because "the Jews" make him "afraid"). Curiously, although Metzner contends that John's conception of "sin" does not pertain to morality and ethics, and that individual offenses for John have no specific sinful quality, Metzner nevertheless argues that John 15:19 identifies "self-love" to be an aspect of the world's "sin" (*Sünde*, 224–9).

[15] 5:44; 7:18; 12:43; cf. 5:41; 8:50. Kanagaraj explains that, for John, "coveting money, praise and fame which are due to others is viewed as the very characteristic of the enemies of Jesus and hence it is not to be entertained among [Jesus's] followers" ("Implied Ethics," 58). Kanagaraj relates this conduct on the part of Jesus's addressees to the tenth commandment in Exod 20: "You will not covet" (v. 17).

[16] In 18:31 "the Jews" declare to Pilate without qualification, "we are not permitted to put anyone to death." That Pilate neither rejects nor disputes this statement even though he would prefer to remain uninvolved in the matter (he responds initially, "take him yourselves and judge him by your own law" [v. 31]), but proceeds to interrogate, torture, and crucify Jesus indicates that the accuracy and truth of this statement by "the Jews" is to be assumed (whether or in what sense this statement is "accurate" historically is beside the point and an altogether different matter). Accordingly, this statement prohibits and condemns the conduct of those who attempt to "murder" Jesus (8:59 [see below]; cf. v. 44), who plot to "murder" Lazarus (12:10–11), and who will in the future "murder" Jesus's followers (even while supposing such conduct ultimately to be commendable; 16:2–3). In 18:39–40, Pilate's audience elects to release not Jesus, but a "bandit" (λῃστής).

[17] 8:44, 55 (see below); cf. 8:40, 45–46.

[18] 5:42; cf. 14:31. On the meaning of the phrase τὴν ἀγάπην τοῦ θεοῦ (5:42) see Chapter 2.

[19] In Luke 10:27 the law is summed up in the commandments to love God and neighbor (see also Matt 22:37–40; Mark 12:29–33); Jesus then says that the one who does this "will live" (v. 28).

[20] Forestell, *Word of the Cross*, 152. Implicit in Forestell's appraisal is what I think needs to be made explicit: sin is love of self rather than God and others (5:42; 12:25), which manifests itself in murder, hatred, lying, and so on.

[21] On the question of whether, for John, πιστεύω + εἰς αὐτόν (v. 30) signifies a different quality of belief than does πιστεύω + αὐτῷ (v. 31), see Bultmann, *John*, 252 n.2. Bultmann concludes, "πιστ. εἰς αὐτόν can be used interchangeably with πιστ. αὐτῷ" (*John*, 252 n.2). Beasley-Murray agrees (*John*, 132), as does Terry Griffith: "No distinction in terms of invalid and valid faith can be made between πιστεύειν taking the dative and πιστεύειν with εἰς. The verb with the dative is used in 5:24 of genuine faith" ("'The Jews Who Had Believed in Him' (John 8:31) and the Motif of Apostasy in the Gospel of John," in Bauckham and Mosser, *John and Christian Theology*, 185 n.8). Concerning the view that "the Jews" cited here do not "truly" believe in Jesus as their dialogue with him commences, see below.

who "remain in his word" (ἐὰν ὑμεῖς μείνητε ...), who *continue* to believe in and follow him, are truly his disciples (v. 31).²² As "sin" was just described as a behavioral pattern and way of life (vv. 21, 23–24), so here Jesus explains that believing in and following him (which is to believe in the one who sent him [12:44]) involves enduring obedience and commitment; it is a way of life. This life, because it is characterized by "truth" (ἀλήθεια [v. 32]; cf. v. 44),²³ culminates not in condemnation and death (as does sin [vv. 21, 24]) but in eternal life (vv. 35, 51) via the resurrection of life (5:29).

What is perhaps most important to observe here, though, with respect to "sin," is the point that people come to believe in Jesus and, yet, are not consequently free of sin's power. After many of Jesus's fellow "Jews" come to believe in him (v. 30), Jesus emphasizes the need for this belief to continue and endure *for the purpose of their liberation from sin* (vv. 31–36), which is here described as a developing or nascent reality that, if these new believers continue to believe, will be realized at some point *in the future*. "If you remain in my word you are truly my disciples," Jesus says to his new adherents, "and you *will* know (γνώσεσθε) the truth, and the truth *will* set you free" (ἐλευθερώσει [vv. 31–32]).²⁴ In this scene Jesus tells people who believe in him that they are not yet "free," which prompts these people to ask subsequently, "How can you say, 'You will become free' (ἐλεύθεροι γενήσεσθε)?" "Sin," which apparently has enslaved these people heretofore, is considered here to be a power that will continue to influence and affect these believers, because liberation from sin is for them not yet realized. It will come about, in accordance with Jesus's liberating work and power (v. 36), through *continuing* to believe in and follow Jesus (vv. 31–32).²⁵ By "remaining" in his word (v. 31; cf. 14:23) and keeping his commandments (cf. 14:15, 21; 15:10–14), they will become his disciples (cf. 15:8: ἵνα... γένησθε ἐμοὶ μαθηταί; cf. also 12:36). Otherwise, like branches that do not bear fruit, they will be cut off from the vine and discarded (15:6).²⁶

---

²² Pascal-Marie Jerumanis finds that, in the Gospel of John, "belief" is a process that must consist of growth and maturation if it is to culminate in its intended goal (*Réaliser la communion avec Dieu: Croire, vivre et demeurer dans l'évangile selon S. Jean*, EBib 2/32 [Paris: Gabalda, 1996], 60–1, 95–9). Hylen reaches a similar conclusion: "The ambiguity in John's characters suggests that belief is a process or spectrum rather than an all-or-nothing affair. Belief mingles with disbelief and misunderstanding through the Gospel. ... Belief, then, appears partial and piecemeal rather than as a singular event" (*Imperfect Believers*, 157).
²³ Jesus later declares to his followers, "when the Spirit comes, the Spirit of truth, he will lead you (ὁδηγήσει ὑμᾶς) into all the truth" (16:13; see also 17:17–19).
²⁴ Note as well the future verbs γενήσεσθε (v. 33) and ἔσεσθε (v. 36).
²⁵ That liberation from sin is considered not to be realized or completed in the moment one comes to believe in Jesus, but to entail something of a process, is implied later during Jesus's farewell prayer: Jesus asks the Father to "sanctify" (ἁγίασον) his followers "in the truth" (ἐν τῇ ἀληθείᾳ; 17:17; cf. ἀλήθεια [2x] in 8:32), which indicates that the sanctification of these believers is not yet completed and, as such, is ongoing (for more on the significance of Jesus's prayer here see Chapter 2). On liberation as an ongoing reality consider also 14:17 (note the future ἔσται), 14:26 (ὑμᾶς διδάξει πάντα), and 16:13 (ὁδηγήσει ὑμᾶς ἐν τῇ ἀληθείᾳ πάσῃ), as well as 17:11 (ἵνα ὦσιν ἓν καθὼς ἡμεῖς) and 17:23 (ἵνα ὦσιν τετελειωμένοι εἰς ἕν). During his farewell discourse Jesus says to his disciples, "I have told you these things to keep you from falling away" (ἵνα μὴ σκανδαλισθῆτε [16:1]).
²⁶ Commenting on John 8:31, Cyril of Alexandria explains that in this passage Jesus "demands of those who believed in him a firm and fixed disposition and a readiness to remain in the good once they have chosen it. This is what faith in him is all about" (*In Jo.* 5.5.533 [trans. Maxwell]). Cyril goes on to say (in connection with John 8:32) that Jesus exhorts these believers "to know 'the truth.' For through

This scene therefore indicates that the problem of "sin" should not be thought of as rectified or resolved for John in the moment one believes, for here people come to believe in Jesus and, yet, are not free of sin's power. Jesus's words here disprove the idea that, in the Fourth Gospel, "sin" is essentially "unbelief." Given that Jesus "knows all things" (21:17),[27] and given the condemnatory words that Jesus proceeds to speak (vv. 37–38, 39b-41a, 42–47), Jesus undoubtedly knows in advance that the belief of these people does not endure, and that their belief will turn into uncertainty and skepticism (vv. 33, 39a), hostility (vv. 41b, 48, 52–53), and even violence (v. 59; cf. 18:31b). Jesus knows that, although his addressees have come to believe in him, his word does not "make progress" (χωρεῖ) in them (v. 37).[28] Jesus's knowledge of what will occur seems to cause his abruptness here: his new followers disagree and quarrel with him over, among other things, the fact of their "slavery," but Jesus knows them better than they know themselves. They will eventually attempt to stone him (v. 59), so Jesus declares to them, "you seek to kill me" (v. 37), although at this juncture they are perhaps oblivious about any such intention (as they are about their "slavery" [v. 33]). The omniscience of Jesus, however, does not erase the initial faith of these people: they "believed in him" (vv. 30–31), but, like many followers who preceded them, they do not abide in Jesus.[29] The power from which these people need to be liberated, "sin" (v. 34), will apparently continue to orient and define them.

Here we should note, though, that this reading is rather controversial. Some argue, for instance, that the people whom Jesus addresses when he speaks about discipleship and liberation from sin (in v. 31 and following) are *not* the people just said to believe in him (v. 30). The latter are cited for their belief, which emerges while Jesus speaks about his reliance on and fidelity to the Father (vv. 25–30), but once these new believers are mentioned nothing more is said about them. Because the dialogue that ensues develops into an impassioned argument, the character of this ensuing dialogue rules out the possibility that, when Jesus begins to speak about discipleship and liberation from sin (v. 31), he speaks to people who believe in him. The people designated as τοὺς πεπιστευκότας αὐτῷ Ἰουδαίους (v. 31) are people different from those just said to believe (v. 30): the participle πεπιστευκότας, while perfect tense in form, is pluperfect in force and signifies people who "had believed" previously but do so no longer. Jesus therefore addresses *unbelievers* when he speaks about discipleship, liberation, and sin

---

this, he says, they will be entirely freed, according to the meaning of his words" (*In Jo.* 5.5.537 [trans. Maxwell]).

[27] In John's Gospel the omniscience of Jesus is frequently described (both implicitly and explicitly) and seems to be an important theological conviction (see 2:4, 19, 24–25; 3:11; 4:17–18, 21; 5:6, 25, 37–42; 6:6, 61–64; etc.).

[28] Brown translates οὐ χωρεῖ ἐν ὑμῖν (v. 37) as "makes no headway in you" (*John (I-XII)*, 352); see further BDAG (1094) and L&N (1:184 [15.13]).

[29] In John 6, after many of Jesus's disciples (πολλοί ... ἐκ τῶν μαθητῶν αὐτοῦ [v. 60]) hear and find to be "difficult" Jesus's words about "the bread of life" and his "flesh and blood" (vv. 32–65), we are told in v. 66 that "many of his disciples (πολλοὶ ἐκ τῶν μαθητῶν αὐτοῦ) turned away and no longer walked with him." Unlike the people to whom Jesus speaks about discipleship and liberation from sin (8:31 and following), though, the people who abandon Jesus here in John 6 are never explicitly said, it appears, to have "believed" in him (but cf. 2:11), although they are repeatedly said to have been "disciples" and, consequently, may be presumed to have believed.

(in v. 31 and following).³⁰ Other interpreters likewise find the nature of the dialogue between Jesus and those designated as τοὺς πεπιστευκότας αὐτῷ Ἰουδαίους (v. 31) to exclude the possibility that Jesus here addresses believers, but these interpreters maintain that "the Jews" to whom Jesus speaks *are* in fact the people just said to believe (v. 30). The intense argument that before long erupts signals that the faith of these people is anything but genuine: their belief is spurious or false.³¹ As in the former reading, then, so here Jesus proceeds to speak about discipleship, liberation, and sin (vv. 31–36) *to people who do not believe.*

Various factors speak against these respective views, however. Concerning the first, there is simply no clear or explicit indication that the people whom Jesus addresses when he speaks about discipleship and liberation from sin (in v. 31 and following) are *not* the people just said to believe in him (v. 30).³² Numerous interpreters render πεπιστευκότας (v. 31) as though it is pluperfect in tense, yet maintain that "the Jews" to whom Jesus speaks are in fact those just said to believe (v. 30). Concerning the second view, to characterize the belief of these "Jews" as "spurious" or "false" is simply

---

³⁰ For this line of interpretation, see, e.g., James Swetnam, "The Meaning of πεπιστευκότας in John 8:31," *Bib* 61 (1980): 106–9; Griffith, "'The Jews,'" 183–92; Hartwig Thyen, *Das Johannesevangelium*, HNT 6 (Tübingen: Mohr Siebeck, 2005), 432–6. Mark W. G. Stibbe also regards Jesus's addressees in v. 31 to be different people from those cited in v. 30, but it is difficult to say whether Stibbe thinks that, at the outset of the dialogue (v. 31), Jesus addresses people who previously believed but do so no longer or, rather, people who currently believe (*John's Gospel*, New Testament Readings [London: Routledge, 1994], 107–31). At one point Stibbe explains that "the Jews" cited in v. 31 "do not believe in Jesus" (116). Stibbe goes on to say, however, that "the Jews mentioned in 8:31 are Jewish disciples of Jesus who are about to apostatize in the ensuing narrative"; "they are Jewish believers who turn out, in the unfolding story, to have no room for Jesus' *logos* (8:37)" (123–4).

³¹ For this line of interpretation, see, e.g., Edwyn Clement Hoskyns, *The Fourth Gospel*, ed. Francis Noel Davey (London: Faber & Faber, 1947), 337–40; Ernst Haenchen, *John: A Commentary on the Gospel of John, Chapters 7–21*, ed. Robert W. Funk and Ulrich Busse, trans. Robert W. Funk, Hermeneia (Philadelphia, PA: Fortress, 1984), 28; D. A. Carson, *The Gospel according to John*, Pillar New Testament Commentary (Grand Rapids, MI: Eerdmans; Leicester: Apollos, 1991), 346–8. Bultmann likewise seems to consider the belief attributed to "the Jews" in vv. 30–31 to be false or not genuine (*John*, 433–43). So do Morris (*John*, 453–6), Lincoln (*Saint John*, 269–70), and Theobald (*Johannes*, 586, 588). Hasitschka makes a distinction between "initial belief" and "true belief," and he seems to conclude that, although "the Jews" cited in 8:30–31 reach the former, they do not reach the latter and, thus, never "truly" or "actually" believe in Jesus (*Befreiung*, 229–39). Similarly, Motyer contends that "the Jews" cited in vv. 30–31 believe in Jesus as "the Prophet," which is "a completely inadequate response" (*Your Father the Devil?*, 166); "these believing Jews are no more prepared to accept Jesus' word than their plotting fellow Jews" (163). Metzner deems the belief of "the Jews" in 8:30–31 to be "superficial" (*Sünde*, 173–4 [cf. 181–3]). See further Paul M. Hoskins, who suggests that the "new Jewish believers" whom Jesus speaks to about discipleship and liberation from sin (in v. 31 and following) do not "truly believe" ("Freedom from Slavery to Sin and the Devil: John 8:31–47 and the Passover Theme of the Gospel of John," *TJ* 31 [2010]: 47–63 [but see in particular 54–5]). Raimo Hakola says that "the faith of these Jews is not real faith at all because, eventually, even they are counted among those who try to kill Jesus" ("The Believing Jews as the Children of the Devil in John 8:44: Similarity as a Threat to Social Identity," in *Evil and the Devil*, ed. Ida Fröhlich and Erkki Koskenniemi, LNTS 481 [London: T&T Clark, 2013], 117).

³² Morris: "there is no indication in the narrative that different groups of people are meant" (*John*, 455). Hakola agrees: "Even though the narrator here [in v. 31] uses slightly different expressions in speaking of believers among the Jews, there is no reason to think that two different groups of believing Jews are meant here" ("The Believing Jews," 116–17). See also C. H. Dodd, "Behind a Johannine Dialogue," in *More New Testament Studies* (Manchester: Manchester University Press, 1968), 42–3.

not accurate, because such characterizations, strictly speaking, contradict what John explicitly says: these people "believed in him" (vv. 30–31). If their belief is "spurious" or "false" (i.e., not real, genuine, or authentic), then it is *not* belief, and thus these people have not believed in Jesus, *ever*.[33] The participle πεπιστευκότας (v. 31) *perhaps* reflects what eventually becomes of these people's belief. That is, the participle *might* signal that at some point these people cease to believe in Jesus (which the subsequent dispute makes clear), but this outcome does not make the belief of these people "spurious" or "false."[34] The fact that the belief of these people turns into "unbelief" does not mean that they did not believe in the first place; it does not follow that they *never* believed. Viewed in light of the story's end and with the knowledge of what will eventually occur, the belief of these people may be characterized as temporary, impermanent, or provisional, but this is not the same as "spurious" or "false."[35] And this distinction is important, because a major factor in these people's *ceasing* to believe becomes clear when their belief is recognized as genuine. Why does their belief not endure and progress? It does not endure and progress, at least in part, *because of sin*, for sin's power is not destroyed for these people in the moment they come to believe in Jesus. The emergence of belief on the part of these "Jews" does not set them "free" (vv. 32–36). As soon as they come to believe (v. 30), Jesus declares that they must *remain* in his word if they are to be liberated from the influence and power, the way of life, that has gripped them heretofore (vv. 31–36).

What most clearly speaks against the two interpretations described above, though, is the point that Jesus's conditional statement in v. 31 assumes his addressees believe in him: "If you remain (μείνητε) in my word," Jesus tells them, "you are truly my disciples." If Jesus's addressees do not believe in him, how can they "remain" or "abide" in his word? For them to "remain" in Jesus's word requires that they have received it and believe in him currently, while Jesus speaks to them.[36] The aspiration or goal of this "remaining," that is, to be Jesus's disciples "truly" (ἀληθῶς), also assumes Jesus's addressees believe

---

[33] Interpreters who describe the belief of "the Jews" in 8:30–31 as "deficient," "inadequate," or "flawed" typically seem to imply by these terms and conclude that this belief is not genuine or authentic (see, e.g., Motyer, *Your Father the Devil?*, 166; Metzner, *Sünde*, 173–4 [cf. 181–3]; Andrew T. Lincoln, *Truth on Trial: The Lawsuit Motif in John's Gospel* [Peabody, MA: Hendrickson, 2000], 83; Lincoln, *Saint John*, 269–70). If the belief of Jesus's addressees here *is* deemed to be simply "deficient" or "inadequate," though, it follows that these "Jews" *do genuinely believe in Jesus* as their dialogue with him commences, but in a way that is imperfect. This would then seem to be the point of Jesus's statement that these believers must *continue* in his word in order to know the truth fully and be set free (vv. 31–32; cf. the work of the Spirit in 16:13). On the matter of "deficient" or "imperfect" belief in John's Gospel see below.

[34] On the sense of τοὺς πεπιστευκότας here in 8:31, though, compare Acts 21:20, in which James and all the elders in Jerusalem say to Paul, "See, brother, how many myriads of believers (τῶν πεπιστευκότων) there are among the Jews" (εἰσὶν ἐν τοῖς Ἰουδαίοις). The participle here refers to the many "Jews" who believe in Jesus currently, that is, while Paul speaks with James and the elders. Cf. also Acts 18:27; 19:18; 21:25; Titus 3:8.

[35] Carson seems to employ "fickle" as a synonym for "spurious": in v. 31 "Jesus now lays down exactly what it is that separates spurious faith from true faith, fickle disciples from genuine disciples" (*John*, 348). The word "fickle," though, would seem appropriate for designating not spurious or phony belief but *a change* in belief—a change of heart. Such consideration perhaps leads Ridderbos to explain that, "in the Fourth Gospel, 'disciple' (μαθητής), like 'believe,' sometimes refers to a provisional, not permanent, decision for Jesus (cf. 6:60, 66)" (*John*, 308 n.172).

[36] Michaels makes a similar point:

in him. Otherwise, of what relevance to them is the goal set before them, namely, to be Jesus's disciples in a *truer* sense? Are we to think that Jesus urges his addressees here to be in actuality and, thus, to a greater extent, something they neither claim nor are considered to be in the first place? What occasions an explanation of true discipleship if Jesus's addressees do not believe in him and, therefore, are not disciples? The subject of Jesus's conditional statement here (v. 31) is not "anyone" (cf. τις [2x] in the conditional statements of vv. 51–52), but "you" (ἐὰν ὑμεῖς μείνητε … ἐστε), that is, the people who "believed in him" (vv. 30–31). "If *you* remain," Jesus tells them. The idea that believers *are* and, also, *become* Jesus's disciples through "remaining" in his word recurs later when Jesus says the following to his disciples during the farewell discourse: "the Father is glorified in this, that you bear much fruit and become (γένησθε) my disciples" (15:8).[37] Jesus says this after encouraging his disciples to "remain" in him (ἐὰν μείνητε ἐν ἐμοί …[15:7]), and Jesus will later pray for the Father to "sanctify" (ἁγίασον) his disciples "in the truth" (17:17).

This brings us to another important point: the belief exhibited by members of "the twelve" in John's Gospel parallels to some extent the belief of "the Jews" whom Jesus addresses here (in 8:31 and following).[38] On several occasions in John's Gospel the belief of Jesus's twelve disciples is shown to be flawed or imperfect, indicating that they have not yet come to know "the truth" (8:32) in full. During Jesus's farewell discourse, for instance, which Jesus begins by exhorting his disciples (who here include members of the twelve) to "believe" (2x [14:1]), Thomas says that he and his fellow disciples know neither where Jesus is going nor "the way" (14:5), despite the fact that Jesus states immediately prior to this, "you know the way where I am going" (14:4). Thomas's confession indicates a degree of dissonance between what Jesus hopes his closest disciples believe and understand (cf. v. 7), on the one hand, and what these disciples do in fact believe and understand, on the other. Jesus's closest disciples exhibit a belief that

> To "dwell on" Jesus' word presupposes that they have in fact "believed him" (that is, believed in him on the basis of his spoken words, v. 31). Jesus is asking them, now that they have believed, to "follow" him (see v. 12) or "walk with him" (see 6:60) in the sense of giving him their allegiance, even to "dwell in him" (6:56) or become united to him in their very being. (*John*, 505)

[37] On John 15:8 Michaels writes: "It comes as something of a shock that at this late date they [i.e., Jesus's disciples] have yet to 'become my disciples'. … Jesus' so-called 'disciples' still have a ways to go" (*John*, 809). Michaels points out that a similar view of discipleship is found in the letters of Ignatius of Antioch (809 n.45). In his *Epistula ad Romanos*, for example, Ignatius explains that he will truly become Jesus's disciple when he undergoes martyrdom: "I am writing all the churches and giving instruction to all, that I am willingly dying for God, unless you hinder me. … Allow me to be bread for the wild beasts. … Then I will truly be a disciple of Jesus Christ" (*Rom.* 4.1-2 [LCL 24:275]). "From Syria to Rome I have been fighting the wild beasts. … But I am becoming more of a disciple by their mistreatment" (*Rom.* 5.1 [LCL 24:275–77]). "Now I am beginning to be a disciple" (*Rom.* 5.3 [LCL 24:277]). Ignatius goes on to say that, insofar as he follows Jesus unto death, he will be truly *human*:

> It is better for me to die in Jesus Christ than to rule the ends of the earth. That is the one I seek, who died on our behalf; that is the one I desire, who arose for us. … Allow me to receive the pure light; when I have arrived there, I will be a human. Allow me to be an imitator of the suffering of my God. (*Rom.* 6.1-3 [LCL 24:277–79])

[38] For "the twelve" in John's Gospel see 6:67–71 and 20:24; cf. Matt 10:1–4; Mark 3:14–19; Luke 6:13–16.

is incomplete and, thus, show belief to be a process. Philip's ensuing request likewise displays deficient or imperfect belief. Following Jesus's reply to Thomas (14:6–7), Philip says, "Lord, show us the Father" (14:8), to which Jesus replies, "Have I been with you for such a long time, Philip, and you do not know me?" (14:9). Jesus goes on to say here, "Do you not believe that I am in the Father and the Father is in me? ... Believe me" (vv. 10–11). This exchange makes clear that, like the believers to whom Jesus speaks about discipleship and liberation from sin (8:31 and following), Jesus's closest disciples believe (cf. 6:69) and, yet, have not come to know "the truth" in full (cf. 8:32). This is undoubtedly an important reason why Jesus later prays for the Father to "sanctify" his disciples in the truth (17:17–19). Among the twelve, imperfect belief is of course exhibited also (and perhaps above all) by Peter, who not only denies being a follower of Jesus (3x) after Jesus is arrested but also lies about being present during Jesus's arrest (18:15–18, 25–27).[39] Other characters in John's Gospel who show belief to be a process could be mentioned as well.[40] For John, the imperfect belief displayed by Jesus's followers in the course of his ministry is presumably due in part to the fact that the Spirit does not come to indwell believers until after Jesus's resurrection (7:39; 14:16–17, 26; 16:7–15; 20:22). Yet the language of the indwelling Spirit "teaching" believers "all things" (ὑμᾶς διδάξει πάντα [14:26]) and "leading" or "guiding" believers "into all the truth" (ὁδηγήσει ὑμᾶς ἐν τῇ ἀληθείᾳ πάσῃ [16:13]) implies that, even after the bestowal of the Spirit, belief and salvation are a process. As those who believe in Jesus both *are* and *will become* his disciples by continuing in his word (15:8), so they both *know* and *will come to know* "the truth" (8:32) through the teaching and leading of the Spirit (14:26; 16:13–15).[41] Let us recall, too, what is said in the prologue: it is to those who believe that Jesus gives power "to become" (γενέσθαι) children of God (1:12).

But there is still another reason for understanding the believers to whom Jesus speaks about discipleship and liberation from sin (8:31 and following) as indeed *believing in him* when their dialogue with him commences. The point that human beings, in the moment they come to believe in Jesus, are not yet liberated from what grips them (8:31–36) is conveyed earlier in John's Gospel when many people in Jerusalem are said to believe in Jesus during Passover (2:23–25). "Many believed in his name (πολλοὶ ἐπίστευσαν εἰς τὸ ὄνομα αὐτοῦ)," John says, "when they saw the

---

[39] Wagener finds that John invites readers (and listeners) to identify with the "highs and lows" Peter experiences and to understand Peter's experience as representative of the development in belief and behavior that the Christian life involves (*Figuren*, 300, 327, 329–32, 338–40). Peter's experience of failure "is viewed as part of being a disciple" (*Figuren*, 331).

[40] On the belief of the Samaritan woman (4:7–30, 39–42), Mary and Martha (11:1–44; 12:1–8), and the Beloved Disciple (13:23–29; 19:26–27; 20:2–10; 21:7, 20–24), see Hylen, *Imperfect Believers*, 41–58, 77–109.

[41] Paul likewise seems to understand belief (and salvation) to be a process. In 1 Corinthians, for instance, Paul tells the Corinthian Christians that, when he was previously with them, he could not address them as "spiritual people," but only as "babes in Christ" (νηπίοις ἐν Χριστῷ), and that he fed them not solid food, but milk, "for you were not ready [for the former] and are still not ready even now, for you are still worldly" (1 Cor 3:1–3). Paul contends that his addressees still think and behave like worldly people (v. 3); as such, they are not yet "mature" (τέλειος [1 Cor 2:6]).

miracles he was doing" (v. 23).⁴² John goes on to explain, however, that Jesus did not entrust himself to these believers because he knew "all people" (πάντας [v. 24]). Jesus needed no one's testimony "concerning human beings, for he himself knew what was in human beings" (αὐτὸς γὰρ ἐγίνωσκεν τί ἦν ἐν τῷ ἀνθρώπῳ [v. 25]). As in the case of the believers to whom Jesus speaks about discipleship and liberation from sin (8:31 and following), so here there is no suggestion that the belief of these people is spurious or not genuine. In fact, unlike in the case of the believers to whom Jesus speaks about discipleship and liberation (8:31 and following), there is no indication that these believers ever become otherwise. That is, there is no indication that at some point these people *cease* to believe.⁴³ What John *does* explain is that Jesus did not entrust himself to these believers because of what was "in" them. Clearly, then, something problematic is still attributed to these people, even though they have come to believe in Jesus (see also 12:42–43). In light of the words about discipleship and liberation that Jesus later speaks to people who have come to believe in him (8:31–36), it seems that what continues to be "in" the believers mentioned here (2:23–25) is "sin."⁴⁴ Jesus will disclose later, during a dialogue with other "Jews" who have come to believe him (8:31 and following), that liberation from sin is a process that comes to fruition through remaining in and keeping his word.⁴⁵

---

⁴² On the issue of a supposed antithesis between "seeing" and "hearing" in John's Gospel, Thompson says the following:

> "Hearing" has long been elevated to supreme rank, while "seeing," at least when used with reference to the signs of Jesus, has been denigrated as an inferior way of knowing God. However, a closer look at the evidence of John suggests that this evaluation ought to be turned completely around. The higher good, one to which Jesus alone may lay claim and that lies in the eschatological future for all others, is the good of *seeing* God. Hearing is in no way inferior to seeing, but it never attains the status of eschatological destiny for those of faith. (*God*, 105; italics original)

⁴³ Concerning the question of whether Nicodemus should be regarded as one of the "many" who are said to believe in Jesus during Passover (2:23), because Nicodemus is introduced (3:1) *not* as one of the believers just mentioned but as a Pharisee and leader of the Jewish people (cf. 8:30–31, in which the belief attributed to "the Jews" in v. 31 identifies them as the believers just mentioned in v. 30), the fact that Jesus explicitly says that Nicodemus is among those who "do not receive our testimony" (3:11), and goes on to imply that Nicodemus does not believe (3:12), suggests that Nicodemus is not to be counted among the "many" just said to believe in Jesus. It seems that, at this juncture, John is introducing readers to the *possibility* of Nicodemus, a Pharisee and "ruler of the Jews," coming to believe in Jesus (cf. 7:50–51; 19:38–42).

⁴⁴ That the problem with the believers cited in 2:23–25 is not a "spurious" or "false" belief on their part is indicated by the scope of the matter at issue: what Jesus finds to be problematic about these new believers pertains to "all people" (πάντας [v. 24]). What afflicts these new believers is "in" human beings as a whole (αὐτὸς γὰρ ἐγίνωσκεν τί ἦν ἐν τῷ ἀνθρώπῳ [v. 25]). The scope of the problem that continues to grip these believers therefore seems, on the one hand, to rule out the possibility that at issue here is a spurious or false belief in Jesus and, on the other hand, to imply that "sin" is the problem at issue, for "sin" is earlier attributed to all human beings when John the Baptist declares Jesus to be the one who takes away "the sin of the world" (1:29; related to the world's "sin" is the "ignorance" of God attributed to the world in, e.g., 1:10–11).

⁴⁵ Modern interpreters who seem to find "the Jews" in 8:30–31 *genuinely* to believe in Jesus as their dialogue with him commences include Schnackenburg (*St. John*, 203–5) and Johannes Beutler (*A Commentary on the Gospel of John*, trans. Michael Tait [Grand Rapids, MI: Eerdmans, 2017], 237–8). Cf. Dodd, "Behind a Johannine Dialogue"; Barrett, *St. John*, 344; Michaels, *John*, 502–5. Hylen understands "the Jews" as a corporate character who both believes and disbelieves: "the Jews may be seen as divided in their response to Jesus. ... This division is not *among* the Jews, but *within* the

The case of "the Jews" who, during Tabernacles, come to believe in Jesus as he speaks about his fidelity to and reliance on the Father (8:30 and following) therefore does indeed disprove the idea that "sin" in John's Gospel amounts to "unbelief." The fact that these people come to believe in Jesus and, then, are told that they are not yet "free" from sin (vv. 30–36) makes clear that sin is not destroyed in the emergence of belief. Liberation from sin is here said to come about through remaining in and keeping Jesus's word, and thus sin is here described as a reality that believers must resist and struggle against as they both are and become Jesus's disciples (cf. 15:8). The scene parallels and clarifies an earlier one in John's Gospel, in which a problematic reality "in human beings" is described as continuing to afflict people who believe in Jesus (2:23–25). The scene also offers an explanation for why many of Jesus's disciples end up abandoning him (see, e.g., 6:60–66), why an important purpose of Jesus's farewell discourse is to keep his disciples from "falling away" (16:1; see also 15:1–10),[46] and why in the course of his farewell prayer Jesus prays for the Father to "sanctify" his disciples "in the truth" (17:17–19; cf. 8:32; 16:13). For John, liberation from sin is not realized in the emergence of belief; rather, it comes about through *continuing* to believe and live in Jesus.

It is also relevant here that, in the course of Jesus's dialogue with his fellow "Jews" during Tabernacles (in 8:12 and following), Jesus attributes to his addressees not only "sin" but also "darkness" (vv. 12–13), ignorance of God (vv. 14–19), "death" (vv. 21–24), and an affiliation with "the world" (v. 23). This association of terms and themes implies that the "sin" of Jesus's fellow "Jews" and "the world" as a whole predates Jesus's advent, for, as we have observed, in John's Gospel Jesus has come into the world so that human beings may pass from "death" into life (5:24–29) and no longer remain in "the darkness" (12:46–47). Jesus has come ultimately not to condemn "the world" (with which Jesus, again, identifies his fellow "Jews") but to save the world. Jesus is the one who takes away "the sin of the world" (1:29). These associations suggest that, for John, the problem of "sin" preexisted and prompted Jesus's advent, which further disproves the idea that "sin" in John's Gospel is essentially a disposition or attitude that arises in response to Jesus (i.e., "unbelief"). "Sin," for John, seems rather to comprise a way or manner of life that, on the one hand, gripped the world prior to Jesus's advent and, on the other, continues to influence human beings subsequent to the emergence of belief. Further consideration of what Jesus says about sin and liberation to "the Jews" who believe in him (8:31–36), and of what Jesus says about sin and liberation elsewhere

---

Jews as a character. The portrayal of the Jews suggests a conflicted or divided character, perhaps even a contradictory character, one who believes in Jesus and also seeks to kill him" (*Imperfect Believers*, 118; italics original). This reading is dissimilar from that of the present study in various ways, one of which is that I find the people who come to believe in Jesus during Tabernacles (in 8:30 and following) to be *some* or *a group of* "the Jews" (cf. 2:23–25; 7:31–32, 43–44; 11:45–47; 12:11–13, 42–43). When these people eventually show by their words and deeds that they believe no longer, they demonstrate that Jesus's word does not "make progress" in them (v. 37) and realign themselves with "the Jews" who do not believe in Jesus. To my knowledge, no one observes or explains the implications of the genuine yet imperfect belief of "the Jews" whom Jesus addresses during Tabernacles (8:31 and following) for John's portrayal of sin, the human predicament, and salvation.

[46] On the sense of σκανδαλίζω in John 16:1 see BDAG (926) and L&N (1:375–76 [31.77–78]).

in John's Gospel (particularly to "the Pharisees" in the scene that follows [9:40–41]), confirms this assessment.

Doing Wrong, Having Guilt, and the Nature of Liberation from Sin

Let us return to Jesus's dialogue with "the Jews" who, during Tabernacles, come to believe in him (8:31 and following). When Jesus reveals that it is "sin" (ἁμαρτία [2x in v. 34]) from which his addressees need to be liberated, what "sin" comprises and the scope of its influence are indicated as well: "every individual who commits sin is a slave of sin" (πᾶς ὁ ποιῶν τὴν ἁμαρτίαν δοῦλός ἐστιν τῆς ἁμαρτίας [v. 34]).[47] The initial occurrence of ἁμαρτία here designates an act that someone "commits" or "does" (ποιῶν), so the sense "sin" or "wrongdoing" is indeed fitting.[48] The remainder of the statement, though, declares that to act in such a way is symptomatic and a sign of the subject's conduct as a whole: every person who does wrong is in fact a "slave" (δοῦλός) *of such behavior* (τῆς ἁμαρτίας), a slave to acting in this way, indicating that to "do wrong" (ποιῶν τὴν ἁμαρτίαν) is symptomatic of an enduring behavioral pattern that grips and coerces the subject, compelling ensuing behavior that is akin to that which has preceded.[49] From this statement (v. 34) we are undoubtedly to infer, consequently,

---

[47] Concerning the syntactic relationship of the genitive τῆς ἁμαρτίας to its head noun δοῦλός, the genitive may be "possessive" in a figurative or metaphorical sense: the one who commits sin is a slave "belonging to" or "owned by" such sin. Or the genitive may be "objective," given the verbal idea implicit in δοῦλός. Still another possibility is that, since Jesus's addressees just asserted, "we have never been slaves to anyone" (v. 33), the genitive τῆς ἁμαρτίας in v. 34 denotes "that in reference to which the noun … to which it stands related [here δοῦλός] is true" (Wallace, *Greek Grammar*, 127). In this respect τῆς ἁμαρτίας is a "genitive of reference" (see also H. E. Dana and Julius R. Mantey, *A Manual Grammar of the Greek New Testament* [New York: Macmillan, 1950], 78). These various nuances are perhaps not mutually exclusive. Whether Jesus's addressees are (or have been) slaves to any actual individual (they say οὐδενί) is beside the point, for Jesus speaks of slavery with respect to sin (cf. Rom 6:16–23; 8:21; 2 Pet 2:19).

[48] The present tense substantival participle here (ποιῶν) seems to be gnomic and convey little aspectual force. Otherwise, the continuous aspect would definitively restrict the generality and applicability of the statement, with δοῦλός applying *only* to those who continually commit sin.

[49] Inasmuch as "sin" is described here as a way of life and power that grips human beings, "sin" in John's Gospel resembles the "evil inclination" or "evil heart" spoken of in Second Temple and rabbinic literature (on this evil inclination see Frank Chamberlin Porter, "The *Yeçer Hara*: A Study in the Jewish Doctrine of Sin," in *Biblical and Semitic Studies: Critical and Historical Essays by the Members of the Semitic and Biblical Faculty of Yale University* [New York: Scribner's Sons, 1901], 91–156; Roland E. Murphy, "*Yēṣer* in the Qumran Literature," *Bib* 39 [1958]: 334–44; Johann Cook, "The Origin of the Tradition of the יצר הטוב and יצר הרע," *JSJ* 38 [2007]: 80–91; Ishay Rosen-Zvi, "Two Rabbinic Inclinations? Rethinking a Scholarly Dogma," *JSJ* 39 [2008]: 513–39; Miryam T. Brand, *Evil Within and Without: The Source of Sin and Its Nature as Portrayed in Second Temple Literature*, Journal of Ancient Judaism Supplements 9 [Göttingen: Vandenhoeck & Ruprecht, 2013]; Benjamin Wold, "Demonizing Sin? The Evil Inclination in 4QInstruction," in *Evil in Second Temple Judaism and Early Christianity*, ed. Chris Keith and Loren T. Stuckenbruck, WUNT 2/417 [Tübingen: Mohr Siebeck, 2016], 34–48). The author of the Damascus Document (CD-A), for example, exhorts "all who enter the covenant" (II, 2) "not to follow the thoughts of a sinful inclination and lustful eyes. For many have gone astray because of such thoughts; brave heroes have stumbled because of them from long ago until now" (II, 16–17; cf. 4Q266 2 II, 16–17). The protagonist of 4 Ezra, after being told by an angel about the eschatological condemnation that looms for most of the world's inhabitants, says

that to commit an act of sin (ποιῶν τὴν ἁμαρτίαν) also contributes to sin's influence and power, since each sinful act is a particular instantiation or realization of one's bondage to sin.[50] Jesus therefore reveals here that "sin" is not committed in a vacuum. On the one hand, an act of sin is both indicative and a product of one's conduct heretofore. On the other, an act of sin is both indicative and conducive of the conduct that will inevitably follow, given sin's influence and power. Sin will continue to enslave and rule over its captives *unless*, that is, the one who is able to liberate from sin (v. 36), and who is himself the way and the truth and the life (14:6), is received and followed. And yet, because Jesus maintains that liberation from sin is still a future reality *for those who have come to believe in him* (vv. 31–36), sin's power is regarded *not* as destroyed in the moment a person believes in Jesus but as persisting subsequent to the emergence of belief (cf. 2:23–25; 12:42–43; 16:1). This point is accentuated by the fact that the belief of Jesus's addressees turns into unbelief.[51] The ongoing influence of sin, it seems, is an important reason why those who come to believe in Jesus must "remain" or "abide" in his word (v. 31; cf. 14:23). In doing so, they remain in the true vine (15:1–17).

Importantly, with respect to the passage at hand (8:31 and following), the true vine discourse (15:1–17) sheds light on more than Jesus's statement about the need for his new adherents to "remain" in his word (v. 31). Given that Jesus's addressees here (v. 31) believe in him and, yet, are not "free" (vv. 32–33), Jesus's ensuing statement that "every person who commits sin is a slave of sin" (v. 34) evidently applies to unbelievers *as well as* to believers. That is, this statement about sin's power (v. 34), given the context, suggests that believers can be enslaved to sin. An interpretive key for understanding this idea is a statement Jesus makes to his disciples during his discourse on the true vine: "apart from me," Jesus says, "you can do nothing" (15:5). Jesus emphasizes here that his disciples do not have the ability *in themselves* to bear fruit (vv. 4–5), which involves doing Jesus's commandments (vv. 7–17). Consequently, the implication that believers can be enslaved to sin (8:34) seems to be based on the idea that believers do

---

the following to his heavenly mediator: "'an evil heart has grown up in us, which has alienated us from God, and has brought us into corruption and the ways of death, and has shown us the paths of perdition and removed us far from life—and that not just a few of us but almost all who have been created!'" (7:48 [*OTP* 1:538]). For additional Second Temple texts that speak of this evil inclination of heart, see, e.g., 1QH^a XIII, 8; XV, 6; 1QS V, 4–5; 4Q417 1 II, 12; 4Q422 I, 12; 4Q436 1 I, 10; 11QPs^a XIX, 15–16; T. Iss. 6:2; T. Ash. 1:3–9; 3:2; cf. 1QH^a IV, 21–37; IX, 23–25; XII, 30–32. Second Temple and rabbinic conceptions of the evil inclination seem to be based on Gen 6:5 ("The Lord saw that the wickedness of human beings was great on the earth, and that every inclination of the thoughts of their hearts was only evil continually") and 8:21 ("the inclination of the human heart is evil from youth"; cf. 4:7). See also, e.g., Jer 7:24; 16:12; 17:9. With respect to John 8:34, Hugo Odeberg finds that "behind this utterance lies the commonly accepted truth of the relation between man's sin and the domination of יצר הרע" (*The Fourth Gospel: Interpreted in Its Relation to Contemporaneous Religious Currents in Palestine and the Hellenistic-Oriental World* [Chicago: Argonaut, 1929], 297). On this point cf. Metzner, *Sünde*, 177.

[50] Barrett reaches a similar conclusion: the one "who actually commits sin demonstrates thereby that he is already the slave of sin; also, by the very sin he commits he makes himself still further a slave" (*St. John*, 345).

[51] John does not seem to indicate when exactly it is that the belief of Jesus's addressees turns into unbelief, so the question of the precise point at which these believers cease to believe does not seem to be a concern for John. What seems to be important, rather, is that (1) Jesus knows in advance that these believers will fall away; and (2) these believers fall away, in part, because of the ongoing influence and problem of sin.

not have the ability, in and of themselves, to fulfill Jesus's commandments, which call believers to disregard themselves for the sake of God and others, out of love for God and others and in faithfulness to God (12:25–26; 13:34–35; 15:12–17; cf. 1:14, 16–17). Believers may be said to be slaves of sin, it seems, with respect to their own moral and ethical capabilities or powers. This implication therefore underscores the point that *it is because of Jesus, living in believers*, that believers have life and are able to bear fruit. Believers have life only insofar as Jesus is "in" them and they are "in" Jesus (6:53–57; 15:4–10). Believers are sanctified in and through Jesus, who sanctifies himself on their behalf (17:19). It seems to be the case, then, that, for John, believers can be enslaved to sin (8:34), have sin "in" them (2:23–25), lack the ability to overcome sin and bear fruit (15:5; cf. 17:19), and at the same time *not* be enslaved to sin, since Jesus lives in them, together with the Father (14:23) and the Spirit (14:17; 20:22).[52]

Jesus's statement about sin's power (v. 34), in conjunction with his words about discipleship and liberation from sin (vv. 31–36), therefore indicates how sin can be an ongoing factor in the lives of believers (which is implied in vv. 32–33). Sin, as that which persists in human beings and continues to influence them following the emergence of belief (cf. again 2:23–25; 12:42–43; 16:1), is a way of life that believers are to resist, a power that believers are to struggle against. Believers do this, that is, struggle against and resist sin, through *abiding in Jesus and his word* (cf. 15:1–10).[53] It is through

---

[52] Hasitschka (*Befreiung*, 242–3) and Metzner (*Sünde*, 178–81) view the "slavery" described in John 8:31–36 to be analogous to the "slavery" spoken of in John 15:15, where Jesus says the following to his disciples: "No longer do I call you slaves (δούλους), because the slave does not know what his master (αὐτοῦ ὁ κύριος) is doing; but I have called you friends, because everything that I heard from my Father I made known to you." On the basis of this statement, both Hasitschka and Metzner seem to conclude that Jesus's disciples are now no longer subject in any way to "sin," because Jesus says here that they are no longer "slaves." However, the "slavery" Jesus speaks of in John 15:15 is altogether different from the slavery Jesus speaks of during Tabernacles (8:31–36). That a distinction is to be made here becomes clear when one observes that, in each case, the "master" of the slaves is different: in 8:31–36 the master of the slaves is "sin," whereas in 15:15 the master or "Lord" of the slaves is Jesus (see also 15:20). In the latter case (15:15), Jesus explains that he no longer calls the disciples slaves "because the slave does not know what his master is doing." Now that Jesus has made known to the disciples what he has heard from the Father, the disciples know their master and Lord in a better sense, and so may be called "friends." If Jesus is thought to speak here of slavery to sin, then the reason the disciples are no longer slaves is that *they now know sin, their master, in a better sense*, which is nonsensical. It is undoubtedly the case, then, that Jesus's statement in John 15:15 (cf. v. 20) pertains not to the relationship of his disciples to "sin" but to the relationship of his disciples *to himself*, their Lord and, now, friend ("if you do what I command" [v. 14], Jesus says). On this point consider also the language of "slave" or "servant" (δοῦλος) and "master" or "Lord" (κύριος) in 13:13–17.

[53] By contrast, according to various Second Temple and rabbinic texts it is through keeping the law that the sinful inclination of human beings is managed and thwarted (cf. Ps 119:9–11). In Sir 21:11, for instance, it is explained that "the one who keeps the law prevails over his impulses" (for the translation of ἐννοήματος here as "impulses" see Patrick W. Skehan and Alexander A. Di Lella, *The Wisdom of Ben Sira: A New Translation with Notes*, AB 39 [New York: Doubleday, 1987], 310. See also Roger A. Bullard and Howard A. Hatton, *A Handbook on Sirach*, United Bible Societies Handbook Series [New York: United Bible Societies, 2008]: Sir 21:11 should be viewed "as a reference to self-control, to keeping our own evil tendencies in check"; the Syriac text "supports the idea that this was the meaning of the lost Hebrew text" [429]). The author of 1QS maintains that it is by observing the law within and in partnership with the community that one's sinful inclination and "stiff neck" are "circumcised" (V, 1–11). The prevalence in Second Temple literature of the belief that the law is the antidote to the sinful inclination is highlighted by Brand:

remaining in Jesus, through continuing to follow the one who is able to liberate from sin (v. 36), that sin's influence is undone. This suggests that what believers *do*, that is, abiding in Jesus and his commandments, fosters liberation from sin. Inasmuch as committing sin promotes sin's influence and power, so also keeping Jesus's word and continuing to follow him (which entails serving others as Jesus did [13:14–15, 34; 15:12]) promotes the abiding presence and activity of both Jesus and the Father: "If a person loves me, this person will keep my word," Jesus says later to his disciples, "and my Father will love this person, and we will come to and dwell within this person" (14:23; cf. 13:17; 15:14).

It is *in Jesus* that liberation comes about because, for John, Jesus is "the way and the truth and the life" (14:6). Jesus is the realization and inauguration in the world of true and everlasting life, and Jesus realizes this life in himself, that is, in his "flesh" (1:3c-4, 14; 17:19), in order to be "the seed" (12:24) that produces this life in others.[54] In contrast to the life of "the world," which is characterized by (among other things) self-love (12:25a), Jesus disregards and offers himself for the sake of God and others (12:25b), even unto death (6:51; 15:12–13). Jesus is therefore the one who offers and keeps his life *par excellence*. By living in Jesus (11:26a), following his example (12:26; 13:15), and receiving his life (6:35–58), believers will be "set free" and, like Jesus, live in the Father's house forever (8:31–36). Inasmuch as believers abide in Jesus and keep his word, believers abide in and are sustained by the true vine (15:1–5). It is this true vine that enables them to "bear fruit" and "become" what they are already called: disciples (15:8) and children of God (1:12).

As noted above, though, the believers to whom Jesus speaks about discipleship and liberation from sin (8:31 and following) do *not* abide in Jesus and his word, unfortunately (cf. 5:34b). The condemnatory words that Jesus proceeds to speak make known in advance this eventual outcome and hasten its realization. Jesus's addressees will continue to "do" the works of someone other than God.[55] Following "the devil" (v. 44), who is the "father" and originator of violence (the devil is said to be a "murderer from the beginning" [v. 44]), they will attempt to murder Jesus (v. 59; cf.

> An idea that is surprisingly strong across nearly all groups of texts explored in this study is that the desire to sin, whether innately human or the result of demonic influence, can be fought with the law. ... The strength of the belief during the Second Temple period that the law combats sin may explain Paul's declarations in Rom 5:20 and 7:7–13. ... Statements in later rabbinic literature that assert that the cure for the "evil inclination" is found in the Torah ... may also stem from the popular idea that the law actively combats the desire to sin. (*Evil Within*, 280–1)

[54] On the mission of Jesus in John's Gospel see Chapter 2. Cyril of Alexandria, while commenting on John the Baptist's confession of Jesus as "the Lamb of God who takes away the sin of the world" (1:29), says that Jesus is "to become the source of all good for human nature, the deliverance from imported corruption, the bestower of eternal life, the basis for transformation into God, the source of piety and righteousness and the road to the kingdom of heaven" (*In Jo.* 2.114 [trans. Maxwell]).

[55] Following his words about discipleship and liberation from sin (vv. 31–36), Jesus repeatedly refers to what his addressees "do," with ποιέω occurring 5x in vv. 38–47. Motyer therefore seems correct that the statements "You are of your father the devil" (v. 44) and "you are not of God" (v. 47) "have an *ethical* and not an *ontological* force" (*Your Father the Devil?*, 185; italics original). Motyer goes on to say that, with respect to John's supposed dualism, "we should abandon talk of 'origin,' lessen the focus on the *moment* of decision, and broaden it out to encompass the whole life-style of "the Jews" so addressed" (194; italics original).

18:31b). Following the devil, the father of "lying" (v. 44), Jesus's addressees are "liars" (v. 55), for, while they continue to claim to know and have God as their Father (vv. 41, 54–55), their behavior shows this claim to be false: if God were their Father they would continue to believe in Jesus. If God were their Father they would love and honor Jesus, like the Father (vv. 42, 54; cf. 3:35; 10:17; 15:9). It is not God's will they prefer (v. 44), perhaps consciously as well as unconsciously (recall the amalgam of willful disobedience and obliviousness attributed to "the Jews" in John 5:39–40). The way in which this scene unfolds and concludes therefore illustrates that belief in Jesus can be fragile, and that it can be fragile *because of sin*. To believe in Jesus in (what may be described as) a moment of "decision" does not in and of itself set one free from sin, so belief in Jesus can turn out to be temporary. Those who come to believe in Jesus must remain in and keep his word if they are to be liberated from the way of life and power that has gripped them heretofore.[56]

So far, then, John presents a conception of "sin" that some might find to be sobering and challenging, inasmuch as John considers sin to be a dilemma that persists for human beings subsequent to the emergence of belief. Believers are not "set free" from sin simply through coming to believe in Jesus. The scene that immediately follows Jesus's dialogue with "the Jews" who believe and fall away (8:31–59), though, indicates that John's conception of sin is multifaceted, and that a certain aspect or effect of "sin" *is resolved* for John when one comes to believe in Jesus.

After Jesus leaves the temple and, in doing so, evades the attempts of his former adherents to stone him (8:59), Jesus encounters a man blind from birth (9:1) and proceeds to dismiss the idea that a person's hardship is always the direct consequence of the "wrongdoing" or "sin" the person (or the person's family) committed (vv. 2–3; Jesus here responds to the question, "who committed sin [τίς ἥμαρτεν]?").[57] Jesus then gives sight to the man (vv. 6–7), which leads those familiar with the man's past circumstances to wonder whether this is the man "who sits and begs" (v. 8). Despite the condemnation of "the Jews" who, after investigating the matter, judge Jesus to be a "sinner" (ἁμαρτωλός [vv. 24–25, 28–29]), the man comes to profess Jesus as "Lord" (v. 38), which is then followed by a brief exchange between Jesus and some of the

---

[56] During his discourse on "the bread of life" Jesus says the following: "All that the Father gives me will come to me, and the person who comes to me I will certainly not drive away. ... The will of the one who sent me is this, that I should not lose what he has given me, but raise it up on the last day" (6:37–39; cf. 17:12; 18:9). These words suggest that those who believe in Jesus do not fall away. However, we have already observed that, during his farewell discourse, Jesus warns of (and so acknowledges) the possibility of believers falling away: "If a person does not remain in me, this person is thrown away like a branch and withers" (15:6; see also v. 2). Jesus speaks these words so as to encourage his disciples to remain in him, keep his commandments, and "become" his disciples (15:1–17). Jesus in fact goes on to explain that an important purpose of his farewell discourse is to keep his disciples from "falling away" (16:1; cf. 17:11). Such a "falling away" is evidently what occurs in the case of "the Jews" who, during Tabernacles, come to believe in Jesus (8:30 and following). In emphasizing that Jesus does not lose those given to him (see also 6:44; 10:28–29) and, yet, showing that believers can in fact fall away, John seems to present the matter of election as a paradox or antinomy, in response to which one may wonder: Is it perhaps the case that, in John's view of things, those who fall away will, in the end, be graciously restored in some way by and to their good shepherd?

[57] Note here that "sin" is again something people "do" (cf. 5:14; 8:21–24, 34).

Pharisees concerning whether the latter perceive and judge rightly (vv. 39–41).[58] Jesus sparks this exchange with the following declaration: "I came into this world for judgment, that those who do not see may see, and that those who see may become blind" (v. 39). When some of the Pharisees ask Jesus, "Are we also blind?" (v. 40), the noun ἁμαρτία occurs twice in Jesus's response (v. 41), which is effectively "no" as well as "yes" (on this see below), but here ἁμαρτία seems to denote a sense different from the one we have noted previously: "If you were blind," Jesus says, "you would not have [ἁμαρτίαν], but now that you say, 'We see,' your [ἁμαρτία] remains'" (v. 41).[59] Here, ἁμαρτία seems to designate not what the Pharisees *do* (cf. 8:34), exactly, but what they "have" (οὐκ ἂν εἴχετε), and what they "have" *as a consequence of* what they do. Note that Jesus's response is a conditional statement (v. 41): if his addressees recognized their predicament and embraced the one who is willing and able to address it (like the man born blind), they would no longer "have" that which otherwise "remains." Their ἁμαρτία "remains" *as a result of* their continued assurance about and assertion of the validity of their judgment, which finds Jesus to be a "sinner" (vv. 24–25, 28–29). Given that ἁμαρτία here designates what these Pharisees continue to *have* as a result of what they continue to *do*, then, ἁμαρτία seems to denote the "guilt" that results from their "sin" or "wrongdoing."[60] If these people believed in Jesus, the guilt they have incurred from their wrongdoing would be removed or wiped away, making them "clean" (καθαρός [13:10; 15:3; cf. 1 John 1:7]).[61] If they followed Jesus, the "wrath of God"

---

[58] In 9:13–34, the designations "the Pharisees" (vv. 13, 15–16) and "the Jews" (vv. 18, 22) seem to be used interchangeably (cf., e.g., 8:13–22), so the people who question the man born blind and judge Jesus to be a "sinner" (they refer to themselves as "disciples of Moses" [v. 28]) seem to represent God's "own" people as a whole (cf. 1:11). As we have observed, John can speak of various groups of "the Jews" (e.g., 8:30–31) as well as of "the Jews" collectively (e.g., 5:15–18).

[59] That Jesus here disputes the idea that his addressees "see" (it is on account of this claim that their ἁμαρτία is said to remain), even though these people evidently are not visually impaired, indicates that the lack of vision of which Jesus here speaks is figurative and refers to a lack of recognition or understanding. Although these Pharisees think they judge and act rightly (vv. 24, 28–29, 34; cf. 5:37–47; 7:14–24; 8:15a), Jesus implies that they in fact do not: they are the figuratively "blind" (τυφλοί) about whom Jesus has just spoken negatively (v. 39d). The protasis of v. 41 ("If you were blind"), then, must imagine for Jesus's addressees a "blindness" *different* from that which they currently possess, a blindness that is in some sense *positive* (since such "blindness" would result in *not* having ἁμαρτίαν). Such a "positive" blindness is exhibited by the man born blind in the sense that he recognizes his predicament and embraces the one who is willing and able to address it. This is evidently the disposition and recognition of those "who do not see" (v. 39c), for whom Jesus "has come into the world" (v. 39b; it is worth mentioning that the positive connotation of blindness here [vv. 39–41] exposes as facile the conclusion of some that "blindness" in John's Gospel is unequivocally a metaphor for "sin," "darkness," and/or "ignorance"). Thus, to the question, "Are we also blind?" (v. 40), Jesus effectively answers "no" ("If you were blind") as well as "yes" ("but now that you say, 'We see'").

[60] Michaels similarly observes that "the expressions 'to have sin' and 'your sin remains' seem to refer to being guilty of sin" (*John*, 576). On this sense of ἁμαρτία see L&N (1:776 [88.310]) and BDAG (50). In the LXX ἁμαρτία seems to denote "guilt" when it occurs with λαμβάνω (Lev 5:1, 17; 7:18; 19:8, 17; 22:9; 24:15; Num 5:31; 9:13; 14:34; 18:1, 22, 32; Ezek 23:49) or φέρω (Isa 53:4). In the MT (cf. the LXX) some distinction between "sin" (or "wrongdoing") and "guilt" may be observed in, e.g., Lev 4:3; 5:17, 21–24 (6:2–5); Pss 32:5; 51:3–16 (1–14); Jer 33:8; 36:3.

[61] For the "stain" or "impurity" that committing sin effects, for which cleansing is required, see, e.g., Lev 16:16; Josh 22:17; Ps 51:1–14; Ezek 22:1–4, 15; 39:23–24; Zech 12:10–13:1 (here cf. John 19:34–37). In John 15:22–24 Jesus seems to refer to "guilt" as well as "sin": "If I had not come and spoken to them, they would not be guilty of sin (lit. 'not have guilt' [ἁμαρτίαν οὐκ εἴχοσαν]), but now they have no excuse for their sin (νῦν δὲ πρόφασιν οὐκ ἔχουσιν περὶ τῆς ἁμαρτίας αὐτῶν) ... If I had not

would no longer "remain" on them (3:36). In continuing to reject and persecute Jesus on account of the conviction that they indeed judge and act rightly (despite Jesus's words and actions to the contrary), though, these people continue to "have guilt" as well as live in the very manner that incurs such guilt.[62]

With respect to the matter of "sin" in John's Gospel, then, two important points come to the fore here. First, sin is indeed a problem that preexisted and prompted Jesus's advent, for Jesus here explains that it is *because* "the Pharisees" and God's own people as a whole claim to think and act rightly when they in fact do not that he "came into the world for judgment" (v. 39). An important purpose of Jesus's advent, as described here (in v. 39), is to expose the misguidedness and waywardness of those who claim to "see." This waywardness on the part of God's covenant people, which again preceded Jesus's advent, undoubtedly has been a major cause of the "guilt" that is said to "remain" for certain Pharisees as a result of their rejection of Jesus (v. 41). Prior to Jesus's advent God's covenant people had an "excuse" (πρόφασις) for their misguidedness and wrongdoing (15:22), but this excuse no longer holds, for Jesus, "the light" (8:12), has come into the world. The guilt of those who reject the light therefore "remains" *so long as* they reject the light (9:41; cf. 3:36). If they were to come to believe in Jesus, their guilt would be removed or taken away (v. 41), making them "clean."

This leads to and further confirms a second point: for John, liberation from sin is a process. When people come to believe in Jesus, they are forgiven of their "sin" or wrongdoing (v. 41).[63] The "stain" of sin they previously bore before God is taken away through coming to believe in the Son of God, whom the Father has sent into the world. The "wrath of God" consequently no longer remains on them (3:36), for they have been washed and made "clean" through receiving Jesus and his word (13:8–10; 15:3). They have been "born of God" (1:12–13; cf. 3:3–8). Importantly, though, liberation from sin, according to John, involves not only the removal of sin's "stain" but also the end of sinful behavior itself. This is suggested here, at the end of Jesus's encounter with the man born blind, by the point that Jesus has come into the world "for judgment" (v. 39). The misguidedness and waywardness on the part of God's own people and the

---

done among them the works that no one else did, they would not be guilty of sin." Jesus's words here indicate that, prior to his advent, God's covenant people (cf. v. 25) had an excuse (πρόφασιν) for their sin or wrongdoing, and so were not reckoned "guilty." However, since the "guilt" of certain Pharisees is said to "remain" (9:41), since God's wrath is said to "remain" on those who disobey the Son (3:36), and since even those who believe in Jesus must be "washed" so as to become "clean" (13:8–10; 15:3), it is evidently the case that, for John, God's covenant people *did* incur "guilt" prior to Jesus's advent, but "guilt" that was in some sense held in abeyance during this time or, as Bultmann says, held "*in suspenso*" (*John*, 159). Commentators who translate John 15:22–24 in a manner similar to that advocated here include Raymond Brown (*The Gospel according to John (XIII-XXI): Introduction, Translation, and Notes*, AB 29A [Garden City, NY: Doubleday, 1970; repr., New Haven, CT: Yale University Press, 2008], 685), Beasley-Murray (*John*, 266), and Carson (*John*, 526–7).

[62] Modern translations that render ἁμαρτία in 9:41 so as to denote or foreground "guilt" include the CEV, ESV, NET, NIV, and RSV; modern commentators include Bultmann (*Theology*, 2:24), Beasley-Murray (*John*, 151), and Carson (*John*, 378). Cf. Brown (*John (I-XII)*, 371).

[63] In the Gospel of John, the verb ἀφίημι is used to signify the idea of "forgiveness" only in 20:23. However, the idea of "forgiveness," which may be defined as the removal of guilt and/or the cessation of anger within the context of personal relationship, is undoubtedly expressed in the statement that "the wrath of God" does not "remain" on those who believe in Jesus (3:36), and in Jesus's words about "guilt" being removed or taken away through coming to believe in him (9:41; cf. 13:8–10; 15:3).

world as a whole (cf. 12:31) is what has prompted this judgment. That this judgment involves bringing sinful behavior to an end is conveyed perhaps most clearly when, earlier in John's Gospel, Jesus says that all those who "do evil" will, on the last day, arise from their graves to "condemnation" (5:28-29; cf. 12:48). Sin as a way or manner of life (8:34) will indeed come to an end (8:35).[64] Whether, for believers in Jesus, it is not *until* this "last day" that liberation from sin is realized, or whether liberation from sin can occur in toto prior to this last day, John does not appear to say. What our foregoing analysis has made clear, though, is that, for John, human beings are not "set free" from sin simply through coming to believe in Jesus. Liberation from sin comes about, rather, through living and remaining in Jesus and his word (8:31-36; cf. 14:23; 15:8-10; 16:13; 17:17-19). Believers in Jesus are to resist the enduring influence of sin as they strive to follow Jesus's example and resemble him in the way they live (12:25-26; 13:15, 34-35; 15:12-14). Like Jesus, believers are to disregard and offer themselves for the sake of God and others, out of love for God and others and in faithfulness to God. In doing so, they both are and become disciples of the one who knows God, loves God, and keeps God's word. By living and remaining in the Son of God, believers receive power to be and become children of God who, as such, reflect the life of the Son of God.

Conclusion

In the Gospel of John the profile of "sin" in some ways matches that of "the darkness," ignorance of God, and "death." Like these other matters, sin pertains to what human beings "do" (8:21, 24, 34; cf. 5:37-47). The problem of sin also preceded and prompted Jesus's advent (9:39-41; 15:22-24; cf. 1:29). In John's Gospel sin is distinguished from such matters as "the darkness," ignorance of God, and "death," though, in the sense that sin comprises both a way of life epitomized by certain wayward acts and "guilt," which results from such behavior (9:41; 15:22-24). For those who reject the light in spite of the light's advent, their "guilt" remains. Additionally, sin is shown to have an ongoing influence in the lives of believers that is somewhat different from that of, for

---

[64] Relevant here is John the Baptist's confession of Jesus as "the Lamb of God who takes away the sin of the world" (1:29). This pronouncement is undoubtedly proleptic in the sense that it anticipates the future and ultimate removal of sin from *the world*. The language of the Baptist's statement (particularly αἴρων) might lead one to conclude that it is the removal of the world's "guilt" (ἁμαρτίαν) that is in focus here (see, e.g., Hoskyns, *The Fourth Gospel*, 176). However, the translation of this instance of ἁμαρτία as "guilt" seems too narrow in scope, given the proleptic and eschatological outlook of the pronouncement (recall again the Gospel's contention that Jesus liberates people from the sinful way of living that grips them [8:31-36]). Additionally, the point that, in John's Gospel, *how* Jesus removes the world's "guilt" is in part by realizing in himself (i.e., in his "flesh") the steadfast love and faithfulness that is true and everlasting life (1:3c-4, 14; 17:19), so as to be the source of new life for the world (1:16-17; 6:51; 11:25-26; 12:24-26), suggests that the Baptist's statement here (1:29) anticipates not merely the removal of the world's "guilt" but the removal or undoing of the *source* of the world's guilt—its sinful mode of existence. One may therefore understand Jesus to "take away the sin of the world" in the sense that Jesus "drives away" (ἐλαύνω) the world's sin in its entirety (Cyril of Alexandria, *In Jo.* 2.114 [PG 73:192b]). In the context of the Baptist's testimony (and of John's narrative more broadly), ὁ αἴρων τὴν ἁμαρτίαν τοῦ κόσμου seems to mean that Jesus "abolishes," "does away with," or "makes an end of" the world's sin (Dodd, *Interpretation*, 237).

example, ignorance of God (see, e.g., 14:4–11) and "death" (see, e.g., 11:25). During Tabernacles, people come to believe in Jesus and, then, are told that they are not yet "free" of sin (8:30–36; cf. 2:23–25; 12:42–43). Sin is here described as a way of life that believers are to resist as they both are and become Jesus's disciples (cf. 15:8). That, for John, liberation from sin is not realized in the emergence of belief, but rather comes about through *continuing* to believe and live in Jesus, explains why many of Jesus's disciples end up abandoning him (6:60–66), why an important purpose of Jesus's farewell discourse is to keep his disciples from falling away (16:1; see also 15:1–10), and why Jesus prays for the Father to "sanctify" his disciples "in the truth" (17:17–19; cf. 8:32; 16:13). For John, people are cleansed of their "guilt" in the moment they come to believe in Jesus; however, liberation from the way of life that has gripped human beings heretofore is not realized in this moment, but is still awaited as a future event. Through living and remaining in Jesus, who is the way and the truth and the life, believers will be "set free" from sin and, like Jesus, will live in the Father's house forever.

5

Conclusions and Reflections

This study began with an assessment of the ways in which the human predicament in John's Gospel is understood in Johannine scholarship. Distinct yet parallel lines of interpretation were uncovered and traced, and each was found to have implications that some, particularly those of the Christian faith, might find to be troubling. The sentiment of Walter Grundmann may serve as an example in this regard: John's portrayal of sin and salvation constitutes "a contradiction to the reality of the Christian community, which in practice is not without sin. Here is a serious problem."[1] A serious problem indeed, for our review of scholarship demonstrated that John's portrayal of sin and the human predicament more broadly is commonly interpreted in ways that lead to one of the following conclusions: the Gospel of John is uninterested in morality and ethics, offers a portrait of the Christian life that is naïve at best, or suggests that something is terribly wrong in the life of the Christian community (for here the problem of sin, for example, should already be resolved).

We then explained that certain Christian theological traditions, one of which is Eastern Orthodox theology, seem to call into question such readings of John's Gospel. This is because, according to Orthodox theology and Christian theological traditions like it, the human predicament pertains to what human beings *do* and *how* they live in relationship with God and one another. Salvation consists of a process of bodily renewal and transformation whereby believers come to resemble God in the way they live. Central to this soteriological perspective is the contention that Jesus, in and through his life, death, and resurrection, fulfills the vocation to which all human beings are called. Jesus makes true and everlasting life an accomplished fact for human beings, and in doing so Jesus reveals the true nature of the predicament from which he saves. The way Jesus lives in relationship with God and others is the "solution," in the light of which is defined the "plight." Although some might dismiss this soteriological perspective as immaterial to the interpretation of John's Gospel, its relevance to the matter at hand becomes clear when one recognizes that this perspective is in part the product of the church's interpretation of and reflection on the Gospel of John. A key factor in the church's development and acceptance of this soteriology (which in Orthodox theology is called "theosis") was and continues to be the church's reading of the Fourth Gospel.

---

[1] Grundmann, *TDNT* 1:307.

On the basis of this last point we then raised the following questions: Has Johannine scholarship satisfactorily traced John's presentation of sin, the human predicament, and salvation? Might John's portrayal of both the plight and its solution indicate that, for John, salvation consists of far more than the emergence of belief in a moment of decision? We have now reached the juncture at which various conclusions may be stated firmly. The human predicament, according to John's delineation of it, is a way or manner of life, a mode of existence that in various ways continues to influence believers as they both are and become, through living in Jesus, "children of God." The "plight" as well as its "solution" pertain for John to ethics and to the quality or condition of human corporeality. Salvation for John does indeed consist of much more than the emergence of belief in a moment of decision, for salvation consists of a process of bodily renewal and transformation. These conclusions follow from John's portrayal of Jesus, on the one hand, and from John's portrayal of such matters as "the darkness," ignorance of God, "illness," "disability," "death," and "sin," on the other.

For John, Jesus is the incarnation and realization in the world of true and everlasting life. This point is introduced in the prologue when it is said that, "in him" (i.e., in the person of Jesus), life "has come into existence" (1:3c–4). This life was and is "light" (vv. 4–5), the brilliance of which is to be identified with—among other things—Jesus's steadfast love and faithfulness (v. 14). Although the law was given through Moses, it was through Jesus that steadfast love and faithfulness came into existence in the world (v. 17). Later in John's Gospel Jesus explains that, for the benefit of "the sheep," he lays down his life (ψυχή) in order to take it up again (10:17–18), which suggests that Jesus is raised from the dead, at least in part, in order to provide the basis for the resurrection of all those who believe and live in him (cf. 6:57; 11:25; 14:19). Also important here (10:17–18) is the point that Jesus's words about his self-offering (see also vv. 11, 15) inform "the good" that is said elsewhere to warrant resurrection to life (5:29). "The sheep," we are told, hear the shepherd's voice and follow him (vv. 3–4, 27). As the hour of his glorification approaches Jesus then speaks of himself as "the seed of wheat" that falls into the earth and dies so as not to remain "alone" (12:24–26): Jesus is the one who denies himself in the world and keeps his life *par excellence*, which Jesus does so as to be the source ("the seed") that produces this life in others (cf. 15:1–17). In the course of his farewell prayer Jesus says that he sanctifies *himself* on behalf of his followers, so that they also may be sanctified in the truth (17:19). All of this indicates that, for John, an essential aspect of Jesus's mission is to realize in himself the way of life that is true and everlasting. This life is "light" and knowledge of God, steadfast love and faithfulness. It is to disregard oneself for the sake of God and others, out of love for God and others and in faithfulness to God. Jesus makes this life an accomplished fact. Consequently, Jesus is for John the measure or point of reference for the way human beings are to live in relationship with God and one another. Jesus is the way and the truth and the life, in the light of which the way of the world is shown and judged to be false.

The problem of the way human beings live, which the advent of Jesus sets in relief, is also introduced in the prologue. The point that, in the person of Jesus, life "has come into existence" (1:3c–4) implies that the world was devoid of life prior to Jesus's advent. But aside from this, the introduction of "the darkness" and its opposition to "the light"

(vv. 4–5; cf. 12:35) attributes waywardness and evil to the world. This waywardness then comes to the fore when, later in the prologue, ignorance of God is attributed to the world and, in particular, to God's "own" people (vv. 10–11). As John's Gospel proceeds the character of this "darkness" (v. 5) and ignorance of God (vv. 10–11) is further clarified. The darkness represents evil deeds and the doing of evil (3:19–20), and it was because of the darkness that human beings (generally speaking) rejected the light upon his advent in the world. This indicates that the darkness preexisted Jesus's advent, which aligns with the point that Jesus has come into the world so that human beings may not remain or continue in the darkness (12:46–47; see also 8:12; 12:35–36). Ignorance of God, as that which characterizes God's own people in particular (1:10–11; cf., e.g., 7:28; 8:19, 55), consists of (among other things) lacking love for God and others (5:42), seeking to glorify oneself rather than God (7:18), not keeping the law (7:19), and living in slavery to sin (8:34–36). John's description of salvation as knowledge of God (17:3) implies that, like the darkness, the world's ignorance of God preexisted and prompted Jesus's advent. Ignorance of God expresses the problem of "the darkness" in different but complementary terms (cf., e.g., Ps 82:5).

Intrinsically related to this problem of the way human beings live is the matter of illness or bodily infirmity in John's Gospel. The case of the man whom Jesus meets at Bethzatha (5:1–15) illustrates the kind of threat that illness can pose, as illness is here shown to have debilitated the man to such an extent that the man's physical mobility was chronically impaired. The healing Jesus brings about not only for this man but also for other people afflicted by illness (4:46–54; 6:2; cf. 11:1–44) makes clear that, for John, physical debilitation or infirmity is problematic. The "miracles" Jesus does for people who are sick indicate that the quality or condition of human corporeality is a focus of Jesus's mission in John's Gospel. With respect to the man at Bethzatha, though, it is important to recognize that the man was afflicted by more than bodily illness. The introduction of the man and his circumstances (5:1–7), together with the point that the man's well-being is shown to involve his physical health (vv. 8–9) *as well as* his inclusion in the religious and communal life of his society (v. 14; cf. v. 1), implicitly indicts the man's society, for it was this social environment that allowed the man to languish in Bethzatha's porticoes (and thus to be religiously and socially disconnected) for a significant portion, if not for the entirety, of the thirty-eight years the man was ill. It was the man's disabling illness, coupled with his lack of a person or people to enable his mobility, that left the man stranded at Bethzatha for the long time the man was there. The portrayal here of the man's social experience of impairment (i.e., of his "disability") therefore further accentuates the problem of the way human beings treat and relate to one another, for "the world" in which Jesus encounters the man (who is found among a "multitude" of people with illnesses and/or disabilities) is depicted as one that disadvantages and marginalizes such people. This implicit indictment of "the world" is developed further in the course of Jesus's encounter with a man blind from birth (9:1–41), whom Jesus delivers from (among other things) a life of begging. The fact that Jesus delivers people from socially disadvantageous circumstances makes clear that such circumstances are indeed problematic.

The matter of "death" in John's Gospel further highlights the problem of the world's way of life. "Death" is both a bodily cessation or end of life that becomes absolute in "the resurrection of condemnation" (5:29; cf. 8:51; 11:25-26; 12:48) and a way or manner of life (5:24-25), the ultimate end of which is "death" in its absolute or eschatological sense. The fact that, through believing in Jesus, people pass "from death into life" (5:24-25) conveys that all human beings were "dead" prior to Jesus's advent. All human beings were living in darkness and ignorance of God. All human beings were enslaved to sin (8:34-36; cf. 1:29; 9:39-41; 15:22-24). The point that salvation from death will culminate on "the last day" when all those who believe and live in Jesus will arise from their graves in "the resurrection of life" (5:29; cf. 6:39-59; 11:25) underscores the corporeal nature of salvation for John. So too does the point that this salvation from death has been realized and inaugurated already for human beings in the person of Jesus, who is himself "the resurrection and the life" (11:25; cf. 2:19-22; 20:1-29). Because Jesus lives, all those who live and remain in him will also live (14:19). Especially when interpreted in the light of Jesus, then, the problem of death makes clear, furthermore, that for John the human predicament is not wholly resolved in the moment one comes to believe in Jesus. The problems of illness (which can cause death) and disability (which in certain respects is the product of "the world" in which people with impairments live) suggest this as well.

Given these findings, it does not seem surprising to discover that the matter of "sin" in John's Gospel likewise indicates that, for John, the human predicament is not wholly resolved in the emergence of belief, but in various and significant ways persists for believers as they both are and become—through living in Jesus—children of God. Sin, for John, comprises both a way of life epitomized by certain wayward acts and "guilt," which results from such behavior. The statement that "every person who commits sin is a slave of sin" (8:34) conveys that sin is not committed in a vacuum. On the one hand, an act of sin is both indicative and a product of one's conduct heretofore. On the other hand, an act of sin is both indicative and conducive of the conduct that, unless one believes and lives in Jesus, will inevitably follow, given sin's influence and power. By means of the juxtaposition of Jesus and all those who oppose him, sin is shown to be love of self rather than God and others (5:42; 12:25), which manifests itself in acts of vainglory (5:44; 12:43), violence (8:44, 59), and falsehood (8:44-46, 55).

From this life of sin Jesus seeks to liberate human beings. Jesus, for John, makes liberation possible, for Jesus makes true and everlasting life an accomplished fact. In and through his coming and going Jesus "sanctifies" himself on behalf of his followers, so that they also may be sanctified in the truth (17:19). Thus, when people come to believe in Jesus their "guilt" is removed or wiped away (9:41; 13:8-10; 15:3), for they have received and now follow the way to the Father. The wrath of God no longer remains on them (3:36). Importantly, though, the case of "the Jews" who come to believe in Jesus and, then, are told that they are not yet "free" of sin (8:30-36) conveys that liberation from sin is a process. This point is introduced earlier in John's Gospel when new believers are said to be untrustworthy because of what is still "in" them (2:23-25; cf. 12:43). Jesus's description of the Spirit as the one who will lead believers "in the truth" (16:13), which is liberative (8:32; cf. 14:6; 17:17-19), conveys as well that liberation is a process. Sin and its power, according to John, therefore remain "in" believers as they live and come to be sanctified *in Jesus*, who, together with the Father and the Spirit, lives *in them* (see, e.g., 14:23; 15:1-17). To the question of whether "sin" is destroyed in the moment one believes, then, John's answer is both "yes" and "no." The "guilt" that people accrue as a result of wrongdoing is removed or cleansed when one comes to believe in Jesus; however, liberation from the wrongdoing that has defined human beings heretofore is not realized in this moment, but is still awaited as a future event. Liberation from sin comes about through living and remaining in Jesus and his word. Believers are to resist the enduring influence of sin as they strive to follow Jesus's example and resemble him in the way they live. In doing so, they both are and become disciples of the one who knows God, loves God, and keeps God's word.

In addition to the implications of these conclusions that have already been highlighted with respect to John's soteriology and theology (e.g., that salvation is for John a process), two further implications will now be suggested for future consideration. These suggestions will bring the present study to a close. First, the Fourth Gospel should not be interpreted in such a way that John's ethics are disconnected from John's soteriology. All too often in scholarship have these two aspects of John's Gospel been isolated from or played off against one another, as though salvation for John does not involve ethics. As we have observed, both the plight and its solution pertain for John to what human beings *do* and *how* they live in relationship with God and one another.[2] Second, John's soteriology and theology are not "dualistic" as much as they are paradoxical.[3] There are of course various antitheses in John's Gospel (e.g., "light" and "darkness"), but our assessment of John's portrayal of sin, the human predicament, and salvation further suggests that, strictly speaking, the Gospel is not dualistic.[4]

---

[2] It is perhaps helpful here to note what Christos Yannaras says about the ascetic struggle that, in certain Christian theological traditions, salvation is found to involve:

> Christian asceticism rejects the deterministic dialectic of effort and result; it presupposes that we hope for nothing from human powers. It expresses and effects the participation of man's freedom in suppressing the rebellion of his nature, but that work itself is grace, a gift of God. Thus human ascetic endeavor does not even aspire to crushing the rebellion of man's nature. It simply seeks to affirm the personal response of man's love to the work of his salvation by Christ, and to accord with divine love and the divine economy, albeit to the infinitesimal extent permitted by the weakness of the nature. (*The Freedom of Morality*, 114)

[3] On the significance of paradoxes or antinomies in Christian theology, see, e.g., Lossky, *Mystical Theology*, 43–66. Lossky contends that theology should be not abstract but contemplative and edifying, "raising the mind to those realities which pass all understanding. This is why the dogmas of the Church often present themselves to the human reason as antinomies, the more difficult to resolve the more sublime the mystery they express" (43).

[4] On the matter of "dualism" in John's Gospel, see, in particular, Jörg Frey, *The Glory of the Crucified One: Christology and Theology in the Gospel of John*, trans. Wayne Coppins and Christoph Heilig, Baylor-Mohr Siebeck Studies in Early Christianity (Waco, TX: Baylor University Press, 2018), 101–67. After a brief review of scholarship and a survey of various dualistic motifs in John's Gospel, Frey asks "whether one can really speak of dualism in John or whether this category as a whole—apart from individual motifs or linguistic elements—must be regarded as inappropriate to the Fourth Gospel" (125). Frey goes on to conclude that, when John's dualistic motifs are interpreted within the context of John's Gospel as a whole, "it no longer appears appropriate to speak of a dualism that underlies the Fourth Gospel" (152). "Of course, there is a remaining opposition between salvation and unsalvation, eschatological life and eschatological ruin. ... So the talk of eschatologically dualistic structures may be justified. To be sure, the whole of early Christianity would then have to be called dualistic in this sense, so that not much is gained with this characterization" (165–6). "Theologically it is clear that in the Gospel of John one can speak only of a soteriologically broken 'dualism' or of soteriologically broken dualistic motifs" (166). See also Miroslav Volf, "Johannine Dualism and Contemporary Pluralism," in Bauckham and Mosser, *John and Christian Theology*, 19–50.

According to John, people can believe in Jesus and, at the same time, be influenced by sin, both internally and externally. People can be "drawn" to Jesus (no one comes to him without the leading of the Father [6:44]) and, then, fall away (6:60–66; 8:30–59; 15:2, 6; 16:1). And yet, Jesus will not lose those whom the Father has given him (6:37–39, 44; cf. 17:12; 18:9). "No one will snatch them out of my hand," Jesus says (10:28). "Paradox" seems far more suitable for describing such aspects of John's Gospel than does "dualism."

Bibliography

Achtemeier, Elizabeth R. "Jesus Christ, the Light of the World: The Biblical Understanding of Light and Darkness." *Int* 17 (1963): 439–49.
Aland, Kurt. "Eine Untersuchung zu Joh 1, 3–4: Über die Bedeutung eines Punktes." *ZNW* 59 (1968): 174–209.
Ashton, John. *Understanding the Fourth Gospel*. 2nd ed. Oxford: Oxford University Press, 2007.
Athanasius of Alexandria. *On the Incarnation*. Translated by John Behr. Popular Patristics Series 44A. Yonkers, NY: St. Vladimir's Seminary Press, 2011.
Athanasius of Alexandria. *The Orations of St. Athanasius against the Arians: According to the Benedictine Text*. Edited by William Bright. 2nd ed. Oxford: Oxford University Press, 1884.
Balás, David L. "Divinization." Pages 338–40 in *Encyclopedia of Early Christianity*. Edited by Everett Ferguson. 2nd ed. New York: Garland, 1997.
Barr, James. *The Semantics of Biblical Language*. London: Oxford University Press, 1961.
Barrett, C. K. *The Gospel according to St. John: An Introduction with Commentary and Notes on the Greek Text*. 2nd ed. Philadelphia, PA: Westminster John Knox, 1978.
Bauckham, Richard. *Gospel of Glory: Major Themes in Johannine Theology*. Grand Rapids, MI: Baker, 2015.
Bauckham, Richard. *The Testimony of the Beloved Disciple: Narrative, History, and Theology in the Gospel of John*. Grand Rapids, MI: Baker, 2007.
Beasley-Murray, George R. *John*. 2nd ed. WBC 36. Nashville, TN: Nelson, 1999.
Behr, John. *The Mystery of Christ: Life in Death*. Crestwood, NY: St. Vladimir's Seminary Press, 2006.
Bennema, Cornelis. *The Power of Saving Wisdom: An Investigation of Spirit and Wisdom in Relation to the Soteriology of the Fourth Gospel*. WUNT 2/148. Tübingen: Mohr Siebeck, 2002.
Bennema, Cornelis. "The Sword of the Messiah and the Concept of Liberation in the Fourth Gospel." *Bib* 86 (2005): 35–58.
Bernard, J. H. *A Critical and Exegetical Commentary on the Gospel according to St. John*. Edited by A. H. McNeile. Vol. 1. ICC. Edinburgh: T&T Clark, 1928.
Beutler, Johannes. *A Commentary on the Gospel of John*. Translated by Michael Tait. Grand Rapids, MI: Eerdmans, 2017.
Bieringer, Reimund, Didier Pollefeyt, and Frederique Vandecasteele-Vanneuville. "Wrestling with Johannine Anti-Judaism: A Hermeneutical Framework for the Analysis of the Current Debate." Pages 3–37 in *Anti-Judaism and the Fourth Gospel*. Edited by Reimund Bieringer, Didier Pollefeyt, and Frederique Vandecasteele-Vanneuville. Louisville, KY: Westminster John Knox, 2001.
Blowers, Paul M. "Introduction." Pages 13–43 in *On the Cosmic Mystery of Jesus Christ: Selected Writings from St Maximus the Confessor*. Translated by Paul M. Blowers and Robert Louis Wilken. Popular Patristics Series 25. Crestwood, NY: St. Vladimir's Seminary Press, 2003.

Brand, Miryam T. *Evil Within and Without: The Source of Sin and Its Nature as Portrayed in Second Temple Literature*. Journal of Ancient Judaism Supplements 9. Göttingen: Vandenhoeck and Ruprecht, 2013.
Brower, Kent. *Holiness in the Gospels*. Kansas City, MO: Beacon Hill, 2005.
Brown, Raymond E. *The Gospel according to John (I-XII): Introduction, Translation, and Notes*. 2nd ed. AB 29. Garden City, NY: Doubleday, 1983.
Brown, Raymond E. *The Gospel according to John (XIII-XXI): Introduction, Translation, and Notes*. AB 29A. Garden City, NY: Doubleday, 1970. Repr., New Haven, CT: Yale University Press, 2008.
Bruce, F. F. *Paul: Apostle of the Heart Set Free*. Grand Rapids, MI: Eerdmans, 1977.
Bruner, Frederick Dale. *The Gospel of John: A Commentary*. Grand Rapids, MI: Eerdmans, 2012.
Bullard, Roger A., and Howard A. Hatton. *A Handbook on Sirach*. United Bible Societies Handbook Series. New York: United Bible Societies, 2008.
Bultmann, Rudolf. *The Gospel of John: A Commentary*. Translated by G. R. Beasley-Murray. Oxford: Blackwell, 1971.
Bultmann, Rudolf. *Theology of the New Testament*. Translated by Kendrick Grobel. 2 vols. New York: Scribner's Sons, 1951–5. Repr., Waco, TX: Baylor University Press, 2007.
Burridge, Richard A. *Imitating Jesus: An Inclusive Approach to New Testament Ethics*. Grand Rapids, MI: Eerdmans, 2007.
Burridge, Richard A. *What Are the Gospels? A Comparison with Greco-Roman Biography*. 2nd ed. The Biblical Resource Series. Grand Rapids, MI: Eerdmans, 2004.
Byers, Andrew J. *Ecclesiology and Theosis in the Gospel of John*. SNTSMS 166. Cambridge: Cambridge University Press, 2017.
Carey, George L. "The Lamb of God and Atonement Theories." *TynBul* 32 (1981): 97–122.
Carson, D. A. *The Gospel according to John*. Pillar New Testament Commentary. Grand Rapids, MI: Eerdmans; Leicester: Apollos, 1991.
Carter, Warren. *John and Empire: Initial Explorations*. New York: T&T Clark, 2008.
Carter, Warren. "'The blind, lame and paralyzed' (John 5:3): John's Gospel, Disability Studies, and Postcolonial Perspectives." Pages 129–50 in *Disability Studies and Biblical Literature*. Edited by Candida R. Moss and Jeremy Schipper. New York: Palgrave Macmillan, 2011.
Ceresko, Anthony R. "The Identity of 'the Blind and the Lame' (*'iwwēr ûpissēaḥḥ*) in 2 Samuel 5:8b." *CBQ* 63 (2001): 23–30.
Christensen, Michael J., and Jeffery A. Wittung, eds. *Partakers of the Divine Nature: The History and Development of Deification in the Christian Traditions*. Grand Rapids, MI: Baker, 2007.
Chrysostom, John. *Commentary on Saint John the Apostle and Evangelist, Homilies 48-88*. Translated by Sister Thomas Aquinas Goggin. FC 41. Washington, DC: Catholic University of America Press, 2000.
Clark-Soles, Jaime. "John, First-Third John, and Revelation." Pages 333–78 in *The Bible and Disability: A Commentary*. Edited by Sarah J. Melcher, Mikeal C. Parsons, and Amos Yong. Studies in Religion, Theology, and Disability. Waco, TX: Baylor University Press, 2017.
Collins, Paul M. *Partaking in Divine Nature: Deification and Communion*. T&T Clark Theology. London: T&T Clark, 2010.
Conzelmann, Hans. "φῶς κτλ." Pages 310–58 in vol. 9 of *Theological Dictionary of the New Testament*. Edited by Gerhard Kittel and Gerhard Friedrich. Translated by Geoffrey W. Bromiley. 10 vols. Grand Rapids, MI: Eerdmans: 1964–76.

Cook, Johann. "The Origin of the Tradition of the יצר הטוב and יצר הרע." *JSJ* 38 (2007): 80–91.
Cooper, Jordan. *Christification: A Lutheran Approach to Theosis.* Eugene, OR: Wipf and Stock, 2014.
Crump, David. "Re-examining the Johannine Trinity: Perichoresis or Deification?" *SJT* 59 (2006): 395–412.
Culpepper, R. Alan. *Anatomy of the Fourth Gospel: A Study in Literary Design.* Philadelphia, PA: Fortress, 1983.
Culpepper, R. Alan. *The Gospel and Letters of John.* Interpreting Biblical Texts. Nashville, TN: Abingdon, 1998.
Cyril of Alexandria. *Commentary on John.* Translated by David R. Maxwell. Edited by Joel C. Elowsky. Vol. 1. Ancient Christian Texts. Downers Grove, IL: IVP Academic, 2013.
Dana, H. E., and Julius R. Mantey. *A Manual Grammar of the Greek New Testament.* New York: Macmillan, 1950.
de la Potterie, Ignace. "Consécration ou sanctification du chrétien d'aprés Jean 17?" Pages 333–49 in *Le Sacré: Études et Recherches; Actes du colloque organisé par le Centre International d'Études Humanistes et par l'Institut d'Études Philosophiques de Rome.* Edited by Enrico Castelli. Paris: Aubier, 1974.
Dennis, John. "Jesus' Death in John's Gospel: A Survey of Research from Bultmann to the Present with Special Reference to the Johannine Hyper-Texts." *CurBR* 4 (2006): 331–63.
Despotis, Athanasios. "From Conversion according to Paul and 'John' to Theosis in the Greek Patristic Tradition." *HBT* 38 (2016): 88–109.
Dodd, C. H. "Behind a Johannine Dialogue." Pages 41–57 in *More New Testament Studies.* Manchester: Manchester Univsersity Press, 1968.
Dodd, C. H. *The Interpretation of the Fourth Gospel.* Cambridge: Cambridge University Press, 1953. Repr., Cambridge: Cambridge University Press, 1988.
Dukes, Jimmy Ward. "Salvation Metaphors Used by John and Paul as a Key to Understanding Their Soteriologies." PhD diss., New Orleans Baptist Theological Seminary, 1983.
Eco, Umberto. *The Role of the Reader: Explorations in the Semiotics of Texts.* London: Hutchinson, 1981.
Eiesland, Nancy L. *The Disabled God: Toward a Liberatory Theology of Disability.* Nashville, TN: Abingdon Press, 1994.
Fanning, Buist M. *Verbal Aspect in New Testament Greek.* Oxford Theological Monographs. Oxford: Clarendon, 1990.
Finlan, Stephen. "Deification in Jesus' Teaching." Pages 21–41 in *Theosis: Deification in Christian Theology.* Edited by Vladimir Kharlamov. Princeton Theological Monograph Series 156. Eugene, OR: Pickwick, 2011.
Finlan, Stephen, and Vladimir Kharlamov, eds. *Theōsis: Deification in Christian Theology.* Princeton Theological Monograph Series 52. Eugene, OR: Pickwick, 2006.
Forestell, J. Terence. *The Word of the Cross: Salvation as Revelation in the Fourth Gospel.* AnBib 57. Rome: Biblical Institute, 1974.
Fox, Michael V. *Proverbs 1–9: A New Translation with Introduction and Commentary.* AB 18A. New York: Doubleday, 2000.
Frey, Jörg. *Die johanneische Eschatologie.* Vol. 1, *Ihre Probleme im Spiegel der Forschung seit Reimarus.* WUNT 96. Tübingen: Mohr Siebeck, 1997.

Frey, Jörg. *Die johanneische Eschatologie*. Vol. 3, *Die eschatologische Verkündigung in den johanneischen Texten*. WUNT 117. Tübingen: Mohr Siebeck, 2000.

Frey, Jörg. "Die *'theologia crucifixi'* des Johannesevangeliums." Pages 169–238 in *Kreuzestheologie im Neuen Testament*. Edited by Andreas Dettwiler and Jean Zumstein. WUNT 151. Tübingen: Mohr Siebeck, 2002.

Frey, Jörg. "Eschatology in the Johannine Circle." Pages 47–82 in *Theology and Christology in the Fourth Gospel: Essays by the Members of the SNTS Johannine Writings Seminar*. Edited by Gilbert van Belle, Jan G. van der Watt, and P. J. Maritz. BETL 184. Leuven: Peeters, 2005.

Frey, Jörg. *The Glory of the Crucified One: Christology and Theology in the Gospel of John*. Translated by Wayne Coppins and Christoph Heilig. Baylor-Mohr Siebeck Studies in Early Christianity. Waco, TX: Baylor University Press, 2018.

Gaffney, James. "Believing and Knowing in the Fourth Gospel." *TS* 26 (1965): 215–41.

Gieschen, Charles A. "The Death of Jesus in the Gospel of John: Atonement for Sin?" *CTQ* 72 (2008): 243–61.

Glicksman, Andrew T. "Beyond Sophia: The Sapiential Portrayal of Jesus in the Fourth Gospel and Its Ethical Implications for the Johannine Community." Pages 83–101 in *Rethinking the Ethics of John: "Implicit Ethics" in the Johannine Writings*. Edited by Jan G. van der Watt and Ruben Zimmermann. WUNT 291. Tübingen: Mohr Siebeck, 2012.

Godet, Frédéric Louis. *Commentary on John's Gospel*. Translated by Timothy Dwight. Kregel Classic Commentary Series. Grand Rapids, MI: Kregel, 1978.

Gorman, Michael J. *Abide and Go: Missional Theosis in the Gospel of John*. Didsbury Lectures Series. Eugene, OR: Cascade, 2018.

Green, Joel B. *Body, Soul, and Human Life: The Nature of Humanity in the Bible*. Studies in Theological Interpretation. Grand Rapids, MI: Baker, 2008.

Gregory of Nyssa. *The Catechetical Oration of St. Gregory of Nyssa*. Translated by J. H. Srawley. Early Church Classics. London: Society for Promoting Christian Knowledge, 1917.

Griffith, Terry. "'The Jews Who Had Believed in Him' (John 8:31) and the Motif of Apostasy in the Gospel of John." Pages 183–92 in *The Gospel of John and Christian Theology*. Edited by Richard Bauckham and Carl Mosser. Grand Rapids, MI: Eerdmans, 2008.

Grigsby, Bruce H. "The Cross as an Expiatory Sacrifice in the Fourth Gospel." *JSNT* 15 (1982): 51–80.

Gross, Jules. *The Divinization of the Christian according to the Greek Fathers*. Translated by Paul A. Onica. Anaheim, CA: A & C Press, 2002. Translation of *La divinization du chrétien d'après les pères grecs: Contribution historique à la doctrine de la grâce*. Paris: Gabalda, 1938.

Grundmann, Walter. "Sin in the NT." Pages 302–16 in vol. 1 of *Theological Dictionary of the New Testament*. Edited by Gerhard Kittel and Gerhard Friedrich. Translated by Geoffrey W. Bromiley. 10 vols. Grand Rapids, MI: Eerdmans, 1964–76.

Gurtner, D. M., and N. Perrin. "Temple." Pages 939–47 in *Dictionary of Jesus and the Gospels*. Edited by Joel B. Green, Jeannine K. Brown, and Nicholas Perrin. 2nd ed. Downers Grove, IL: Intervarsity Press, 2013.

Habets, Myk. "Reforming Theōsis." Pages 146–67 in *Theōsis: Deification in Christian Theology*. Edited by Stephen Finlan and Vladimir Kharlamov. Princeton Theological Monograph Series 52. Eugene, OR: Pickwick, 2006.

Habets, Myk. *Theosis in the Theology of Thomas Torrance*. Ashgate New Critical Thinking in Religion, Theology, and Biblical Studies. Burlington, VT: Ashgate, 2009.

Haenchen, Ernst. *John: A Commentary on the Gospel of John, Chapters 1–6*. Edited by Robert W. Funk and Ulrich Busse. Translated by Robert W. Funk. Hermeneia. Philadelphia, PA: Fortress, 1984.

Haenchen, Ernst. *John: A Commentary on the Gospel of John, Chapters 7–21*. Edited by Robert W. Funk and Ulrich Busse. Translated by Robert W. Funk. Hermeneia. Philadelphia: Fortress, 1984.

Hakola, Raimo. "The Believing Jews as the Children of the Devil in John 8:44: Similarity as a Threat to Social Identity." Pages 116–26 in *Evil and the Devil*. Edited by Ida Fröhlich and Erkki Koskenniemi. LNTS 481. London: T&T Clark, 2013.

Hasitschka, Martin. *Befreiung von Sünde nach dem Johannesevangelium: Eine bibeltheologische Untersuchung*. Innsbrucker theologische Studien 27. Innsbruck: Tyrolia, 1989.

Hasitschka, Martin. "Befreiung von Sünde nach dem Johannesevangelium." Pages 92–107 in *Sünde und Erlösung im Neuen Testament*. Edited by Hubert Frankemölle. QD 161. Freiburg: Herder, 1996.

Hays, Richard B. *The Moral Vision of the New Testament: A Contemporary Introduction to New Testament Ethics*. San Francisco, CA: HarperOne, 1996.

Hengel, Martin. "The Prologue of the Gospel of John as the Gateway to Christological Truth." Pages 265–94 in *The Gospel of John and Christian Theology*. Edited by Richard Bauckham and Carl Mosser. Grand Rapids, MI: Eerdmans, 2008.

Hoskins, Paul M. "Freedom from Slavery to Sin and the Devil: John 8:31–47 and the Passover Theme of the Gospel of John." *TJ* 31 (2010): 47–63.

Hoskyns, Edwyn Clement. *The Fourth Gospel*. Edited by Francis Noel Davey. London: Faber & Faber, 1947.

Hylen, Susan E. *Imperfect Believers: Ambiguous Characters in the Gospel of John*. Louisville, KY: Westminster John Knox, 2009.

Jerumanis, Pascal-Marie. *Réaliser la communion avec Dieu: Croire, vivre et demeurer dans l'évangile selon S. Jean*. EBib 2/32. Paris: Gabalda, 1996.

Kanagaraj, Jey J. "The Implied Ethics of the Fourth Gospel: A Reinterpretation of the Decalogue." *TynBul* 52 (2001): 33–60.

Kärkkäinen, Veli-Matti. *One with God: Salvation as Deification and Justification*. Collegeville, MN: Liturgical Press, 2004.

Käsemann, Ernst. *The Testament of Jesus: A Study of the Gospel of John in Light of Chapter 17*. Translated by Gerhard Krodel. Philadelphia, PA: Fortress, 1968.

Kharlamov, Vladimir, ed. *Theosis: Deification in Christian Theology*. Vol. 2 of *Theosis: Deification in Christian Theology*. Princeton Theological Monograph Series 156. Eugene, OR: Pickwick, 2011.

Kierspel, Lars. *The Jews and the World in the Fourth Gospel: Parallelism, Function, and Context*. WUNT 2/220. Tübingen: Mohr Siebeck, 2006.

Knöppler, Thomas. *Die theologia crucis des Johannesevangeliums: Das Verständnis des Todes Jesu im Rahmen der johanneischen Inkarnations- und Erhöhungschristologie*. WMANT 69. Neukirchener Verlag: Neukirchen-Vluyn, 1994.

Koester, Craig R. "'The Savior of the World' (John 4:42)." *JBL* 109 (1990): 665–80.

Koester, Craig R. *Symbolism in the Fourth Gospel: Meaning, Mystery, Community*. 2nd ed. Minneapolis, MN: Fortress, 2003.

Koester, Craig R. "What Does It Mean to Be Human? Imagery and the Human Condition in John's Gospel." Pages 403–20 in *Imagery in the Gospel of John: Terms, Forms, Themes, and Theology of Johannine Figurative Language*. Edited by Jörg Frey, Jan G. van der Watt, and Ruben Zimmermann. WUNT 200. Tübingen: Mohr Siebeck, 2006.

Koester, Craig R. *The Word of Life: A Theology of John's Gospel*. Grand Rapids, MI: Eerdmans, 2008.

Köstenberger, Andreas J. *A Theology of John's Gospel and Letters: Biblical Theology of the New Testament*. Grand Rapids, MI: Zondervan: 2009.

Kuyper, Lester J. "Grace and Truth: An Old Testament Description of God, and Its Use in the Johannine Gospel." *Int* 18 (1964): 3–19.

Labahn, Michael. "'It's Only Love'—Is That All? Limits and Potentials of Johannine 'Ethic'—A Critical Evaluation of Research." Pages 3–43 in *Rethinking the Ethics of John: "Implicit Ethics" in the Johannine Writings*. Edited by Jan G. van der Watt and Ruben Zimmermann. WUNT 291. Tübingen: Mohr Siebeck, 2012.

Lawrence, Louise J. *Sense and Stigma in the Gospels: Depictions of Sensory-Disabled Characters*. Biblical Refigurations. Oxford: Oxford University Press, 2013.

Lee, Dorothy. *Flesh and Glory: Symbol, Gender, and Theology in the Gospel of John*. New York: Crossroad, 2002.

Lincoln, Andrew T. *The Gospel according to Saint John*. BNTC 4. Peabody, MA: Hendrickson, 2005.

Lincoln, Andrew T. *Truth on Trial: The Lawsuit Motif in John's Gospel*. Peabody, MA: Hendrickson, 2000.

Loader, William. *Jesus in John's Gospel: Structure and Issues in Johannine Christology*. Grand Rapids, MI: Eerdmans, 2017.

Lossky, Vladimir. *In the Image and Likeness of God*. Crestwood, NY: St. Vladimir's Seminary Press, 1974.

Lossky, Vladimir. *The Mystical Theology of the Eastern Church*. Crestwood, NY: St Vladimir's Seminary Press, 1997.

Lot-Borodine, Myrrha. *La Déification de l'homme selon la doctrine des Pères grecs*. Paris: Cerf, 1970. Repr., Paris: Cerf, 2011.

Louth, Andrew. "The Place of Theosis in Orthodox Theology." Pages 32–44 in *Partakers of the Divine Nature: The History and Development of Deification in the Christian Traditions*. Edited by Michael J. Christensen and Jeffery A. Wittung. Grand Rapids, MI: Baker, 2007.

Mantzaridis, Georgios I. *The Deification of Man: Saint Gregory Palamas and the Orthodox Tradition*. Translated by Liadain Sherrard. Contemporary Greek Theologians 2. Crestwood, NY: St. Vladimir's Seminary Press, 1984.

Marrow, Stanley B. "Κόσμος in John." *CBQ* 64 (2002): 90–102.

Maximus the Confessor. *On the Cosmic Mystery of Jesus Christ: Selected Writings from St Maximus the Confessor*. Translated by Paul M. Blowers and Robert Louis Wilken. Popular Patristics Series 25. Crestwood, NY: St. Vladimir's Seminary Press, 2003.

Medley, Mark S. "Participation in God: The Appropriation of Theosis by Contemporary Baptist Theologians." Pages in 205–46 in *Theosis: Deification in Christian Theology*. Edited by Vladimir Kharlamov. Princeton Theological Monograph Series 156. Eugene, OR: Pickwick, 2011.

Meeks, Wayne A. "The Ethics of the Fourth Evangelist." Pages 317–26 in *Exploring the Gospel of John: In Honor of D. Moody Smith*. Edited by R. Alan Culpepper and C. Clifton Black. Louisville, KY: Westminster John Knox, 1996.

Meeks, Wayne A. "The Man from Heaven in Johannine Sectarianism." *JBL* 91 (1972): 44–72.
Metzger, Bruce M. *A Textual Commentary on the Greek New Testament*. 2nd ed. Stuttgart: Deutsche Bibelgesellschaft/United Bible Societies, 1994.
Metzner, Rainer. *Das Verständnis der Sünde im Johannesevangelium*. WUNT 122. Tübingen: Mohr Siebeck, 2000.
Meyendorff, John. *A Study of Gregory Palamas*. Translated by George Lawrence. Crestwood, NY: St. Vladimir's Seminary Press, 1998.
Michaels, J. Ramsey. *The Gospel of John*. NICNT. Grand Rapids, MI: Eerdmans, 2010.
Miller, Ed L. *Salvation-History in the Prologue of John: The Significance of John 1:3/4*. NovTSup 60. Leiden: Brill, 1989.
Moloney, Francis J. *Love in the Gospel of John: An Exegetical, Theological, and Literary Study*. Grand Rapids, MI: Baker, 2013.
Montgomery, James A. "Hebrew *Hesed* and Greek *Charis*." *HTR* 32 (1939): 97–102.
Morris, Leon. "The Atonement in John's Gospel." *CTR* 3 (1988): 49–64.
Morris, Leon. *The Gospel according to John: The English Text with Introduction, Exposition, and Notes*. NICNT. Grand Rapids, MI: Eerdmans, 1971.
Moss, Candida R. "The Marks of the Nails: Scars, Wounds, and the Resurrection of Jesus in John." *Early Christianity* 8 (2017): 48–68.
Motyer, Stephen. *Your Father the Devil? A New Approach to John and 'the Jews.'* Paternoster Biblical and Theological Monographs. Carlisle: Paternoster, 1997.
Müller, Theophil E. *Das Heilsgeschehen im Johannesevangelium: Eine exegetische Studie, zugleich der Versuch einer Antwort an Rudolf Bultmann*. Zürich: Gotthelf-Verlag, 1961.
Murphy, Roland E. "Yēṣer in the Qumran Literature." *Bib* 39 (1958): 334–44.
Mussner, Franz. *ZΩH: Die Anschauung vom "Leben" im Vierten Evangelium, unter Berücksichtigung der Johannesbriefe*. Münchener theologische Studien, historische Abteilung. München: Karl Zink, 1952.
Nellas, Panayiotis. *Deification in Christ: Orthodox Perspectives on the Nature of the Human Person*. Translated by Norman Russell. Contemporary Greek Theologians 5. Crestwood, NY: St. Vladimir's Seminary Press, 1987.
Odeberg, Hugo. *The Fourth Gospel: Interpreted in Its Relation to Contemporaneous Religious Currents in Palestine and the Hellenistic-Oriental World*. Chicago: Argonaut, 1929.
Olyan, Saul M. *Disability in the Hebrew Bible: Interpreting Mental and Physical Differences*. Cambridge: Cambridge University Press, 2008.
Painter, John. "The Prologue as an Hermeneutical Key to Reading the Fourth Gospel." Pages 37–60 in *Studies in the Gospel of John and its Christology: Festschrift Gilbert Van Belle*. Edited by Joseph Verheyden et al. BETL 265. Leuven: Peeters, 2014.
Pamment, Margaret. "The Meaning of *Doxa* in the Fourth Gospel." *ZNW* 74 (1983): 12–16.
Pazdan, Mary Margaret. "Discipleship as the Appropriation of Eschatological Salvation in the Fourth Gospel." PhD diss., University of St. Michael's College, 1982.
Porter, Frank Chamberlin. "The *Yeçer Hara*: A Study in the Jewish Doctrine of Sin." Pages 91–156 in *Biblical and Semitic Studies: Critical and Historical Essays by the Members of the Semitic and Biblical Faculty of Yale University*. New York: Scribner's Sons, 1901.
Reynolds, Benjamin E. "The Anthropology of John and the Johannine Epistles: A Relational Anthropology." Pages 121–39 in *Anthropology and New Testament Theology*. Edited by Jason Maston and Benjamin E. Reynolds. LNTS 529. London: T&T Clark, 2018.

Ridderbos, Herman N. *The Gospel according to John: A Theological Commentary*. Translated by John Vriend. Grand Rapids, MI: Eerdmans: 1997.
Rosen-Zvi, Ishay. "Two Rabbinic Inclinations? Rethinking a Scholarly Dogma." *JSJ* 39 (2008): 513–39.
Russell, Norman. *The Doctrine of Deification in the Greek Patristic Tradition*. OECS. Oxford: Oxford University Press, 2009.
Russell, Norman. *Fellow Workers with God: Orthodox Thinking on Theosis*. Foundations Series 5. Crestwood, NY: St. Vladimir's Seminary Press, 2009.
Sanders, E. P. *Judaism: Practice and Belief, 63 BCE-66 CE*. London: SCM Press; Philadelphia, PA: Trinity Press International, 1992.
Sanders, Jack T. *Ethics in the New Testament*. Philadelphia, PA: Fortress, 1975.
Schelkle, Karl. "John's Theology of Man and the World." Pages 127–40 in *A Companion to John: Readings in Johannine Theology (John's Gospel and Epistles)*. Edited by Michael J. Taylor S.J. New York: Alba House, 1977.
Schipper, Jeremy. *Disability and Isaiah's Suffering Servant*. Biblical Refigurations. Oxford: Oxford University Press, 2011.
Schipper, Jeremy. "Reconsidering the Imagery of Disability in 2 Samuel 5:8b." *CBQ* 67 (2005): 422–34.
Schnackenburg, Rudolf. *The Gospel according to St. John: Commentary on Chapters 5-12*. Translated by Cecily Hastings, Francis McDonagh, David Smith, and Richard Foley, S.J. New York: Crossroad, 1990.
Schnelle, Udo. *The Human Condition: Anthropology in the Teachings of Jesus, Paul, and John*. Translated by O. C. Dean, Jr. Minneapolis, MN: Fortress, 1996.
Schnelle, Udo. *Theology of the New Testament*. Translated by M. Eugene Boring. Grand Rapids, MI: Baker, 2009.
Schwankl, Otto. "Die Metaphorik von Licht und Finsternis im johanneischen Schrifttum." Pages 135–67 in *Metaphorik und Mythos im Neuen Testament*. Edited by Karl Kertelge. QD 126. Freiburg im Breisgau: Herder, 1990.
Schwankl, Otto. *Licht und Finsternis: Ein metaphorisches Paradigma in den johanneischen Schriften*. Herders Biblische Studien 5. Freiburg im Breisgau: Herder, 1995.
Scott, E. F. *The Fourth Gospel: Its Purpose and Theology*. Edinburgh: T&T Clark, 1908.
Scrutton, Anastasia. "'The Truth Will Set You Free': Salvation as Revelation." Pages 359–68 in *The Gospel of John and Christian Theology*. Edited by Richard Bauckham and Carl Mosser. Grand Rapids, MI: Eerdmans, 2008.
Skehan, Patrick W., and Alexander A. Di Lella. *The Wisdom of Ben Sira: A New Translation with Notes*. AB 39. New York: Doubleday, 1987.
Skinner, Christopher W. "Misunderstanding, Christology, and Johannine Characterization: Reading John's Characters through the Lens of the Prologue." Pages 111–25 in *Characters and Characterization in the Gospel of John*. Edited by Christopher W. Skinner. LNTS 461. London: T&T Clark, 2013.
Smith, D. Moody. *The Theology of the Gospel of John*. New Testament Theology. Cambridge: Cambridge University Press, 1995.
Snyder, Sharon L., and David T. Mitchell. *Cultural Locations of Disability*. Chicago: University of Chicago Press, 2006.
Stevens, George Barker. *The Theology of the New Testament*. New York: Scribner's Sons, 1899.
Stibbe, Mark W. G. *John's Gospel*. New Testament Readings. London: Routledge, 1994.
Stimpfle, Alois. "'Ihr seid schon rein durch das Wort' (Joh 15,3a): Hermeneutische und methodische Überlegungen zur Frage nach 'Sünde' und 'Vergebung' im

Johannesevangelium." Pages 108–22 in *Sünde und Erlösung im Neuen Testament*. Edited by Hubert Frankemölle. QD 161. Freiburg: Herder, 1996.

Suggit, John. "Jesus the Gardener: The Atonement in the Fourth Gospel as Re-Creation." *Neot* 33 (1999): 161–8.

Swetnam, James. "The Meaning of πεπιστευκότας in John 8:31." *Bib* 61 (1980): 106–9.

Talbert, Charles H. "The Fourth Gospel's Soteriology between New Birth and Resurrection." Pages 176–91 in *Getting "Saved": The Whole Story of Salvation in the New Testament*. Edited by Charles H. Talbert and Jason A. Whitlark. Grand Rapids, MI: Eerdmans: 2011.

Theobald, Michael. *Das Evangelium nach Johannes: Kapitel 1–12*. RNT. Regensburg: Friedrich Pustet, 2009.

Theobald, Michael. "Theologie und Anthropologie: Fundamentaltheologische Aspekte des johanneischen Offenbarungsverständnisses." *ZKT* 141 (2019): 44–63.

Theodorou, Andreas. "Die Lehre von der Vergottung des Menschen bei den griechischen Kirchenvätern." *KD* 7 (1961): 283–310.

Thomas, Stephen. *Deification in the Eastern Orthodox Tradition: A Biblical Perspective*. Gorgias Eastern Christian Studies 2. Piscataway, NJ: Gorgias Press, 2007.

Thompson, Marianne Meye. *The God of the Gospel of John*. Grand Rapids, MI: Eerdmans, 2001.

Thompson, Marianne Meye. *John: A Commentary*. NTL. Louisville, KY: Westminster John Knox, 2015.

Thompson, Marianne Meye. "'Light' (φῶς): The Philosophical Content of the Term and the Gospel of John." Pages 273–83 in *The Prologue of the Gospel of John: Its Literary, Theological, and Philosophical Contexts. Papers Read at the Colloquium Ioanneum 2013*. Edited by Jan G. van der Watt, R. Alan Culpepper, and Udo Schnelle. WUNT 359. Tübingen: Mohr Siebeck, 2016.

Thompson, Marianne Meye. "When the Ending Is Not the End." Pages 65–75 in *The Ending of Mark and the Ends of God: Essays in Memory of Donald Harrisville Juel*. Edited by Beverly Roberts Gaventa and Patrick D. Miller. Louisville, KY: Westminster John Knox, 2005.

Thyen, Hartwig. *Das Johannesevangelium*. HNT 6. Tübingen: Mohr Siebeck, 2005.

Turner, George Allen. "Soteriology in the Gospel of John." *JETS* 19 (1976): 271–7.

Turner, Max. "Atonement and the Death of Jesus in John—Some Questions to Bultmann and Forestell." *EvQ* 62 (1990): 99–122.

Urban, Christina. *Das Menschenbild nach dem Johannesevangelium: Grundlagen johanneischer Anthropologie*. WUNT 2/137. Tübingen: Mohr Siebeck, 2001.

VanderKam, James C. *An Introduction to Early Judaism*. Grand Rapids, MI: Eerdmans, 2001.

van der Watt, Jan G. "Ethics Alive in Imagery." Pages 421–48 in *Imagery in the Gospel of John: Terms, Forms, Themes, and Theology of Johannine Figurative Language*. Edited by Jörg Frey, Jan G. van der Watt, and Ruben Zimmermann. WUNT 200. Tübingen: Mohr Siebeck, 2006.

van der Watt, Jan G. "Ethics of/and the Opponents of Jesus in John's Gospel." Pages 175–91 in *Rethinking the Ethics of John: "Implicit Ethics" in the Johannine Writings*. Edited by Jan G. van der Watt and Ruben Zimmermann. WUNT 291. Tübingen: Mohr Siebeck, 2012.

van der Watt, Jan G. *Family of the King: Dynamics of Metaphor in the Gospel according to John*. Leiden: Brill, 2000.

van der Watt, Jan G. "Salvation in the Gospel according to John." Pages 101–31 in *Salvation in the New Testament: Perspectives on Soteriology*. Edited by Jan G. van der Watt. NovTSup 121. Leiden: Brill, 2005.

Vawter, Bruce. "What Came to Be in Him Was Life (Jn 1,3b-4a)." *CBQ* 25 (1963): 401–6.

Vellanickal, Matthew. *The Divine Sonship of Christians in the Johannine Writings*. AnBib 72. Rome: Biblical Institute Press, 1977.

Volf, Miroslav. "Johannine Dualism and Contemporary Pluralism." Pages 19–50 in *The Gospel of John and Christian Theology*. Edited by Richard Bauckham and Carl Mosser. Grand Rapids, MI: Eerdmans, 2008.

von Wahlde, Urban C. "Archeology and John's Gospel." Pages 523–86 in *Jesus and Archeology*. Edited by James H. Charlesworth. Grand Rapids, MI: Eerdmans, 2006.

Wagener, Fredrik. *Figuren als Handlungsmodelle: Simon Petrus, die samaritische Frau, Judas und Thomas als Zugänge zu einer narrativen Ethik des Johannesevangeliums*. WUNT 2/408. Tübingen: Mohr Siebeck, 2015.

Wallace, Daniel B. *Greek Grammar Beyond the Basics: An Exegetical Syntax of the New Testament*. Grand Rapids, MI: Zondervan, 1996.

Westcott, Brooke Foss. *The Gospel according to St. John: The Greek Text, with Introduction and Notes*. Edited by A. Westcott. Grand Rapids, MI: Eerdmans, 1954.

Wiles, Maurice F. *The Spiritual Gospel: The Interpretation of the Fourth Gospel in the Early Church*. Cambridge: Cambridge University Press, 1960.

Wold, Benjamin. "Demonizing Sin? The Evil Inclination in 4QInstruction." Pages 34–48 in *Evil in Second Temple Judaism and Early Christianity*. Edited by Chris Keith and Loren T. Stuckenbruck. WUNT 2/417. Tübingen: Mohr Siebeck, 2016.

Yannaras, Christos. *Elements of Faith: An Introduction to Orthodox Theology*. Translated by Keith Schram. Edinburgh, Scotland: T&T Clark, 1991.

Yannaras, Christos. *The Freedom of Morality*. Translated by Elizabeth Briere. Contemporary Greek Theologians 3. Crestwood, NY: St. Vladimir's Seminary Press, 1984.

Yannaras, Christos. *Person and Eros*. Translated by Norman Russell. Brookline, MA: Holy Cross Orthodox Press, 2007.

Yong, Amos. *The Bible, Disability, and the Church: A New Vision of the People of God*. Grand Rapids, MI: Eerdmans, 2011.

Zahn, Theodor. *Das Evangelium des Johannes*. 5th and 6th ed. Leipzig: Deichert, 1921.

Zimmerman, Ruben. "Is There Ethics in the Gospel of John? Challenging an Outdated Consensus." Pages 44–80 in *Rethinking the Ethics of John: "Implicit Ethics" in the Johannine Writings*. Edited by Jan G. van der Watt and Ruben Zimmermann. WUNT 291. Tübingen: Mohr Siebeck, 2012.

Zizioulas, John D. *Being as Communion: Studies in Personhood and the Church*. Contemporary Greek Theologians 4. Crestwood, NY: St. Vladimir's Seminary Press, 1985.

Zizioulas, John D. *Communion and Otherness: Further Studies in Personhood and the Church*. Edited by Paul McPartlan. London: T&T Clark, 2006.

Zumstein, Jean. "The Purpose of the Ministry and Death of Jesus in the Gospel of John." Pages 331–46 in *The Oxford Handbook of Johannine Studies*. Edited by Judith M. Lieu and Martinus C. de Boer. Oxford: Oxford University Press, 2018.

Index of Modern Authors

Achtemeier, Elizabeth R. 26 n.16
Aland, Kurt 23 n.5
Ashton, John 33 n.43

Balás, David L. 12 n.55
Barr, James 18 n.71
Barrett, C. K. 43 n.83, 59 n.24, 73 n.5,
  84 n.45, 87 n.50
Bauckham, Richard 17 n.69, 29 n.33,
  46 n.93
Beasley-Murray, George R. 23 n.5, 68 n.47,
  73 n.5, 77 n.21, 91 n.61, 92 n.62
Behr, John 11 n.52, 15 n.63
Bennema, Cornelis 1, 2 n.6, 33 n.43,
  57 n.21
Bernard, J. H. 23 n.5
Beutler, Johannes 84 n.45
Bieringer, Reimund 41 n.72
Blowers, Paul M. 14 n.60, 14 n.61
Brand, Miryam T. 86 n.49, 88 n.53
Brower, Kent 15 n.64
Brown, Raymond E. 5, 23 n.3, 23 n.5, 28
  n.26, 44 n.84, 46 n.94, 55 n.15, 68 n.47,
  74 n.7, 75 n.10, 79 n.28, 91 n.61, 92 n.62
Bruce, F. F. 66 n.42
Bruner, Dale 23 n.5, 57 n.19
Bullard, Roger A. 88 n.53
Bultmann, Rudolph 1, 6, 18 n.72, 23 n.5,
  31 n.41, 33 n.43, 33 n.46, 38 n.62, 41
  n.69, 57 n.19, 74 n.7, 75 n.12, 77 n.21,
  80 n.31, 91 n.61, 92 n.62
Burridge, Richard A. 17 n.69
Byers, Andrew J. 15 n.64

Carey, George L. 33 n.44
Carson, D. A. 80 n.31, 81 n.35, 91 n.61,
  92 n.62
Carter, Warren 1 n.1, 62 n.30
Ceresko, Anthony R. 59 n.23
Clark-Soles, Jaime 58 n.22
Collins, Paul M. 11 n.52, 12 n.55

Conzelmann, Hans 27 n.19
Cook, Johann 86 n.49
Cooper, Jordan 11 n.52
Crump, David 15 n.64
Culpepper, R Alan 23 n.5, 33 n.43

Dana, H. E. 86 n.47
de la Potterie, Ignace 37 n.58, 39 n.63
Dennis, John 33 n.44
Despotis, Athanasios 12 n.55
Di Lella, Alexander A. 88 n.53
Dodd, C. H. 17 n.67, 27 n.20, 34, 43 n.83,
  44 n.87, 44 n.88, 80 n.32, 84 n.45,
  93 n.64
Dukes, Jimmy Ward 2 n.6, 47 n.96

Eco, Umberto 17 n.68
Eiesland, Nancy L. 64 n.36

Fanning, Buist M. 38 n.61
Finlan, Stephen 12 n.55
Forestell, J. Terence 7–8, 30 n.36, 30 n.37,
  33 n.43, 34 n.48, 67 n.43, 77
Fox, Michael V. 75 n.11
Frey, Jörg 5 n.22, 7 n.37, 33 n.44,
  68 n.47, 99 n.4

Gaffney, James 43 n.83, 44 n.87
Gieschen, Charles A. 33 n.44
Glicksman, Andrew T. 30 n.35
Godet, Frédéric Louis 39 n.66
Gorman, Michael J. 15 n.64, 64 n.35
Green, Joel B. 7 n.33, 66 n.42
Griffith, Terry 77 n.21, 80 n.30
Grigsby, Bruce H. 33 n.44
Gross, Jules 11 n.52, 12 n.55
Grundmann, Walter 6 n.31, 9–10, 95
Gurtner, D. M. 53 n.11

Habets, Myk 11 n.52
Haenchen, Ernst 57 n.19, 80 n.31

Hakola, Raimo 80 n.31, 80 n.32
Hasitschka, Martin 8–9, 17 n.67, 34 n.50, 75 n.12, 76 n.13, 80 n.31, 88 n.52
Hatton, Howard A. 88 n.53
Hays, Richard B. 10 n.48
Hengel, Martin 18 n.70
Hoskins, Paul M. 80 n.31
Hoskyns, Edwyn Clement 80 n.31, 93 n.64
Hylen, Susan E. 2 n.9, 41 n.72, 78 n.22, 83 n.40, 84 n.45

Jerumanis, Pascal-Marie 78 n.22

Kanagaraj, Jey J. 44 n.84, 77 n.15
Kärkkäinen, Veli-Matti 11 n.52
Käsemann, Ernst 33 n.43
Kierspel, Lars 41 n.69, 41 n.72
Knöppler, Thomas 3, 33 n.44
Koester, Craig R. 1, 5, 10, 27 n.20, 31 n.41, 44 n.88, 67 n.44
Köstenberger, Andreas J. 31 n.41, 41 n.69
Kuyper, Lester J. 28 n.26

Labahn, Michael 4
Lawrence, Louise J. 63 n.33
Lee, Dorothy 5–6, 27 n.20, 29 n.33
Lincoln, Andrew T. 28 n.26, 68 n.47, 80 n.31, 81 n.33
Loader, William 33 n.42, 34, 40 n.68
Lossky, Vladimir 11 n.52, 15 n.63, 99 n.3
Lot-Borodine, Myrrha 11 n.52
Louth, Andrew 10 n.51, 11 n.52, 12 n.53

Mantey, Julius R. 86 n.47
Mantzaridis, Georgios I. 11 n.52
Marrow, Stanley B. 41 n.69
Medley, Mark S. 11 n.52
Meeks, Wayne A. 17 n.67, 33 n.43
Metzger, Bruce 52 n.7
Metzner, Rainer 2 n.10, 3, 33 n.44, 76 n.13, 77 n.14, 80 n.31, 81 n.33, 86 n.49, 88 n.52
Meyendorff, John 11 n.52
Michaels, J. Ramsey 23 n.4, 33 n.43, 55 n.14, 68 n.47, 81 n.36, 82 n.37, 84 n.45, 91 n.60
Miller, Ed L. 22 n.2, 23 n.5, 23 n.8, 24 n.9, 25 n.13
Mitchell, David T. 51 n.3, 51 n.4

Moloney, Francis J. 33 n.43, 34 n.48, 37 n.59
Montgomery, James A. 28 n.26
Morris, Leon 33 n.44, 74 n.7, 80 n.31, 80 n.32
Moss, Candida R. 65 n.37
Motyer, Stephen 41 n.72, 80 n.31, 81 n.33, 89 n.55
Müller, Theophil E. 33 n.44
Murphy, Roland E. 86 n.49
Mussner, Franz 17 n.67, 31 n.41, 34 n.50

Nellas, Panayiotis 11 n.52

Odeberg, Hugo 86 n.49
Olyan, Saul M. 52 n.8

Painter, John 18 n.70
Pamment, Margaret 29 n.33
Pazdan, Mary Margaret 2 n.6
Perrin, N. 53 n.11
Pollefeyt, Didier 41 n.72
Porter, Frank Chamberlin 86 n.49

Reynolds, Benjamin E. 6 n.31
Ridderbos, Herman N. 73 n.5, 74 n.6, 81 n.35
Rosen-Zvi, Ishay 86 n.49
Russell, Norman 11 n.52, 12 n.55, 12 n.56

Sanders, E. P. 54 n.13
Sanders, Jack T. 4 n.20
Schelkle, Karl 6 n.31
Schipper, Jeremy 50–1, 59 n.23
Schnackenburg, Rudolf 57 n.19, 84 n.45
Schnelle, Udo 4, 5 n.23, 17 n.67, 27 n.20, 30 n.34, 34 n.50
Schwankl, Otto 26 n.15, 27 n.20, 29 n.31
Scott, E. F. 3, 30 n.37, 33 n.43
Scrutton, Anastasia 8–9
Skehan, Patrick W. 88 n.53
Skinner, Christopher W. 18 n.70
Smith, D. Moody 2 n.8, 2 n.9, 31 n.41, 33 n.43, 41 n.69
Snyder, Sharon L. 51 n.3, 51 n.,4
Stevens, George Barker 31 n.41
Stibbe, Mark W. G. 80 n.30
Stimpfle, Alois 3
Suggit, John 34 n.50
Swetnam, James 80 n.30

Talbert, Charles H. 2 n.7
Theobald, Michael 4, 18 n.72, 80 n.31
Theodorou, Andreas 11 n.52, 12 n.55
Thomas, Stephen 12 n.55
Thompson, Marianne Meye 16 n.65, 17 n.69, 27 n.20, 28 n.26, 30 n.35, 44 n.88, 57 n.19, 59 n.23, 68 n.47, 84 n.42
Thyen, Hartwig 80 n.30
Turner, George Allen 1 n.1
Turner, Max 33 n.44

Urban, Christina 3–4, 5 n.25

Vandecasteele-Vanneuville, Frederique 41 n.72
VanderKam, James C. 53 n.11
van der Watt, Jan G. 5, 6 n.32, 24 n.11, 27 n.20, 29 n.30, 30 n.36, 33 n.43, 36 n.52, 45 n.90
Vawter, Bruce 23 n.5

Vellanickal, Matthew 2 n.8, 8 n.43, 17 n.67, 34 n.50, 46 n.94
Volf, Miroslav 99 n.4
von Wahlde, Urban C. 52 n.6

Wagener, Fredrik 17 n.67, 83 n.39
Wallace, Daniel B. 38 n.61, 55 n.14, 86 n.47
Westcott, Brooke Foss 23 n.5, 39 n.64
Wiles, Maurice F. 12 n.55
Wold, Benjamin 86 n.49

Yannaras, Christos 11 n.52, 99 n.2
Yong, Amos 50 n.1

Zahn, Theodor 47 n.95
Zimmerman, Ruben 3 n.11, 39 n.65
Zizioulas, John D. 11 n.52, 15 n.63
Zumstein, Jean 18 n.72, 33 n.43

Index of Ancient Sources

ISRAEL'S SCRIPTURES/OLD TESTAMENT

Genesis
1	23
2:4	23 n.7
4:7	86 n.49
6:5	86 n.49
8:21	86 n.49
24:27	28 n.26
24:49	28 n.26
27:1	52 n.8
32:11	28 n.26
47:29	28 n.26
48:10	52 n.8

Exodus
5:2	42 n.74
15:25	62
19:5	41 n.71
19:5–6	43 n.81
19:10–23 LXX	37 n.56
21:24–26	52 n.8
23:24–25	43 n.81
29:1–46 LXX	37 n.56
29:38–42	54 n.12
29:45–46 LXX	43
31:12–16 LXX	37 n.57
31:13	43 n.80
32:1–24	43 n.81
34:6	28 n.26

Leviticus
1–7	54 n.12
4:3	91 n.60
5:1 LXX	91 n.60
5:17	91 n.60
5:21–24 (6:2–5)	91 n.60
7:18 LXX	91 n.60
8:1–30 LXX	37 n.56
11:41–45 LXX	37 n.57
11:44–45	45 n.90, 46 n.92
16:16	91 n.61
18:1–5	43 n.81
18:24–30	43 n.81
19:1–20:26 LXX	37 n.57
19:2	44 n.84
19:8 LXX	91 n.60
19:17 LXX	91 n.60
19:18	28, 44 n.84, 75 n.9
20:7–8	45 n.90, 46 n.92
20:22–26	43 n.81
21:16–23	52 n.8, 59 n.23
22:9 LXX	91 n.60
22:31–33 LXX	37 n.57
23	54 n.12
24:15 LXX	91 n.60
24:19–20	52 n.8

Numbers
5:31 LXX	91 n.60
6:10–12 LXX	37 n.56
6:24–26	26, 30 n.35
9:13 LXX	91 n.60
10:10	54 n.12
14:1–35	43 n.81
14:34 LXX	91 n.60
18:1 LXX	91 n.60
18:22 LXX	91 n.60
18:32 LXX	91 n.60
23:10	68 n.45
28–29	54 n.12

Deuteronomy
4:5–6	43 n.80
4:32–40	43 n.80
6:1–15	43 n.81
6:5	28, 44 n.84, 75 n.9
7:6	43 n.81
10:12	44 n.84
10:14	41 n.71
12:29–30	43 n.81
14:1	46 n.92

18:13 LXX	37 n.57	*Nehemiah*	
28:9 LXX	37 n.57	3:1	52 n.6
28:27	62 n.31	3:32	52 n.6
30:15–20	68 n.45	7:73–8:8	54 n.12
31:17–18	30 n.35	12:39	52 n.6
32:4–27	43 n.81		
32:39	62 n.31	*Job*	
		5:18	62 n.31
Joshua		18:21	42 n.74
2:14	28 n.26	19:13 LXX	43 n.79
7:13 LXX	37 n.56	21:14	42 n.74
22:17	91 n.61	24:11–13	42 n.74
		24:13	26
Judges		27:14 LXX	60 n.26
2:10–13	42 n.74	36:12	42 n.74
1 Samuel/1 Kingdoms		*Psalms*	
2:10	LXX 43	4:6	30 n.35
2:12	42 n.74	6:2	62 n.31
4:15	52 n.8	14:2–4 (13:2–4 LXX)	42 n.74
7:1 LXX	37 n.56	24:1	41 n.71
8:4–22	43 n.81	25:10	28 n.26
16:5 LXX	37 n.56	27:1	(26:1 LXX) 26, 30 n.35
2 Samuel		30:2	62 n.31
2:6	28 n.26	31:16	26, 30 n.35
4:4	52 n.8	32:5	91 n.60
5:8	59 n.23	36:11 (10)	43
9:13	52 n.8	37:3–6 (36:3–6 LXX)	26 n.16
14:25	52 n.8	40:11 (10)	28 n.26
15:20	28 n.26	43:3 (42:3 LXX)	26 n.16
		44:3	30 n.35
1 Kings/3 Kingdoms		46:11 (10)	43
8:43	43	51:3–16 (1–14)	91 n.60, 91 n.61
8:61 LXX	37 n 57		
14:4	52 n.8	71:22 (70:22 LXX)	28 n.28
		78:1–72	43 n.81
2 Kings		79:6–7 (78:6–7 LXX)	42 n.74
20:5	62 n.31	80:3	30 n.35
25:7	52 n.8	81:8–16	43 n.81
		82:1–7 (81:1–7 LXX)	42–3
1 Chronicles		82:5	45, 97
23:4–5	54 n.12	86:15	28 n.26
23:30–31	54 n.12	89:14–16 (88:14–16 LXX)	26
28:9	43	91:14	43
		91:14–15	43 n.80
2 Chronicles		95:8–11 (94:8–11 LXX)	42 n.74
29:20–30:27	54 n.12		
30:20	62 n.31		

97:10–11 (96:10–11 LXX)	26 n.16	48:4–8	42 n.74
103:2–3	62 n.31	48:17–18 LXX	37 n.57
106:1–48	43 n.81	49:6	26 n.16
107:17–20	62 n.31	49:7 LXX	28 n.28
109:10	60 n.26	53:4 LXX	91 n.60
112:4 (111:4 LXX)	26 n.16	53:10–12	68 n.45
115:1	28 n.26	56:7	54 n.12
116:15	68 n.45	56:11	42 n.74
116:17–19 (115:8–10 LXX)	54 n.12	57:18–19	62 n.31
119:9–11	88 n.53	59:8	42 n.74
119:105 (118:105 LXX)	26	60:19–20	26
		62:1 LXX	26 n.16

Proverbs

1–9	75 n.11	*Jeremiah*	
1:20–33	74 n.8	1:5 LXX	37 n.56, 37 n.60
2:16–18	75 n.11	2:1–3:5	43 n.81
2:16–19	68 n.45	2:8	42 n.74
3:3	28 n.26	3:22	62 n.31
4:18–19 LXX	26	4:11 LXX	37 n.57
5:6	75 n.11	4:22	42 n.74
6:23 LXX	26	7:24	86 n.49
7:14–19	75 n.11	9:1–5 (2–6)	42
8:35–36	68 n.45	16:12	86 n.49
20:28	28 n.26	17:9	86 n.49
		17:14	62 n.31
Ecclesiastes		21:8–10	68 n.45
2:13	26 n.16	22:16 LXX	42
		24:7	43 n.80
Song of Songs		28:27–28 LXX	37 n.56
4:7	52 n.8	30:17	62
		31:31–34	43 n.80, 46 n.92
Isaiah		33:6	62 n.31
1:2–4	42	33:8	91 n.60
1:2–31	43 n.81	36:3	91 n.60
2:2–5	26 n.16		
5:13	42 n.74	*Ezekiel*	
5:20	26 n.16	18:30–32	68 n.45
6:10	62 n.31	20:10–13 LXX	37 n.57
9:2 (1)	26 n.16	22:1–4	91 n.61
9:6–7 (5–6)	26 n.16	22:15	91 n.61
19:21	43 n.80	23:49 LXX	91 n.60
19:22	62 n.31	33:10–11	68 n.45
26:9 LXX	26	37:21–28 LXX	37 n.57
30:26	62 n.31	39:23–24	91 n.61
35:8 LXX	37 n.57		
42:6	26	*Daniel*	
42:6–7	26 n.16	1:4	52 n.8
42:16	26 n.16	11:32	43
45:20	42 n.74		

Hosea		24:27	26 n.18
1:10	46 n.92	34:20	62 n.31
2:21–22 (19–20)	43 n.80	38:9	62 n.31
4:1	28 n.26	40:28–30	60
4:1–2	42 n.74	49:7	37 n.56, 37 n.60
4:1–19	43 n.81	50:12–21	54 n.12
6:1	62 n.31		
6:1–3	43 n.80	*Baruch*	
6:4–7	42 n.74	2:30–35	43 n.80
8:1–4	42 n.74	4:12–13	42 n.74, 43
10:12 LXX	26 n.16		
14:4	62 n.31	*1 Esdras*	
		1:3	37 n.56
Joel			
2:15–16 LXX	37 n.56	*2 Esdras*	
		1:28–29	46 n.92
Amos		7:48	68 n.45
1:2-2:16	43 n.81		

OLD TESTAMENT PSEUDEPIGRAPHA

Micah		*Apocryphon of Ezekiel*	
7:9	26 n.16	1:20	52 n.8
7:20	28 n.26		
		1 Enoch	
Zephaniah		3:6–8	26 n.18
1:7 LXX	37 n.56	108:14–15	26 n.18, 27
3:5 LXX	43 n.82		
		4 Ezra	
Zechariah		7:48	86 n.49
7:9	28 n.26		
11:17	52 n.8	*Jubilees*	
12:10–13:1	91 n.61	1:22–25	46 n.92

DEUTEROCANONICAL WORKS

		Letter of Aristeas	
Judith		88	54 n.12
8:17–20	43 n.80	92–95	54 n.12
Wisdom of Solomon		*3 Maccabees*	
5:5	46 n.92	6:28–30	46 n.92
5:6	26 n.18	7:6	46 n.92
7:26	26 n.18		
15:3	43 n.80	*4 Maccabees*	
16:10–12	62 n.31	16:23	43 n.80
16:16	42 n.74		
		Psalms of Solomon	
Sirach		2:31	42 n.74
15:15–17	68 n.45	17:26	46 n.92
21:11	88 n.53	17:27	42 n.74

Sibylline Oracles
2:51	43 n.80
8:399–401	68 n.45
13:4	68 n.45
14:4–9	26 n.18

Testament of Asher
1:3–9	86 n.49
3:2	86 n.49

Testament of Benjamin
5:3	26 n.18, 27

Testament of Gad
5:1	26 n.18

Testament of Issachar
6:2	86 n.49

Testament of Joseph
10:3	26 n.18
20:2	26 n.18

Testament of Levi
9:10	52 n.8
14:4	26 n.18
19:1	26 n.18, 27

Testament of Naphtali
2:10	26 n.18

Testament of Zebulun
9:8	26, 30 n.35

Testament of Job
43:6	26 n.18

DEAD SEA SCROLLS

$1QH^a$
IV, 21–37	86 n.49
IX, 23–25	86 n.49
XII, 30–32	86 n.49
XIII, 8	86 n.49
XV, 6	86 n.49

1QM
VII, 4–5	52 n.8
XIII, 1–16	26 n.18

1QS
II, 24-III, 7	26 n.18
III, 13	26
III, 13–23	26 n.18
III, 20–21	26
V, 1–11	88 n.53
V, 4–5	86 n.49

1QSa
II, 3–10	52 n.8

CD-A
II, 2	86 n.49
II, 16–17	86 n.49

4Q266
2 II, 16–17	86 n.49

4Q417
1 II, 12	86 n.49

4Q422
I, 12	86 n.49

4Q436
1 I, 10	86 n.49

11QPsa
XIX, 15–16	86 n.49

PHILO

De agricultura
130	52 n.8

De ebrietate
157	26 n.18

De providentia
2.64	54 n.13

De specialibus legibus
1.69–70	54
1.117	52 n.8
1.167–193	54 n.12
1.242	52 n.8

Index of Ancient Sources

De vita Mosis
1.90–91   62 n.29
1.95   62 n.29

Legum allegoriae
1.17–18   26 n.18
1.46–47   26 n.18
2.97   52 n.8

Quod deterius potiori insidari soleat
101   26 n.18

Quod Deus sit immutabilis
3.122–123   26 n.18

JOSEPHUS

Against Apion
1.233–234   52 n.8
2.193–198   54 n.12

Jewish Antiquities
1.267   52 n.8
3.237–257   54 n.12
4.203   54 n.13
7.61   52 n.8
7.113   52 n.8
14.366   52 n.8
20.167–168   62 n.29

Jewish War
5.228–229   52 n.8

NEW TESTAMENT

Matthew
4:23–24   62 n.32
5:14–16   29 n.32
5:23–24   54 n.12
5:29–30   4 n.21
5:48   37 n.57
6:22–23   4 n.21
8:4   54 n.12
8:16   62 n.32
8:22   68 n.45
9:2–7   56 n.18
9:35   62 n.32
10:1   62 n.32
10:1–4   82 n.38
10:7–8   62 n.32
11:1–6   62 n.32
14:14   62 n.32
16:24–28   36 n.52
18:8   52 n.8
19:21   37 n.57
21:12–14   59 n.23
21:15   59 n.23
22:31–32   66 n.41
22:37–40   77 n.19
24:24   62 n.29

Mark
1:34   62 n.32
2:3–12   56 n.18
3:10   62 n.32
3:14–19   82 n.38
6:13   62 n.32
6:55–56   56 n.18
8:34–38   36 n.52
9:45   52 n.8
10:46–52   60 n.26
12:26–27   66 n.41
12:29–33   77 n.19
13:22   62 n.29

Luke
1:10   54 n.12
2:22–38   54 n.12
5:15   62 n.32
5:17–19   56 n.18
5:24   56 n.18
6:13–16   82 n.38
6:18–19   62 n.32
7:18–23   62 n.32
8:43–48   62 n.32
9:1–2   62 n.32
9:6   62 n.32
9:11   62 n.32
9:23–26   36 n.52
10:9   62 n.32
10:27–28   77 n.19
11:33–36   4 n.21, 29 n.32
15:24   68 n.45
15:32   68 n.45
16:3   60
18:35–43   60 n.26
20:36   45 n.90
20:37–38   66 n.41

21:1–4	54 n.12	1:44	52 n.7
24:53	54 n.12	1:45–49	41 n.72
		1:49	64
John		2:4	79 n.27
1:1	24, 25 n.12, 39	2:11	79 n.29
1:1–2	23–4	2:13	53
1:1-3b	22–4	2:13–25	53 n.9
1:1–4	37 n.60	2:18–20	53 n.10
1:1–18	18	2:19	79 n.27
1:3	23–4, 41	2:19–22	29 n.30, 35, 40, 98
1:3c-4	22–30, 32, 35, 36 n.53, 41, 45, 46, 47, 89, 93 n.64, 96	2:21	29 n.29
		2:23–25	83–4, 85, 87, 88, 94, 98
1:4	22, 23 n.3, 25	2:24–25	79 n.27
1:4–5	23, 29, 96, 97	3:1	84 n.43
1:4–18	18	3:1–8	46 n.92, 71
1:5	22, 23 n.3, 25, 27, 29, 30 n.36, 41, 47	3:3–5	64
		3:3–7	29
1:6–8	41	3:3–8	45 n.91, 46, 92
1:9–10	25, 41	3:11	79 n.27, 84 n.43
1:9–13	46	3:12	84 n.43
1:10	41–2	3:15–16	25
1:10–11	28 n.23, 41–5, 48, 84 n.44, 97	3:16	31, 44 n.84
		3:16–18	28
1:11	41–2, 44, 46 n.92, 65, 75 n.9, 76, 91 n.58	3:17	1 n.1, 25, 27, 31, 45, 48
		3:19–20	47, 71, 76, 97
1:12	28, 45–7, 70, 83, 89	3:19–21	24, 27–28, 29, 32
		3:35	90
1:12–13	29, 35, 40, 48, 71, 92	3:36	25, 32, 45 n.89, 75, 91–2, 98
1:12–17	47	4:7–30	83 n.40
1:13	45, 46 n.92	4:9	41 n.72
1:14	13, 24, 25, 28 n.26, 29, 35, 36 n.53, 37 n.60, 39, 45, 8, 89, 93 n.64, 96	4:17–18	79 n.27
		4:21	79 n.27
		4:22	28 n.23, 41 n.72
		4:34	28 n.25, 65 n.38
		4:35–38	38
1:14–18	30 n.35	4:39–42	83 n.40
1:16	35	4:42	1 n.1
1:16–17	28 n.26, 36 n.53, 39, 41 n.72, 45–6, 88, 93 n.64	4:45	53 n.10
		4:46–54	49, 52, 59 n.24, 62, 63, 65, 97
1:17	35, 41 n.72, 76, 96	4:47	62
1:18	25, 37 n.60, 39, 65	4:48	62
1:19–23	41 n.72	4:49	62
1:29	19, 31, 72, 84 n.44, 85, 89 n.54, 93 n.64, 98	4:50	62 n.29
		4:54	53
		5:1	52, 53, 54, 57, 59

5:1–15	49–50, 51, 52–60, 63, 66, 69, 97	5:37–47	75 n.11, 91 n.59, 93
5:1–29	18	5:39	41 n.72
5:2–3	52, 54–5	5:39–40	74–5, 90
5:3	52 n.8, 55 n.14, 55 n.15, 58	5:40	75
		5:41	77 n.15
5:3–4	56, 96	5:42	28, 44, 75 n.9, 76 n.13, 77 n.18, 77 n.20, 97, 98
5:3–12	56 n.18		
5:4	55		
5:5	52 n.8, 55–8	5:42–47	75
5:5–9	62	5:44	44, 75 n.9, 76 n.13, 77 n.15, 98
5:6	55–9, 79 n.27		
5:7	52 n.8, 55–8	5:45–47	75 n.9
5:7–8	55	6:1–71	53 n.9
5:8	56–8	6:2	59 n.24, 62, 63, 97
5:8–13	57	6:4	53
5:9	56	6:6	79 n.27
5:9–10	38 n.62, 65	6:31–33	41 n.72
5:10	57 n.20	6:32–35	24
5:10–15	77 n.14	6:32–65	79 n.29
5:14	19, 53, 57, 59, 60, 72, 90 n.57	6:33–34	74
		6:33–35	25
5:15–18	91 n.58	6:35	29 n.30, 67
5:16	65	6:35–58	69, 89
5:16–18	37 n.60, 38 n.62, 41 n.72, 65	6:37–39	90 n.56, 100
		6:38	28 n.25, 65 n.38
5:16–29	50, 65–9	6:39–40	7 n.37, 51, 64
5:17	57, 65	6:39–59	66, 67, 98
5:18	65	6:40	25
5:19	28 n.25	6:44	7 n.37, 32 n.42, 38, 64, 90 n.56, 100
5:19–20	65		
5:21	57, 62, 65–7, 69		
5:21–29	65	6:48	75
5:24	67, 68 n.45	6:48–51	25 n.13, 30 n.35
5:24–25	36 n 53, 67, 69, 73, 75, 98	6:48–55	24
		6:50	76
5:24–29	71, 85	6:50–51	25, 67, 69
5:25	66–7, 76, 79 n.27	6:51	25 n.12, 29, 31, 38, 40, 89, 93 n.64
5:25–26	62		
5:26	24, 25, 29 n.30	6:52–71	72
5:27	96	6:53	25 n.14
5:28–29	7 n.37, 35–6, 51, 64 n.34, 66–7, 69, 73, 74 n.8, 76, 93	6:53–57	88
		6:54	7 n.37, 64
		6:57	24, 25, 35, 50, 68, 96
5:29	49, 50, 64, 68, 69, 71, 78, 96, 98		
		6:58	25
5:30	28 n.25, 65	6:60–66	16 n.65, 68, 79 n.29, 85, 94, 100
5:34	44 n.84, 89		
5:37–42	71, 79 n.27	6:61–64	79 n.27

6:63	40	8:25–30	79
6:67–71	82 n.38	8:26	76
6:68	40	8:28–29	28 n.25
6:69	28 n.28, 83	8:29	65 n.38
7:1–7	42, 44	8:30	72, 77–85
7:1–8:59	53 n.9	8:30–31	77–85, 91 n.58
7:2	53, 72	8:30–36	94, 98
7:7	28, 31 n.40	8:30–59	100
7:10–14	72	8:31	19, 28, 77–85, 87
7:11–31	53 n.10	8:31–32	44, 78
7:14–24	91 n.59	8:31–36	44, 72, 77–89, 93
7:14–28	71	8:31–59	77–90
7:16–18	65 n.38	8:32	8, 78, 82, 83,
7:18	44, 77 n.15, 97		85, 94, 98
7:19	38 n.62, 41	8:32–33	87, 88
	n.72, 44, 97	8:32–36	81
7:21–24	65	8:33	41 n.72, 78, 79,
7:22–23	41 n.72		86 n.47
7:23	38 n.62	8:34	44, 79, 86–8, 90
7:28	28 n.23, 44, 48, 97		n.57, 91, 93, 98
7:29	28 n.24, 40	8:34–36	46 n.92, 97, 98
7:30–31	72	8:35	78, 93
7:31–32	84 n.45	8:36	13, 78, 87, 89
7:33–34	73	8:37	41 n.72, 72, 79,
7:34	73–5		84 n.45
7:35–36	73	8:37–38	79
7:39	83	8:38–44	31 n.40
7:40–44	72	8:38–47	89 n.55
7:43–44	84 n.45	8:39	45 n.90, 79
7:50–51	84 n.43	8:39–41	79
8:7	72 n.2	8:39–42	46 n.92
8:12	24, 25 n.12, 28,	8:40	77 n.17
	29, 30 n.36,	8:41	79, 90
	31, 47, 69, 72,	8:42	25, 28, 44 n.86, 90
	76, 92, 97	8:42–47	79
8:12–13	85	8:44	31, 75, 77 n.16,
8:12–20	53 n.10, 76		77 n.17, 78, 89–
8:13–22	91 n.58		90, 98
8:14–19	85	8:45–46	77 n.17, 98
8:15	91 n.59	8:46	29
8:19	28 n.23, 44, 48, 97	8:47	89 n.55
8:21	73–6, 78, 93	8:48	72, 79
8:21–24	85, 90 n.57	8:49	28 n.24
8:21–59	19, 68–69,	8:50	77 n.15
	72, 73–90	8:51	28, 67, 69,
8:23	41 n.72, 42, 44,		76, 78, 98
	76, 78, 85	8:51–52	82
8:24	75, 76, 78, 93	8:52	72
8:25–29	77	8:52–53	79

8:54–55	90	10:17–18	28 n.25, 29, 35, 36, 40, 48, 67, 96
8:55	28 n.23, 28 n.24, 40, 44, 48, 65 n.38, 76 n.13, 77 n.17, 90, 97, 98	10:18	29 n.30
		10:22–23	53 n.9
		10:22–39	37 n.60, 53 n.10
		10:26–27	28
8:58	25 n.12, 37 n.60	10:28	25, 100
8:59	72, 77 n.16, 79, 89–90, 98	10:28–29	90 n.56
		10:30	65 n.38
9:1	38 n.62, 60, 90	10:30–38	44 n.86
9:1–41	51, 52 n.8, 60–1, 63, 90–3, 97	10:34	13
		10:36	37, 38
9:2	60	11:1–6	52 n.8
9:2–3	90	11:1–44	59 n.24, 61–2, 63, 83 n.40, 97
9:3	60, 63		
9:3–4	38 n.62	11:9–10	24
9:5	24	11:13–14	66
9:6–7	61, 62 n.29, 90	11:19	62
9:6–14	38 n.62	11:22	62 n.28
9:7	61, 63	11:23–26	35, 50, 62
9:8	60–1, 90	11:24	62 n.28, 64 n.34, 66
9:11	61, 63		
9:13	91 n.58	11:25	24, 25, 29 n.30, 30 n.35, 35, 47, 66–7, 69, 75, 94, 96, 98
9:14	38 n.62		
9:15	61, 63, 91 n.58		
9:16	38 n.62, 91 n.58	11:25–26	66, 68, 93 n.64, 98
9:17	61	11:26	66, 69, 89
9:18	91 n.58	11:27	25
9:22	61, 91 n.58	11:31	62
9:24	91 n.59	11:33	62
9:24–25	90, 91	11:33–35	62
9:27–33	61	11:38	62
9:28	91 n.58	11:38–44	65
9:28–29	90, 91	11:39–40	62
9:31	28 n.27	11:41–42	28 n.27
9:34	60, 61, 91 n.59	11:45–47	84 n.45
9:35–38	61	11:50–52	38
9:36	63	11:51–52	46 n.92
9:38	90	11:55–56	53 n.10
9:39–41	32, 45 n.89, 90–2, 93, 98	12:1–8	83 n.40
		12:1–19:42	53 n.9
9:40–41	86, 91–2	12:4–6	77 n.14
9:41	91–2, 93, 98	12:10–11	77 n.16
10:10	62, 77 n.14	12:11–13	84 n.45
10:11	29, 35, 36, 96	12:12	53 n.10
10:11–18	38	12:13–15	64
10:15	28 n.24, 29, 35, 36, 96	12:20	53 n.10, 54 n.12
		12:20–23	36
10:17	45, 50, 90	12:24	89

12:24–25	45	13:37–38	29 n.30
12:24–26	36–7, 89, 93 n.64, 96	14:1	82
		14:1–4	36
12:25	29, 35, 36 n.52, 38 n.62, 48, 77 n.20, 89, 98	14:4	82
		14:4–6	28, 36
		14:4–11	94
12:25–26	46 n.92, 64, 67, 68, 72, 77 n.14, 88, 93	14:5	82
		14:6	24, 25 n.13, 29 n.30, 30 n.35, 48, 68, 75, 76, 87, 89, 98
12:27–33	36		
12:28	28 n.27		
12:31	31, 64, 70, 93	14:6–7	83
12:35	27, 28, 29, 45, 47, 48, 97	14:7	82
		14:7–9	68 n.46
12:35–36	24, 28, 31, 47, 97	14:7–11	25, 44 n.86
12:36	25, 28, 29, 40, 48, 78	14:8	83
		14:9	83
12:41	25 n.12	14:10–11	83
12:42–43	84, 87, 88, 94	14:15	28, 78
12:43	77 n.15, 98	14:16–17	83
12:44	78	14:17	78 n.25, 88
12:44–45	44 n.86	14:18–20	35
12:45	68 n.46	14:19	24, 25, 35, 46 n.92, 50, 66, 68, 69, 96, 98
12:46	22, 24, 25, 27, 29, 30–31, 32 n.42, 45, 47		
		14:21	28, 78
12:46–47	31, 71, 76, 85, 97	14:23	78, 87, 88, 89, 93, 98
12:47	1 n.1, 31, 45, 48		
12:48	7 n.37, 64, 66, 67, 69, 74 n.8, 76, 93, 98	14:23–24	28
		14:26	78 n.25, 83
		14:30	31 n.40
12:49–50	28 n.25	14:31	28 n.24, 40, 44, 65 n.38, 77 n.18
13:2	31 n.40		
13:3–11	32 n.42	15:1–5	89
13:8	38	15:1–10	85, 88, 94
13:8–10	91 n.61, 92, 98	15:1–17	36, 87, 90 n.56, 96, 98
13:10	91		
13:13–17	36, 88 n.52	15:2	90 n.56, 100
13:14–15	89	15:2–6	68
13:15	28, 89, 93	15:3	32 n.42, 38, 91, 92, 98
13:17	89		
13:18	38	15:4–5	87
13:23–29	83 n.40	15:4–10	88
13:27	16 n.65, 31 n.40	15:5 87–8	
13:33	73	15:6	66, 67, 69, 78, 90 n.56, 100
13:34	89		
13:34–35	28, 36, 38, 64, 88, 93	15:7	82
		15:7–17	87
13:36-14:6	75		

Index of Ancient Sources 125

15:8	29, 47, 78, 82, 83, 85, 89, 94	17:11–15	68
		17:12	90 n.56, 100
15:8–10	93	17:15	31 n.40, 64
15:9	90	17:17	78 n.25, 82
15:9–10	64	17:17–19	37–40, 46 n.92, 78 n.23, 83, 85, 93, 94, 98
15:10	28, 44, 65 n.38		
15:10–14	78		
15:12	89	17:18	38
15:12–13	64, 89	17:19	30 n.35, 38–9, 45, 48, 68, 69, 88, 89, 93 n.64, 96, 98
15:12–14	28, 36, 93		
15:12–17	88		
15:13	29, 38	17:20–23	38
15:14	89	17:21	31
15:15	88 n.52	17:21–23	64
15:16	38	17:23	78 n.25
15:18–20	64	17:25	28 n.23, 28 n.24, 37, 40, 44, 48, 69
15:19	31, 38, 77 n.14		
15:20	88 n.52	18:9	90 n.56, 100
15:21	28 n.23, 44, 48	18:14	38
15:22	92	18:15–18	83
15:22–24	32, 45 n.89, 91 n.61, 93, 98	18:20	53, 57
		18:25–27	83
16:1	68, 78 n.25, 85, 87, 88, 90 n.56, 94, 100	18:28-19:16	41 n.72
		18:31	77 n.16, 79, 90
		18:35	41 n.72
16:2	66, 67	18:36	64
16:2–3	44, 64, 77 n.16	18:38	77 n.14
16:3	28 n.23, 44, 48	18:39–40	77 n.16
16:7–15	83	19:4	77 n.14
16:8–11	64	19:6	77 n.14
16:11	31 n.40	19:8–16	77 n.14
16:13	78 n.23, 78 n.25, 81 n.33, 83, 85, 93, 94, 98	19:12	77 n.14
		19:19–22	41 n.72
		19:26–27	83 n.40
16:13–15	83	19:28–30	38
16:27	28	19:30	29 n.30, 65 n.38
16:28	25 n.12	19:34–37	91 n.61
16:33	64, 70	19:38	29 n.29
17:2–5	45	19:38–40	29 n.30
17:3	22, 40, 44 n.86, 48, 97	19:38–42	84 n.43
		19:40	29 n.29
17:4	65 n.38	19:41-20:8	66
17:5	25 n.12, 37 n.60	20:1–29	35, 36, 69, 98
17:6	31, 38	20:2–10	83 n.40
17:8	40	20:9	29 n.30
17:9–26	37–8	20:12	29 n.29
17:10	37	20:20	29 n.30
17:11	37, 78 n.25, 90 n.56	20:22	46 n.92, 83, 88
		20:23	32 n.42, 92 n.63

20:24	82 n.38	*2 Corinthians*	
20:25	64	4:3	68 n.45
20:26–28	25		
20:27	29 n.30, 52, 64	*Ephesians*	
20:28	25 n.12, 37 n.60, 39	1:4	37 n.57
		2:1–5	68 n.45
20:30–31	1 n.1	5:1–2	45 n.90
21:7	83 n.40	5:8–11	29 n.32
21:15–17	28		
21:17	79	*Philippians*	
21:19	66, 67	2:3–11	36 n.52
21:20–24	83 n.40	2:15	45 n.90
21:22–23	66, 67		
		Colossians	
Acts		2:13	68 n.45
3:1	54 n.12		
4:30	62 n.32	*Titus*	
5:12–16	62 n.32	3:8	81 n.34
5:15	56 n.18		
9:32–35	62 n.32	*James*	
9:33–35	56 n.18	1:15	68 n.45
10:38	62 n.32	5:16	62 n.32
18:27	81 n.34		
19:18	81 n.34	*1 Peter*	
21:20	81 n.34	1:13–17	37 n.57
21:25	81 n.34	1:14–16	45 n.90
26:18	29 n.32	2:9	29 n.32
28:8–9	62 n.32		
		2 Peter	
Romans		2:19	86 n.47
6:16–23	86 n.47	3:11	37 n.57
7:9–10	68 n.45		
8:1–30	45 n.90	*1 John*	
8:6	68 n.45	1:2	25
8:10	68 n.45	1:2–3	24
8:21	86 n.47	1:6–7	29
12:1	4 n.21, 37 n.57	1:7	91
12:2	37 n.57	2:1	29, 45 n.91
13:11–14	29 n.32	2:29	29, 45 n.91
		3:1–2	45 n.90
1 Corinthians		3:5	29
1:18	68 n.45	3:7–10	45 n.90
2:6	83 n.41	3:8	24
3:1–3	83 n.41	3:9	45 n.91
6:12–20	4 n.21	3:10	46 n.92
12:9	62 n.32	3:14	68 n.45
12:28	62 n.32	4:7–8	45 n.91

4:9	45 n.91	*Epistulae ad Serapionem*	
5:11	24	1.24	12 n.54
5:18	45 n.91		
		Orationes contra Arianos	
Revelation		1.9	12 n.54
3:1	68 n.45	2.69–70	12 n.54
14:12	37 n.57	3.19–23	15 n.63
		3.20	12 n.54
		3.34	12 n.54, 40 n.67

RABBINIC LITERATURE

Augustine
Sermones

Mishnah		31.6	15 n.63
Pesaḥim		77.9	15 n.63
5:5–10	54 n.12		

Clement of Alexandria
Paedagogus

Sukkah		1.2	61 n.27
5:1–7	54 n.12	1.5	12 n.54
		1.6	12 n.54
Tamid		1.12	12 n.54
3:8	54 n.12	3.1	12 n.54
4:1–5:1	54 n.12		
5:6–7:4	54 n.12	*Protrepticus*	
		1	12 n.54
		11–12	12 n.54

APOSTOLIC FATHERS

Stromateis

Ignatius		5.10	12 n.54
Epistula ad Romanos		7.16	12 n.54
4.1-2	82 n.37		
5.1	82 n.37	Cyril of Alexandria	
5.3	82 n.37	*Commentarius in Joannem*	
6.1-3	82 n.37	1.9.91	47 n.96

OTHER ANCIENT CHRISTIAN WRITINGS

		1.9,91-93	12 n.54, 15 n.63
Athanasius		2.114	89 n.54, 93 n.64
De decretis		4.2.363	12 n.54
14	12 n.54	5.5.533	78 n.26
		5.5.537	78 n.26
De incarnatione		12.1.1088	12 n.54
9	12 n.54		
13	12 n.54, 68 n.46	*De Trinitate dialogi*	
14	15 n.63	7.639–644	12 n.54
16	12 n.54		
54	12 n.54, 40 n.67	Dionysius the Areopagite	
		De ecclesiastica hierarchia	
De synodis		1.3	12 n.54
51	12 n.54	2.1	15 n.63

Epistula ad Adelphium
4   12 n.54

2.2.1	12 n.54, 15 n.63	3.18.1	12 n.54
3.3.11-12	12 n.54	3.19.1	12 n.54, 13
		4.38.4	12 n.54
Gregory of Nazianzus		5	14 n.58, 40 n.67
Epistulae		5.1.1	12 n.54
101	12 n.54	5.1.3	13
		5.16.1	14
Orationes		5.16.2	12 n.54, 14
1.5	12 n.54		
		John Chrysostom	
Gregory of Nyssa		*Homiliae in Joannem*	
Antirrheticus adversus Apollinarium		11.1	15 n.63
11	12 n.54	67	37 n.54
53	12 n.54		
		Maximus the Confessor	
De beatitudinibus		*Ambiguorum Liber*	
5	12 n.54	7	12 n.54, 66 n.39
		42	12 n.54
De oratione dominica			
5	12 n.54	*Expositio orationis dominicae*	
		5	12 n.54
De vita Moysis			
2	12 n.54	*Quaestiones ad Thalassium*	
		2	12 n.54, 15 n.63
Oratio catechetica magna		6	15 n.63
25–26	12 n.54	21–22	12 n.54
32	12 n.54	54	12 n.54
35	12 n.54, 33 n.45, 37 n.55	64	12 n.54, 14–15
37	12 n.54	Origen	
		Commentarii in evangelium Joannis	
Irenaeus		19.1	15 n.63
Adversus haereses			
3.4.2	12 n.54	Thomas Aquinas	
3.6.1	12 n.54	*Super evangelium S. Ioannis lectura*	
3.16.9	12 n.54	15.2	15 n.63

Index of Subjects

ascetic struggle 10–11, 48, 73, 85, 93, 99
atonement 21, 33–5
   see also Jesus, mission of

belief 3–16, 28, 40, 46, 48, 49, 64, 66, 68,
   69–70, 72, 78–9, 81, 82–3, 85, 87–8,
   90, 94, 96, 98
Bethzatha 52–3, 54–5
   man at 55–60, 63, 97

children of God 40, 45–7, 48, 64, 68, 70, 71,
   73, 83, 89, 93, 96, 98

darkness 3, 6, 8, 9, 10, 16–17, 18, 22–32, 41,
   43, 45, 47–8, 69, 71, 76, 85, 93, 96–8
death 1–5, 7–8, 9, 10, 13, 16–17, 18, 22, 32,
   35, 36, 49–50, 61–2, 64, 65–70, 71, 73,
   76, 85, 93–4, 97–8
devil 31, 89–90
disability 16–17, 18, 49–65, 69–70, 91,
   97–8
disciples 31, 37–9, 47, 78–9, 82–3, 85, 94
discipleship 28–9, 36, 64, 73, 78, 82–3, 85,
   87–90, 93, 94, 99
   see also ethics
dualism 6, 10, 89, 99–100

election 46, 71, 90, 100
ethics 3–17, 21–2, 25–30, 32, 36–40, 42–5,
   48, 49, 60, 63–4, 70, 71, 75–7, 87–90,
   93, 95–9

glory 29–30, 36, 64

human corporeality/embodiment 3–17,
   18, 21, 33, 35, 39–40, 49–50, 57, 63,
   65–70, 72, 95–8
human predicament 1–100

ignorance of God 3–10, 16–17, 18, 21–2,
   32, 41–5, 48, 69, 71, 85, 93–4, 97–8

illness 16–17, 18, 32, 49–64, 65, 69–70,
   97–8

Jerusalem temple 53–4, 55, 57, 59
Jesus
   mission of 1–17, 18, 21–2, 24–31, 32–40,
     44–5, 47–8, 50, 62–4, 65–7, 68–70,
     71–2, 76, 85, 88, 89, 92–3, 95, 96,
     98, 100
   person of 11, 12–15, 24–5, 28–9, 37,
     39–40, 44, 52, 59, 62, 64–5, 75, 79,
     88–9, 93, 96, 98, 100

kingdom of God 62, 64–5
knowledge of God 3, 10, 16–17, 21–2, 28,
   34, 40, 43–5, 47–8, 96

last day 64, 66–70, 73–4, 98
law of Moses 4, 26, 35, 43–4, 46, 71, 76–7,
   88–9, 96, 97
life 3–17, 18, 21–30, 32, 33–40, 45–6, 47–8,
   49, 50, 57, 62, 64, 65–70, 71, 74–5, 78,
   88–9, 94, 96, 98
light 3, 8, 10, 16–17, 18, 21–30, 31–2, 40–1,
   47–8, 76, 92, 96

man born blind 60–1, 63, 90, 97
miracles 18–19, 50, 62, 63, 65, 83–4, 97

ontology 4, 5

paradox 90, 99–100

resurrection 7, 21, 24–5, 35–6, 49–50, 51,
   64, 66–7, 68–70, 96, 98
revelation 2–9, 11, 18–19, 21, 25, 27, 30,
   31–2, 33–4, 40, 50, 74

salvation 1–100
sanctification 7, 37–40, 48, 78, 82–3, 85,
   87–9, 94, 96, 98

see also ethics; Jesus, mission of; sin
sin 1–17, 19, 22, 32, 35, 40, 42–3, 59, 60, 61, 67, 68–9, 71–94, 98–9
   liberation from 78–9, 81, 83–4, 85, 87–93, 94, 98–9
   see also sanctification

"the Jews" 28, 41–2, 44–6, 48, 53, 57, 65, 72, 73–93, 98
theosis 10–17, 33, 40, 95

world 1–3, 6, 16–17, 21–2, 25, 30–1, 34, 38, 41, 44–5, 51–2, 60, 63–4, 66–7, 68–70, 85, 93, 96–8

www.ingramcontent.com/pod-product-compliance
Lightning Source LLC
Chambersburg PA
CBHW061844300426
44115CB00013B/2498